E-Government and its Implications for Administrative Law

For other titles in the Series see p. 225

INFORMATION TECHNOLOGY & LAW SERIES (1)

E-GOVERNMENT AND ITS IMPLICATIONS FOR ADMINISTRATIVE LAW

Regulatory Initiatives in France, Germany, Norway and the United States

edited by

J.E.J. Prins

M.M. Eifert
C. Girot
M. Groothuis
W.J.M. Voermans

T•M•C• ASSER PRESS
The Hague

The *Information Technology & Law Series* is published
for ITeR by T·M·C·Asser press
P.O. Box 16163, 2500 BD The Hague, The Netherlands
www.asserpress.nl

The *Information Technology & Law Series* is an initiative of ITeR, the National Programme for Information Technology and Law, which is a research programme set up by the Dutch government and the Netherlands Organisation for Scientific Research (NWO) in The Hague. Since 1995 ITeR has published all of its research results in its own book series. In 2002 *ITeR* launched the present internationally orientated and English language *Information Technology & Law Series.* This series deals with the implications of information technology for legal systems and institutions. It is not restricted to publishing ITeR's research results. Hence, authors are invited and encouraged to submit their manuscripts for inclusion. Manuscripts and related correspondence can be sent to the Series' Editorial Office, which will also gladly provide more information concerning editorial standards and procedures.

Editorial Office
NWO/ITeR
P.O. Box 93461
2509 AL The Hague, The Netherlands
Tel. +31(0)70-3440950; Fax +31(0)70-3832841
E-mail: iter@nwo.nl
Web site: www.nwo.nl/iter

Single Copies and Standing Orders
The books in the *Information Technology & Law Series* can either be purchased as single copies at the regular retail price or through a standing order at a discount. For more information see www.asserpress.nl/cata/ITLaw/fra.htm.

ISBN 90-6704-141-6
ISSN 1570-2782

Cover and lay-out: Oasis Productions, Nieuwerkerk a/d IJssel, The Netherlands

PREFACE

In April 2001 the Dutch government issued a draft text to amend the Public Administration Act.[1] Once in force, it will adapt Dutch administrative law to the digital era and will facilitate the use of electronic communications in administrative procedures. At present, Dutch administrative law formally requires the use of traditional media (paper), which is increasingly felt to be anachronistic in the era of electronic commerce and electronic government.

The Netherlands is not the only country to design a framework for electronic administrative communication. The current pressure to provide an adequate legal framework is high in various countries. Many countries have started to work on new provisions in administrative law in order to remove legal impediments that bar electronic services from public administrations. Some have recently enacted such provisions. Finland, for example, implemented the Act on Electronic Services in the Administration on January 1, 2000.[2]

This study provides an overview and an analysis of these legislative developments in four selected countries. As explained in chapter 1, these countries are: France, Germany, Norway and the United States. What approach has been taken in these countries? What specific requirements have been formulated to facilitate electronic administrative communication and at what level? What can we learn from the regulatory projects in these countries?

Before embarking on the analysis we would like to thank Mr. Frank van Ommeren of the Dutch Ministry of Justice for his valuable comments on the framework of this study, Professor Dag Wiese Schartum, Mr. Rolf Riisnæs of the Norwegian Research Center for Computers and Law

[1] Voorontwerp van Wet Aanvulling van de Algemene wet bestuursrecht met regels over verkeer tussen burgers en bestuursorganen langs elektronische weg (Wet elektronisch bestuurlijk verkeer). The text can be found at: <http://www.minjust.nl/a_beleid/thema/digiwet/>.

[2] <http://www.om.fi/2838.htm>.

(Oslo), Mr. Ørnulf Røhnebæk (Ministry of Justice, Norway), Mr. Thomas Myhr (Ministry of Trade and Industry, Norway), Mr. Michael Mundaca of the United States Internal Revenue Service and Ms. Kim Byars of the United States Patent and Trade Mark Office. Finally, we express our gratitude to Vivian Carter and Bastiaan Garnier for their tremendous help with the editing of the English text.

Tilburg, The Netherlands, September 2001

CORIEN PRINS
MARTIN EIFERT
CLARISSE GIROT
MARGA GROOTHUIS
WIM VOERMANS

TABLE OF CONTENTS

Chapter 1
TAKING ADMINISTRATIVE LAW INTO THE DIGITAL ERA

Chapter 1
TAKING ADMINISTRATIVE LAW INTO THE DIGITAL ERA

1.1 ELECTRONIC GOVERNMENT

In May 2001, an interesting article appeared in the newspapers: the US government was reported to be more successful in its sales on the Internet than Amazon.com. Whereas the US government was reported to have a turnover of 3.6 billion dollars on the Internet, the sales of Amazon.com amounted to only 2.8 million dollars.[1] The news suggests that the concept of electronic government has expanded enormously in the United States. A closer look, however, reveals that there is still a long way to go before efficient on-line services for US citizens and enterprises are available.

Nevertheless, important steps have clearly been taken to pave the way towards a digitised government. Not only in the US, but in various countries around the world governments have recognised the potential of new information and communication technologies (ICT) to bring about fundamental renewal, not only in their functioning but also in their presence towards other organisations, societal groups or individuals. Both in their relationship with the citizen (for instance, democratic processes, public service delivery, or policy implementation), inter-organisational arrangements (for instance, policy coordination, policy implementation, or public service delivery), and in intra-organisational activities (for instance, policy development, operational activities, or knowledge management), ICT promises enormous opportunities to increase efficiency and effectiveness in all kinds of policy sectors.[2]

---

[1] <http://www.webwereld.nl/nieuws/7647.phtml>.

[2] See extensively the various chapters in: J.E.J. Prins (ed.), *Designing E-Government. On the Crossroads of Technological Innovation and Institutional Change*, The Hague/Boston: Kluwer Law International 2001.

J.E.J. Prins (Ed.), E-Government and its Implications for Administrative Law

In 1993, the US government was the first to launch an e-goverment initiative.[3] Subsequently agendas were issued in the United Kingdom (the Green Paper entitled "*government.direct*")[4], Australia (entitled "*Clients First*")[5], Canada[6] and many other countries, including The Netherlands.[7] International organisations such as the G8[8] and the European Commission also addressed the issue. The Commission launched the *eEurope* initiative, which focuses, among other things, on government on-line. It is the Commission's intention to ensure that citizens have easy access to government information, services and decision-making procedures on-line.[9] The European Council adopted the initiative during the Lisbon summit in March 2000.

In the meantime, the US government has already greatly expanded citizen access to on-line government information and services and proposed initiatives to build on the 1993 Administration's efforts, led by Vice President Gore. On 24 June 2000, the US government unveiled a series of new initiatives to give the American people – what President Clinton in his first ever Saturday webcast addressed to the Nation claimed to be – "the 'Information Age' government they deserve". Clinton stated that the new initiatives will cut red tape, make the government more responsive to the needs of citizens, and expand opportunities for participation in our democracy.[10] By the end of 2000:

---

[3] National Performance Review, Washington 1993. See also: Office of the Vice President, *Re-engineering Government Through IT*, Accompanying Report to the National Performance Review, Government Printing Office, Washington DC, 1993 <http://www.npr.gov/library/reports/it.html>.

[4] Office of Public Service, *Government.direct. A Green Paper on the Electronic Delivery of Government Services*, Cm 3438, HMSO, London, November 1996. Available at: <http://www.citu.gov.uk/greenpaper.htm>. See for a discussion: Ch. Bellamy, J.A. Taylor, *Understanding government.direct*, *Information Infrastructure and Policy* 6 (1997/1998), p. 3.

[5] *Clients First. The Challenge for Government Information Technology*, 1 March 1995. Available at: <http://www.nla.gov.au/gov/itreview/final/itrg-tc.html>.

[6] *Blueprint for Renewing Government Services Using Information Technology.* Available at: <http://www.ifla.org/documents/infopol/canada/tb-bp.txt>.

[7] *Actieprogramma Elektronische Overheid*, *Kamerstukken II* 1998/1999, 26 387. Available at: <http://www.minbzk.nl/e-overheid>.

[8] See: <http://www.open.gov.uk>.

[9] Available at: <http://europa.eu.int/information_society/eeurope>.

[10] See: <http://www.whitehouse.gov/WH/New/html/e-government.html>.

- Citizens must be able to search all on-line resources offered by the federal government from a single web site called <firstgov.gov>;
- Citizens, small businesses and community groups must have one-stop access to roughly $500 billion in grants and procurement opportunities.

Not only at a national level, but also at a European Union level the need to develop efficient on-line services for European citizens and enterprises is felt as well. In June 2001, the Swedish Presidency of the European Union organised the conference entitled "eGovernment in the service of European citizens and enterprises what is required at the European level". The conference was organised within the overall framework of the eEurope 2002 Action Plan. The main objective of the conference was to identify and promote e-government services at the European level for citizens and enterprises, to examine what needs to be done and how it should be done, at the European level, and the impact on the Member States. The eEurope 2002 Action Plan, drafted by the Council of Ministers and the European Commission, and adopted by the June 2000 Feira European Council, stresses the need for both the EU institutions and the Member States' public administrations to make every effort to develop efficient on-line services for European citizens and enterprises.

It was stressed by European representatives that all Member States are now launching e-government services aimed at citizens and enterprises by public administrations via digital and internet-based technologies. However, these services are mainly aimed at the country's own citizens and enterprises, and they are devised within country-specific administrative traditions and culture. Within the single market citizens and enterprises in other Member States are also potential customers of these e-government services. Examples include on-line public procurement, company registration, change of residence, etc. The challenge for Europe's public administrations, therefore, is to ensure that e-government services are open to other Member States' citizens and enterprises, to ensure the respect of single market principles.

If citizens and enterprises are to communicate electronically with public administrations, they need to know what this entails, what they have to do, what the benefits of on-line dialogue will be – and how their concerns (for example in the areas of trust, privacy and the protection of personal information) will be addressed. If public administrations introduce electronic working tools and methods, they also need to devise Draft Regulations, 'user manuals', roadmaps, etc. to explain to citizens and enterprises, both at the national level and in other countries, what they have to do to make the most of e-services.

At the June conference the following general conclusions were reached[11]:

- Europe's public administrations need to develop a common vision of how e-government services will develop, and subsequently be committed to the implementation. This should be based on decentralised responsibilities with a clear outline of the roles of the Member States, the European Commission and other Institutions;
- The vision should include what public administration will do to ensure that citizens and enterprises are confident about electronic ways of working (e.g. privacy and security issues);
- It should also include measures to ensure greater openness and citizens' involvement in the EU and national administrations' regulatory processes;
- Public administrations are not solely responsible for electronic communications. The private sector should also be involved (e.g. possibly through public private partnerships, involvement of chambers of commerce, etc.);
- It is not just an issue of providing technical solutions. For e-government to work the bulk of changes are required at the organisational level;
- There is no single solution. It is recommended that administrations provide a multi-channel approach (e.g. PCs, kiosks, digital television, GSM, SMS, WAP, etc.) to services.

The aforementioned accelerating development towards realising an electronic government has heightened the pressure on legislatures in various countries to provide an adequate legal framework for electronic administrative communication. Thus, various countries have passed, or have started working on, a revision of provisions in administrative law which impede the electronic services of public administrations.

---

[11] See: <http://europa.eu.int/ISPO/ida/>.

1.2 Electronic administrative procedures

Now that the potential of electronic communication for public administration is becoming apparent, this has prompted discussions as regards the appropriate legal framework. An *electronic* government requires administrative communication and administrative procedures to be handled electronically.

A brief glance at the relevant legal framework, however, teaches us that when dealing with administrative communications electronically, we come up against certain legal impediments and uncertainties. Generally, many rules and regulations require communication in paper-based writing, often accompanied by a handwritten signature. Furthermore, requirements of physical presence (for example handing over certain documents or registration purposes) are not suitable for an electronic government. Finally, in certain situations the submission of specific documents is required, such as the submission of the original documents in procedural matters. Thus, a scanned version of such documents is not acceptable.

In the face of these legal impediments, governments are considering amendments to administrative procedure laws in order to allow electronic communication. However, by favouring the introduction of electronic communication, the question arises whether government agencies are obliged to enter into a digital world. Or is it still at the discretion of the public administration to decide whether it allows electronic communication? And, can administrations in return limit their communication to electronic forms of communication?

Clearly, the question also arises as to how to proceed in amending the relevant laws and regulations. Should governments aim at a comprehensive adaptation of all relevant statutes and provisions, or should they opt for a limited effort and establish some general basic rules concerning electronic communication under administrative procedural law? Once this question has been decided, many other questions emerge. What specific requirements in administrative law need to be introduced for electronic communication? What issues should be regulated at the general level of administrative procedure law and what issues should be dealt with in specific regulations or Draft Regulations? Should specific requirements be introduced regarding electronic signatures? Should there be differnces between traditional forms of communication and electronic communications, etc.?

An interesting point when considering the answer to the above questions is the possible interplay between public law and civil law. For in the light of the e-commerce related legislative developments in civil law, the question is whether civil law stipulations can be applied within the framework of public law when a regulation has been issued for the concerns of the private sector, but no equivalent regulation exists concerning the public sector. To what extent can e-commerce related private law and case law influence the interpretation of public law?

1.3 A SURVEY OF REGULATORY INITIATIVES

As mentioned in the Preface, in April 2001, the Dutch government issued a draft text which is to amend the Public Administration Act.[12] Once in force this text will adapt Dutch administrative law to the digital era and authorise and facilitate the use of electronic communications for the performance of administrative procedures.

The Dutch legislature is not the only one to amend the administrative procedural system to facilitate electronic communication by public organisations. From the following chapters of this study it becomes clear that several other countries are eager to embark upon legislative reform in this area. We will discuss four such countries in this study: France, Germany, Norway and the United States. The reason for analysing the situation in these specific countries is that, on the one hand, all four countries have issued various policy documents and Internet-related initiatives to implement e-government ambitions while, on the other hand, the legal climate for facilitating these ambitions appears to be strikingly different. As will become clear, this situation has everything to do with the legal and administrative tradition of the respective countries. For example, the French administration is renowned for its reluctance towards organisational change and innovation, whereas the United States has been

[12] Voorontwerp van Wet "Aanvulling van de Algemene wet bestuursrecht met regels over verkeer tussen burgers en bestuursorganen langs elektronische weg (Wet elektronisch bestuurlijk verkeer)". The text can be found at: <http://www.minjust.nl/a_beleid/thema/digiwet/>.

widely acknowledged as a leading country when it comes to developments related to on-line communication.

Another reason for selecting the four countries mentioned is that their system of administrative law works with different characteristics and concepts. Thus, it is of interest to see to what extent these characteristics influence the proposed amendments of the administrative law system. Finally, from the analysis in the different chapters it becomes clear that the respective countries are all dealing with the characteristics of electronic communication in different ways and thus introduce different rules on careful electronic communication.

Chapter 2
FRANCE

Chapter 2
FRANCE

2.1 INTRODUCTION

At present the French administration is unable to deliver an official decree in an electronic form. It is quite striking that the discussions concerning France's entry to the Information Society have not dealt with this aspect of the development of the electronic dimension of the French administration. This does not preclude such a development in the future, of course, but the French administration is renowned for its reluctance towards organisational change and innovation. It is presumed that very strong political incentives will be needed in this respect. However, some important changes will have already taken place once measures have been taken to simplify the citizen's access to administrative documents and procedures. It is reasonable to infer that the possibility of issuing electronic decisions will eventually be derived from these developments, although it is difficult to predict a time period for such an evolution.

2.1.1 **Present practice**

An important document was released on 16 January 1998 by the French government, called the "Programme d'action gouvernemental pour l'entrée de la France dans la Société de l'Information" (PAGSI). The aims of this governmental action programme are, among others, the dematerialization of administrative procedures as a fundamental field of action.[1]

[1] See the original text of the PAGSI at: <http://www.internet.gouv.fr/francais/textesref/modern.htm>, (1 August 2001, English version available). Regular information on the implementation of the programme is available at: <http://www.internet.gouv.fr>.

The essential motive for implementing dematerialised procedures is to improve the service rendered to the user. As regards business users, this simplification would allow a price reduction in the costs incurred by these procedures.

Two essential goals can be noted in this respect. The first is the availability of all administrative forms on the Internet. The second is that, eventually, all of these procedures can be fully carried out on-line without having to print out forms and fill them in by hand. PAGSI defined these procedures, called *"téléprocédures"*, as "dematerialised procedures between the public authorities and their partners or users".

PAGSI's aim was for all administrative forms in use to be available on the Internet before the end of 1998. From a survey released on 20 October 2000 it appeared, however, that only 613 of the 1656 forms in use were available on-line.[2] Of the 613 forms, only 102 could be completed on-line, while 473 had to be printed out and sent by post to the Administration once completed. An example of forms available on-line but which have to be printed out and completed are, for instance, an application for vehicle registration,[3] a request for a grant for higher education,[4] application forms for the registration of patents or trademarks,[5] or the registration of travel agencies.[6] The final decisions regarding these procedures are only communicated by post.

A few *téléprocédures* are already available. They generally focus on saving the citizen's time and effort in having to personally carry out administrative procedures. Occasionally these procedures are aimed at simplifying the Administration's processing of the resulting files. In this respect, one of the most recent examples of such a *téléprocédure* is the possibility for companies to pay or receive a VAT refund electronically. Every company that has freely subscribed to the service can pay its yearly VAT through the Internet. Their account is then directly debited or credited with the corresponding amount. This procedure makes it necessary for companies to resort to electronic signatures and certification services. This will be discussed later on.

---

[2] The site where these e-forms may be downloaded is <http://www.service-public.fr>, and more specifically from <http://www.cerfa.gouv.fr> (1 August 2001).

[3] See: <http://www.interieur.gouv.fr/cerfa/flash/choix.html> (1 August 2001).

[4] See: <http://www.education.gouv.fr/prat/formul/defaultb.htm> (1 August 2001).

[5] See: <http://www.inpi.fr/inpi/html/proteger/formdepo/indexbis.htm> (1 August 2001).

[6] See: <http://www.equipement.gouv.fr/formulaires> (1 August 2001).

Furthermore, at the end of 2000 an assessment report was released on the development of *téléprocédures* for business users.[7] The report essentially describes the goals which the Administration should achieve when developing *téléprocédures*, but it can also be used to help to anticipate certain regulatory issues as set out in the following paragraphs.

2.1.2 Present regulatory developments and expectations

The development of initiatives relating to the electronic development of administrative procedures is a specific follow-up to Decree No. 98-1083 dated 2 December 1998 concerning administrative simplifications. As a result of this Decree a Commission was created to guarantee administrative simplifications (*Commission pour les simplifications administratives*, or COSA).[8] This Commission may occasionally resort to the interministerial mission for technical support for the development of information and communication technology in the administration (*Mission interministérielle pour le développement du soutien technique au développement des technologies de l'information et de communication dans l'administration*, or MTIC).[9] COSA must ensure that the contents of all administrative forms are harmonised, normalised and simplified. All developments concerning the on-line availability of administrative forms are related to the overruling ambition to simplify.

As a result, since the Decree of 2 February 1999 it is compulsory to make all administrative forms accessible on-line[10] This Decree requires that all the forms deemed necessary for formalities or to assert one's

---

[7] *Evolution des téléprocédures à destination des enterprises*, preliminary report presented by G. Corré and J.-F. Lesné to the Conseil Général des Technologies de l'Information, December 2000, available at: <http://www.mtic.pm.gouv.fr/programmes/teleprocedures/index.html> (25 March 2001).

[8] "Décret No. 98-1083 du 2 décembre 1998 relative aux simplifications administratives", JORF/LD No. 280, 3 December 1998, p. 18124, also available at: <http://admi.net/jo/19981203/PRMX9803301D.html> (25 March 2001).

[9] Information about the development of *téléprocédures* in the French administration is available on the site of the MTIC at: <http://www.mtic.pm.gouv.fr/programmes/teleprocedures>.

[10] "Décret No. 99-68 du 2 février 1999 relatif à la mise en ligne des formulaires administratifs", JORF/LD No. 29, 4 February 1999, p. 1775, also available at: <http://admi.net/jo/19990204/PRMX9903385D.html> (1 August 2001).

rights against an administration or a public establishment must be available for free on the Internet site "admifrance.fr" or any other site which has a list defined by an official decision ("*arrêté*") made by the Prime Minister. It also imposes the obligation that the different administrative services of the State may not refuse to examine requests presented by means of these electronic forms.

Similarly, a recent Law of 14 April 2000 determined that any person who is obliged to comply with a deadline to initiate any sort of administrative procedure may fulfil this obligation by sending the relevant documents on time, not only by post, but also "by any validated telematic or computer process that enables them to meet the deadline".[11]

Two other texts are relevant, which are informal, non-binding documents issued by the Prime Minister in 1999 to provide guidance to administrative services on the relevance of the Internet to their activities ("*circulaires*"). The first *circulaire* concerned the Internet sites of the State Administration.[12] This document refers to the goal of each ministry to generalise the on-line availability of public data, to improve the information and the service provided to the user as well as the efficiency of its administration. The general principles to be derived from this text are that the content and presentation of public authorities' sites should be reliable, accessible and interactive. This implies, in the case of the latter, that administrative services should create electronic mailboxes so that citizens can receive an answer within 7 days of submitting their request. A supplementary document is also available to provide a step by step guide to each administrative service.[13]

The second *circulaire* provides instructions for the administration regarding the development of *téléprocédures* and also indicates their technical and legal reliability.[14] Prior to their publication on-line, these forms

[11] Art. 16 of the Law 2000-231 of 12 April 2000 relative to the right of citizens with the administration, available at: <http://www.legifrance.com/texteconsolide/PPEDQ.htm> (1 August 2001).

[12] Circulaire du 7 octobre 1999 relative aux sites Internet des services et de l'administration de l'Etat, published in the Code de la communication, Dalloz 2001, p. 792.

[13] See: <http://www.fonction-publique.gouv.fr>.

[14] Circulaire du 31 décembre 1999 relative à l'aide aux démarches administratives sur l'Internet, JORF/LD No. 5 du 7 janvier 1999, p. 279, also available at: <http://www.adminet.com/jo/20000107/PRMX0003923C.html> (25 March 2001).

are subject to examination by COSA. This requirement is in line with the universal goal to improve the organisation of the relations between the French administration and French citizens. The *circulaire* also acknowledges that civil servants who have daily contacts with citizens are in a better position to develop on-line services that meet the public's requirements and expectations. However, local developments should not lead to contradictory interpretations of the law or to an unequal position between users concerning access to the administration. Therefore, the Prime Minister recommends that these local services should respect the principles set out in a "Charter" appended to the *circulaire*. For instance, local sites should refer to national sites when they are available on the issue concerned, and national forms should be referred to instead of the local ones, if the former exist. As regards *téléprocédures*, *i.e.*, fully automated services, the *circulaire* recommends that formalities on local sites should not add any requirement, formality or additional relevant document to those mentioned in the form issued at the national level.

It does not appear that any specific action will be taken at a legislative level. Such a regulatory intervention will probably only be necessary if the step is ever taken to favour the on-line communication of administrative decisions. So far, the government's only aim is to simplify administrative procedures and to avoid the physical presence of citizens or that of a company agent who could implement such procedures. The issue of whether or not a final administrative decision should be communicated on-line does not, in this respect, seem to be of fundamental importance. As will be mentioned underneath, the draft Information Society Law, issued in July 2001, does not contain any specific provisions to facilitate administrative electronic transactions.

2.2 The administrative system and problems in the light of electronic transactions

2.2.1 General characteristics of the administrative system

The organisation of the administrative system in France can be typified as extremely specific due to the importance given to the power of the State and to central administrative services.[15] Historically, it was considered that there was a radical difference between private and public activities: public authorities care for the public interest while individuals only care for their own. As a consequence, the Administration was subject to specific jurisdiction and rules. This specific order of jurisdiction progressively led to the creation of a distinct set of rules for all administrative legal issues so that they could be clearly distinguished from private law issues. As a result, the sources of administrative law in France are extremely specific. Administrative law is, in fact, French "Common Law", due to the traditional importance of the case law determined by the administrative courts and, essentially, by the Conseil d'Etat, the Supreme Court in this field. Specific regulations and statutes are also relevant, of course. It appears as though even the importance of administrative case law is being diminished as a method against the influx of all sorts of legislative and regulatory texts. On the whole, French administrative law is extremely complex. This complexity is unsatisfactory, in as much as it slows down the process of decision-making and French citizens are unfamiliar with the rules on administrative matters.[16] It also makes it difficult to predict the evolution of certain rules, among which is the evolution of the Administration in an electronic environment.

2.2.2 Interaction between administrative and civil law

As a consequence of the general characteristics of French administrative law, official interaction between administrative law and civil law is impossible. In fact, one of the most difficult issues in French administrative law is to determine which set of rules is relevant to a given case. In other words, both sets of rules are always seen as *alternatives*, and not as *complementary*. However, the greater acceptance of electronic elements as means of evidence in civil and commercial law, for instance, and the general development of electronic commerce will certainly prevent administrative law from remaining immune to technological developments.

Furthermore, the distinction between private and public law seems to be minimal on certain occasions. For instance, when a regulation has been

[15] Debbasch, *Institutions et droit administratifs*, Part 2, L'action et le contrôle de l'Administration, PUF, 4th ed., 1998, p. 34.

[16] Debbasch, p. 37.

issued apparently for the concerns of the private sector, but no equivalent regulation exists concerning the public sector, it might be possible to infer that the same developments will eventually characterise the latter. A requirement is then that the original objective concerning the protection of specific interests of the Administration is not involved. Such a point, however, does not result from the law, but from a commitment to realism. For our specific purposes, this suggestion seems to apply to the case of electronic signatures which is dealt with below.

2.2.3 **Requirements of the administrative system relevant for electronic communication**

Although there are no rules as to whether an administrative decision can be communicated electronically or not, certain rules must be considered as relevant in this respect. Administrative acts should always respect certain formal rules of procedure as a condition for their validity. Some of these rules might cause problems when applied in the electronic context.

Basically, the law distinguishes between essential and non-essential formalities. Non-essential formalities result from customs and their non-fulfilment has no effect on their validity (mentioning a date on a document, for instance), while essential formalities are sanctioned by the illegality of the act.

An essential requirement, to start with, is that administrative acts which unilaterally deal with an individual's position ("*actes administratifs unilatéraux*") might have to be "justified": the agent taking the final decision should specifically provide the legal or factual reasons that have led him/her to take this decision.[17] More specifically, the requirement of "justification" means that a text of reference should be referred to in the final decision. The (judicial) rule of principle is that administrative decisions should not be 'justified', while exceptions should exclusively correspond to a situation settled by an administrative regulation. In practice, however, these exceptions have become very numerous. Furthermore, since the Law of 11 July 1979 relative to the "justification" of administrative acts and to the improvement of relations between the Administration and citi-

[17] Debbasch, p. 260, Morand-Deviller, *Cours de Droit Administratif*, Montchrestien, 6th ed., 1999, p. 349, de Forges, *Droit Administratif*, PUF, 4th ed., 1998, p. 57.

zens, the legislator has also brought important exceptions to the principle of 'non-justification'.[18] Different types of decisions should correspondingly be justified in order to satisfy this essential formality:

- individual decisions that have been taken in derogation of general regulations;
- individual decisions that are unfavourable to the addressee;
- decisions that restrain the implementation of a public liberty;
- decisions which impose a sanction;
- individual decisions which restrain or cancel another decision that had awarded a right to the addressee;
- individual decisions that refuse to grant an authorisation to the addressee.

These specific decisions should be communicated in writing and should mention the factual or legal considerations that form the basis of the decision. This obligation could be derogated from three different circumstances: 'an absolute emergency', medical confidentiality, and in cases of national defence.[19] Furthermore, when this requirement of justification applies, the administrative agent's justifications should be precise and complete. On the other hand, when this requirement of justification does not apply, the administration may make its decisions very informally.[20]

Secondly, administrative acts should be officially made public. The decision must be published when it concerns administrative acts for general application. As for administrative acts for individual application, the decision should be specifically notified to the person concerned with an acknowledgement of receipt. Once such an act has been published or notified, it is binding for the addressee and for all others concerned. Here again, it is not known whether sending an e-mail can be considered as a fulfilment of this requirement of notification or whether the requirement of acknowledgement of receipt can be fulfilled with an electronic version.

Other requirements also apply when the decision is communicated to the addressee. The decision should mention a date, the name and the sig-

---

[18] See the text of the Law at: <http://www.legifrance.gouv.fr/textes/html/fic79587111979.htm> (1 August 2001).

[19] Morand-Deviller, p. 349.

[20] Chapus, *Droit Administratif Général*, Part 1, Domat Droit Public, 14th ed. 2000, p. 494-495.

nature of the administrative agent who has communicated the decision. Since the recent Law of 14 April 2000, citizens have the right to know the name, first name, the title and the administrative address of the person who is dealing with their case.[21] The 2000 report on the evolution of *téléprocédures* in administration also implies that the agent's e-mail address should be given.[22] Such measures would raise the user's confidence in the fact that their case is being dealt with and enable them to enquire about the follow-up. This, however, implies that all administrative agents have an e-mail address, which is not the case at the moment.

All these elements must be mentioned in the correspondence which citizens receive from the Administration. Exceptions to the rule may relate to matters of public safety or individual security. Furthermore, any decision taken by an administrative authority should mention in perfectly legible text, the agent's signature, his/her name, first name, and title (Art. 4 of the Law). Finally, if it is compulsory, the intervention of other authorities should be mentioned in the text of the final decision as well.[23] The requirement that an administrative act should be signed, might again cause problems of interpretation in an electronic context. This requirement is exceedingly important, however, as it is qualified as an "essential formality", which implies that the act will be void if this formality has not been respected.[24]

2.2.4 Problems with electronic communication

As can be seen from the above developments, matters of interpretation may arise as to the transposition of several requirements of validity of administrative acts in an electronic context.

The first of these is that certain types of act should be 'justified', which implies that a written document on paper should be communicated to the

[21] Law 2000-231 of 12 April 2000 relative to the right of citizens with the administration, available at: <http://www.legifrance.com/texteconsolide/PPEDQ.htm> (1 August 2001).

[22] *Evolution des téléprocédures à destination des entreprises*, preliminary report presented by G. Corré and J.-F. Lesné to the Conseil Général des Technologies de l'Information, December 2000, p. 7.

[23] Debbasch, p. 261.

[24] Jurisclasseur Droit Administratif, "Ediction de l'acte administratif – Auteurs, formes, procédures", 1998, fasc. 107-20, No. 46-47.

addressee of the decision. The second is that administrative acts should be notified to the addressee accompanied by a confirmation of receipt. The third is that the agent taking the decision should always append his signature to the corresponding administrative act.

In all three cases, it is not clear whether electronic mail can sufficiently fulfil these requirements. However, the general policy concerning *télé-procédures*, if not the on-line communication of administrative decisions, is that the relations between citizens and the administration should be increasingly simplified by such electronic communication.

2.2.5 Solutions under case law?

There is no case law available in administrative law that formally indicates such a liberal understanding of the communication of an administrative act. However, and as indicated above, an administrative act may be dealt with in more ways than in writing.

For instance, an administrative decision sent by telex is considered valid,[25] as well as the refusal of a request for extradition which has been communicated orally.[26] On the other hand, a decision of the Conseil d'Etat has explicitly stipulated that the signature required on an administrative act should be 'handwritten'.[27] As a result, it is difficult to derive any safe inference from these few judicial examples to acknowledge the validity of administrative acts communicated electronically.

2.2.6 Influence of other legal domains in addressing the problems

The current situation under French law is to accept the validity of electronic documents in private law, particularly concerning requirements of proof. As indicated above, the distinction between private and public law in France is very strong. However, recent modifications to the French Civil Code in order to accept the validity of electronic evidence and of

[25] Conseil d'Etat, *Syndicat National de l'Enseignement Supérieur*, 30 June 1978, Revue de Droit Public 1979, p. 557.

[26] Conseil d'Etat, *Confédération Helvétique*, Actualités Juridiques de Droit Administratif 1995, p. 56.

[27] Conseil d'Etat, *Torras*, Recueil Lebon 1990, p. 665.

electronic signatures could lead to the presumption that these modifications could eventually be applied to the administrative sector. The earlier mentioned report issued on the evolution of *téléprocédures* in France seems to take this point for granted, but caution is required since this report does not pay attention to the legal dimensions of the discussion.[28]

French Parliament has recently drafted a law to adapt the law of evidence to meet the needs of information technology. This covers electronic signatures the provisions of which have been incorporated into the relevant sections of the French Civil Code.[29] More specifically, Art. 1316-1 of the Civil Code acknowledges that "a writing (*écrit*) in electronic form is now accepted as valid evidence in the same way as a written document, providing that the person who produced it can be identified and that the document can be kept and stored in such conditions that its authenticity is warranted". As for Art. 1316-3 of the Civil Code, it further specifies "a writing via an electronic medium has the same evidentiary value as a written document".

This statute strengthens the position of some courts which have recently taken innovative positions in relation to evidentiary requirements. For instance, a decision in 1997 by the French Supreme Court (*Cour de cassation*) accepted that a written act (an *écrit*) could be stored on any medium (including a fax) for evidentiary matters, provided that "its integrity and the imputability of its contents to its author are checked or are not contested".[30] This position specifically concerned the commercial assignment of a recoverable debt between merchants. The requirements of proof have always been liberal in the commercial sector, as follows from Art. 109 of the French Commercial Code, which provides that acts between merchants may be proven by any means.

However, discussion has arisen as to the judicial admissibility of such electronic evidence in practice. As a matter of fact, a group of experts on matters of security in IT have challenged the reliability of such evi-

[28] Report entitled *Evolution des téléprocédures à destination des entreprises*, December 2000, p. 11.

[29] Law No. 2000-230 of 13 March 2000, adapting the law of evidence to Information Technology and relative to electronic signatures, JORF 14 March 2000, p. 3968, also available at: <http://www.adminet.com/jo/20000314/JUSX9900020L.html> (1 August 2001).

[30] Cass. com. 2 December 1997, bull. civ. 1997, 4th part, No. 315.

dence.[31] They argue that the condition in Art. 1316-1, which states that the author of a document should be fully identifiable, cannot be complied with when a document is sent electronically. The screen, which shows the number of an incoming call on the recipient's machine, can be diverted, so that the identification of the person calling is not revealed. These experts conclude that the evidentiary value of such an electronic evidence could be challenged in court because it would be impossible to assert the identity of the author using the present communications hardware provided by France Télécom. No case law, however, has so far confirmed this fear.

Be that as it may, it has not been definitely established whether these developments in civil law can be applied to the administrative sector. The Minister of Justice has given no specific indications regarding this so it can be presumed that the special circumstances, which apply to the administrative sector, ought to be maintained and be granted to administrative and to civil acts.[32] However, it seems more realistic to infer that the same developments will eventually characterise both the public and the private sector.

2.2.7 **Conclusion**

The general evolution of French law towards the admission of electronic evidence and of electronic signatures for the purposes of private law offers a sharp contrast to the absence of any similar initiative in the public sector. It seems reasonable to presume that the administrations will eventually 'go electronic', even when the legislator has remained surprisingly silent on the legal issues implied by the development of electronic communication between the administration and citizens. However, it is possible to anticipate that these issues will eventually be tackled on the same model as in private law. This is in line with the different policies that tend to develop electronic initiatives in this sector with the aim being to sim-

[31] The conclusions of the expert group are summed up in "Audit sur le degré probatoire de la qualité de l'auteur d'un écrit électronique", Bull. Act. Lamy Droit de l'Informatique, No. 130 G, November 2000, p. 123.

[32] In the latter sense, Chatillon, "Le régime français de la cryptologie: comment le déchiffrer?", special issue of the Bull. Act. Lamy Droit de l'Informatique, No. 129 F, October 2000, p. 13.

plify access by the citizen to administrative services. For instance, one of the ambitions of the legislator is to provide every administrative agent with an electronic mailbox to communicate with citizens. This might have an impact, however, on the law of administrative procedure.

2.3 Amending administrative procedure law to allow for electronic transactions

2.3.1 **General observations**

Strikingly, the long-awaited omnibus law on the information society, issued by the French cabinet on 13 June 2001, does not seize the opportunity to propose legislative changes in the administrative procedure law to allow for electronic communication. The draft Information Society Law (*Project de Loi sur la Société de l'Information*) comprises 50 articles, divided into five principal chapters: 1) assuring citizens' access to digital information; 2) assuring freedom in on-line communication; 3) promoting electronic commerce; 4) assuring the development of the digital network; 5) the prevention of cyber crime.[33]

Considering the absence of any project on the development of electronic "decisions" in France at the moment, there can be no discussion on the need to amend the administrative procedure law in order to adapt the latter to an electronic context. However, it is possible to anticipate that if this was the case, the following would apply.

Due to the fact that the French administrative system is essentially regulated by judge-made law, and more specifically by the decisions handed down by the Conseil d'Etat, a first possibility could be that the Conseil d'Etat itself would accept the electronic communication of administrative decisions. It has done so in relation to decisions communicated by telex, for instance, which is a frequent event in daily administrative practice.

In principle, the legislator might not be competent to acknowledge this point concerning administrative decisions taken by local authorities, in as much as it is only competent to determine "the fundamental principles of

---

33 Available at: <http://www.lsi.industrie.gouv.fr>.

the free administration of local authorities, of their competencies and of their resources" (Art. 34 of the Constitution). By default, the executive is competent for any other matters falling outside the scope of Art. 34 (Art. 37 of the Constitution). It seems difficult, considering the French understanding of the notion of "fundamental principle", that the acknowledgement of the possibility to communicate the decisions of local authorities electronically could be interpreted as one such fundamental principle. On the contrary, it seems plausible that such a decision is more likely to result from a decision taken by the Prime Minister, concerning the decisions taken by local as well as central administrative authorities.

This would be coherent with the regulatory developments on the online communication of administrative forms. For instance, the *circulaire* of 7 October 1999 (see above) provides that the forms necessary to carry out a formality or to claim a right against the administration should be provided free of charge through the official site <http://www.service-public.fr> or on one of the sites listed as a result of a decision by the Prime Minister.[34] Each ministry is responsible for the development of its Website and for the improvement of the corresponding services to the citizens. However, these individual initiatives should not contradict general decisions taken at the national level. As a result, any local initiative that corresponds to another national initiative should be exclusively transitory before it is generalised. As for the services of assistance to the fulfilment of administrative formalities, they should be carried out in cooperation with the competent interministerial mission. The objective, in this specific case, consists of ensuring that all investments are shared by the services concerned. Furthermore, this corresponds to the ambition to standardise on-line administrative forms as confirmed in the 2000 report on the evolution of *téléprocédures* in France, aiming at simplifying their use by citizens and companies.[35]

Otherwise said, for legal, organisational as well as financial reasons, it seems likely that the acknowledgement of electronic 'decisions' will

[34] For the present, the list has been set by an Arrêté of 16 June 2000, "portant habilitation des sites de l'Etat à diffuser des formulaires administratifs", J.O. 18 June 2000, No. 140, p. 9189, also at <http://www.legifrance.com> (1 August 2001).

[35] Report *Evolution des téléprocédures à destination des entreprises*, December 2000, p. 13.

eventually be taken at the general level, even if this does not preclude local or individual initiatives from being the first to be taken in practice. Practice shows that local authorities actually vary concerning electronic communication between themselves and citizens, but those authorities having decided to 'go electronic' usually do so in a very modern and proactive way. They often provide a good example to be followed by national authorities.

At present it is impossible to answer questions 3.3 and 3.4 considering the absence of any substantial development on electronic administrative procedures in France.

2.3.2 **Rules on safe electronic communication**

While the development of careful electronic communication has become increasingly important in the private sector in France, the issue has completely eluded the public sector. Development has been focused on electronic commerce rather than on the development of the electronic administration, despite many declarations in favour of the latter. As a result, there is no such thing as a requirement for safe electronic communication in French law concerning electronic 'decisions'.

A general rule does not exist for private law either. An important law is being prepared within the framework of the second step of the governmental action programme on the participation of France in the Information Society (PAGSI). The project "Law on the Information Society" (LSI) has as an essential goal which is to "look out for the security and the fairness of on-line transactions", which specifically implies "to ensure the transparency of networks" and "to institute the freedom to use means of cryptography".[36] However, this project does not mention anything about a requirement for safe electronic communications, and even less so in relation to administrative decisions.

2.3.2.1 *Electronic signatures*

The same sort of comment applies to the issue of electronic signatures. The European Directive on digital signatures was implemented in France

[36] A summary of the project is available at: <http://www.internet.gouv.fr/francais/textesref/pagsi2/synthese.htm> (1 August 2001).

through the same law which acknowledges the legal value of electronic evidence.[37] A project for a Decree has been made available for public discussion, which specifies under which conditions an electronic signature can be presumed to be reliable, in accordance with Art. 4 of Law No. 2000-230 of 13 March 2000.[38] The conditions for the reliability of electronic signatures were to be further defined in a decree.

The text of the Law basically follows the text of the Directive. However, it does not follow the possibility offered by Art. 3 (7) of the Directive to allow for additional requirements for digital signatures in the public sector. Generally speaking, the Law and the proposed Decree remain completely silent on the issue of digital signatures in the public sector. However, the 2000 report on the evolution of *téléprocédures* in France seems to take the point for granted that these regulatory developments concern the public sector, although the Law has formally only modified the Civil Code. The justification of the authors of the report on this point is that the issues at stake (computer security, etc.) are the same for the public sector as in electronic commerce transactions.[39]

The public consultation on the contents of the Decree was officially terminated in September 2000, but it took until 30 March 2001 before the final text of the Decree (no. 2001-272) was published.[40] Prior to the final publication of the Decree, its absence proved quite problematic in practice. In October 2000, the Court of Appeal of Besançon concluded that no official text recognised the validity of digital signatures in legal acts.[41] The case concerned a discussion on the validity of the "computer signa-

---

[37] Law No. 2000-230 of 13 March 2000, adapting the law of evidence to Information Technology and relative to electronic signatures, JORF 14 March 2000, p. 3968, see above.

[38] This article now completes Art. 1316-4 Para. 2 of the *Code civil*, which provides that electronic signatures have the same value as handwritten signatures from the moment that they comply with specific conditions set by a Decree taken after the opinion of the Council of State.

[39] Report entitled *Evolution des téléprocédures à destination des entreprises*, December 2000, p. 12.

[40] Premier décret d'application de la loi du 13 mars 2000 "portant adaptation du droit de la preuve aux technologies de l'information et relative à la signature éléctronique", No. 2001-272, 30 mars 2001.

[41] CA Besançon, chambre sociale, 20 October 2000, Sarl Chalets Boisson / Bernard G., available at: <http://www.legalis.net> (25 March 2001).

ture" ("*signature informatique*") of the defendant's counsel. The latter lost the case at first instance, and the individual's counsel initiated an appeal procedure on April 1st, 2000, to which the defendant appended a signature by using a specific code on his computer. The case was decided by determining whether this signature would render this procedural act of appeal invalid. The court considered that the litigated act had been established before the enactment of Law No. 2000-230 of 13 March 2000. As a result, the provisions of this Law were deemed inapplicable in this case, "all the more so as the Decree that is due to determine the conditions of reliability of the identification of the person appending such a signature to a legal act has not been published at the time of the oral debates in the court. As a result, the court is not in a position to appreciate the degree of reliability of the process involved in the case as against the text whose publication is expected." The key point in the decision of the court was that the identification of the person who has used this "computer signature" is very uncertain. Now, with the publication of the 30 March 2001 Decree, the status of digital signatures in France has become more certain, both in the private and in the public sector.

2.3.2.2 *Who specifies the requirements?*

Considering the absence of any discussion on the point, it is impossible to determine who will specify such requirements. However, it seems that if such were the case, the usual procedure would apply: a Law would determine the general rules of the requirements for safe electronic communication, while a Decree would determine the specific conditions under which this requirement could be fulfilled.

2.3.3 **Conclusion**

It is difficult, for the time being, to talk about the possible modification of French law as regards administrative procedure so as to adapt it to an electronic context, when no policy exists as yet to develop electronic "decisions" in administrative law. It is not certain, however, that the introduction of the possibility to issue such decisions electronically would actually represent a revolution for French administrative procedure law. It probably implies a change in the administration's mentality, as well as substantial financial investments.

2.4 Electronic communication versus traditional communication

2.4.1 Do differences remain between both forms of communication?

All the initiatives taken in relation to electronic documents and electronic signatures have resulted in the official recognition of the equivalence of both mediums. For instance, Art. 1613-3 of the *Code civil* now provides that "writing on an electronic medium has the same evidentiary value as writing on paper". Art. 1614-2 Para. 2 has the same impact in the field of electronic signatures. Therefore, the status of electronic documents and signatures in the light of civil law is that both mediums are, at least in theory, equivalent (as in the specific case illustrated by the decision of the Court of Appeal of Besançon mentioned above).

As far as administrative law is concerned, however, it is still hazardous to predict whether an administrative decision communicated electronically will have the same status as a decision communicated on paper, since no such procedure exists at the moment. It seems absurd if this were not the case. If we look at the initiatives which already exist to develop electronic communications between the administration and the citizen, *i.e.*, the unilateral forms of communication described above, some elements already tend to presume this equivalence. A few examples can be provided in this respect.

Art. 16 of Law 2000-231 of 12 April 2000 relative to citizens' rights concerning the administration, for instance, puts both mediums on a par concerning the communication of documents by citizens to the administration when this communication occurs within a given time period. In that case, the communication of these documents by post is deemed to be equivalent to their communication by means of telematics or computers, provided that the date when these documents were sent through the latter method can be determined.

Also, Art. 4 of Decree No. 99-68 of 2 February 1999 relative to the online communication of administrative forms provides that an administration may not refuse to examine requests submitted by users through forms printed from an official Internet site of the administration when these forms are duly signed and have not been altered from the information available on the site.

Finally, the 2000 report on the evolution of *téléprocédures* in France takes this point for granted on multiple occasions. This document, however, considers technical policies only, and does not specifically pay attention to the legal issues that may result from these technical choices.

At any rate, traditional and electronic means of access are considered to be complementary rather than competitive.

2.4.2 **Is it possible to discriminate between means of access?**

Here again, this point is difficult to answer under French administrative law.

Theoretically, one of the general principles of French administrative law is that of equality, meaning that all citizens as well as legal entities must be similarly treated by the administration. As a consequence, a decision by the administration to limit its communications to individuals or companies to on-line forms of communication might contradict this principle of equality, as it may operate in a discriminatory way.

Concerning the French practice of *téléprocédures*, however, the situation is ambivalent. The 2000 report on the evolution of *téléprocédures* in France takes it for granted that it is undesirable to discriminate between both forms of communication. *Téléprocédures* should firstly be competitive as against traditional forms of communication. In other words, it should always be up to the citizen to choose to use traditional forms of communication or a *téléprocédure* and not because of being able to have recourse to a materialised procedure. Secondly, the report argues, maintaining paper-based procedures should prevent citizens and companies from being excluded from participating in the use of *téléprocédures*.[42]

On the other hand, from May 1st, 2001, it is now compulsory for companies with a turnover of at least FF 100 million to make exclusive use of *téléprocédures* for the transmission of their company tax and their VAT returns, as well as for the payment of VAT.[43] This is one of the most important examples of *téléprocédures* available in France at the moment. As

---

[42] Report entitled *Evolution des téléprocédures à destination des entreprises*, December 2000, p. 6 and 11.

[43] The corresponding document of the Ministry of Economy and Finance is available at: <http://www.minefi.gouv.fr/minefi/entreprise/> (1 August 2001).

for companies which do not match this turnover requirement, they can opt for this system as well. It is not really surprising that such a procedure can be exclusively performed on-line by such companies. The risk of discrimination then seems to be quite small for companies with turnovers which are high enough to presume that they will avail themselves of the necessary computer systems to carry out this transmission.

The logic, therefore, seems to be that both mediums of communication should remain available when exclusion or unfairness might result from making electronic communication the exclusive means of communicating with the administration. On the other hand, if no such risk of exclusion applies, the rule may be to impose electronic communication as the exclusive method of communication. Here again, there is no decisive rule on this point.

2.4.3 **Conclusion**

As elsewhere in this national report, it is difficult to provide a decisive answer as to the relation between paper-based and electronic communication. Paper-based communication certainly remains the most important mode of communication for the French administration. However, there does not seem to be any fundamental legal obstacle to the development of electronic communication. An important issue in this respect, however, is the risk of detrimental discrimination, which could result from the imposition of electronic forms for communication only. This relates to the fact that, within Western European countries, France has clearly been lagging behind in terms of computer equipment and access to the Internet, although it is catching up with its neighbours.[44] The risk of discrimination, therefore, could be quite realistic, at least among individuals. However, it is expected that strong political incentives to develop Internet-related initiatives will eventually bear fruit, even in the conservative French administration.

---

[44] In December 2000, about 13% of households would have been connected to the Internet (source Médiamétrie).

2.5 General conclusion

The main finding of this national report is that, strictly speaking, the electronic communication of administrative decisions does not exist in France. The administration's only experience with electronic communication concerns downloading citizens' electronic forms and, possibly, the electronic communication of documents by the latter. It is therefore impossible, at the moment, to talk about the existence of electronic *exchanges* between the administration and the citizen.

However, various policies have been introduced over the past 3 years which indicate that this might change in the future. The eventual communication of administrative decisions by electronic means is never mentioned as an official goal. However, one of the aims of these policies is to provide all administrative agents with an e-mail account so that citizens are kept informed regarding the progress of their case. In the longer term, if this objective were to be achieved, the French administration would be a step nearer to communicating its decisions electronically.

The legal framework involving such a communication would probably require some clarification. The existing rules on the communication of administrative decisions and the corresponding formalities of these acts are not, as such, inadequate in an electronic dimension. However, it would be desirable for some points to be clarified. For instance, the absence of official complementarity between private and public law formally prevents the new civil rules on electronic evidence and electronic signatures from applying to the administrative sector as a matter of course. It would be absurd, on the other hand, to introduce such changes in the private sector while refusing to apply them in the public sector. It would be desirable, as a consequence, that such ambiguities should be cleared.

The main conclusion of this report, however, is not of a legal nature. The absence of any substantive discussion on the development of electronic decisions in the French administration is in fact quite emblematic of its specific position. An appropriate legal framework is but the second step to implement the electronic taking of administrative decisions. The first necessary step is a strong political will to commit administrative agents to adapt to modern changes and technology. Only such a will can overcome the difficulty for the French administration to consider the citizen as a 'client' rather than as a person in dependence. It is quite a new concept here that the improvement of the position of citizens should be the driving force of administrative concerns. In this respect, the French administration, although it is trying to improve its relations with citizens, is still far from achieving the official goals it has set out in general policies.

Chapter 3
GERMANY

Chapter 3
GERMANY

3.1 Introduction

Until now electronic communications have not yet been the subject of specific legal stipulations except for two state-laws that have no practical relevance and are described below. Consequently, at present, electronic communications are governed by general rules that sometimes allow the integration of a new means of communication by interpretation and sometimes become an impediment when used. There are plenty of legislative actions planned which will, in the very near future, result in such stipulations and internal Draft Regulations (see below 3.5)[1].

However, administrative communication and administrative procedure is exempted from formalities to a large degree and is therefore generally open to electronic communications. § 10 VwVfG (Federal Public Administration Act, cf. Section 3.2.1 for details) explicitly states that administrative procedures are not subject to formal requirements unless otherwise stipulated and requires simple, functional and efficient execution. Public administration may use its own discretion with respect to the appropriate procedure for an individual case and electronic communications can be an appropriate means in many cases.[2] Even in the case of a formal requirement concerning a final administrative decision, all the other steps in the procedure allow electronic communications.[3]

---

[1] For examples and a sample of those internal Draft Regulations see www.staedtetag.de/mitgliederservice/dez8/umfrage_email/index.html.

[2] Cf. Holznagel, B., Krahn, C. & Werthmann; C.: Electronic Government auf kommunaler Ebene – Die Zulässigkeit von Transaktionsdiensten im Internet, Deutsches Verwaltungsblatt (DVBl.) 1999, p. 1481.

[3] Cf. Rosenbach, H.J.: Verfahrensrechtliche Rahmenbedingungen für den Einsatz der elektronischen Datenverarbeitung in der Verwaltung, Nordrhein-Westfälische Verwaltungsblätter (NWVBl.) 1997, p. 123 concerning an administrative act ("Verwaltungsakt") in writing.

Even though this is the general rule, there are several thousand provisions which explicitly or implicitly require paper-based communication or a handwritten signature.[4] Most scholars assume that every provision in administrative law, which requires communication in writing, excludes electronic communications. However, referring inter alia to the case law on the use of modern means of communication in e.g. Civil Procedure Law (which will be reported in 2.5), it has also been stated that a functional interpretation of the respective provision is necessary and very often leads to different results, especially concerning applications. [5] But, so far, internal Draft Regulations often prohibit the use of e-mail communication when written communication or transmission of personal data[6] is necessary. They also oblige public out the irregularity in form.[7]

There are also several possible interpretations with regard to the conditions under which terms a final formal decision, regulating an individual case in the field of administrative law (Verwaltungsakt) can be issued electronically. Since § 37 sub. 2 VwVfG states that an administrative act can be issued "in writing, by word of mouth or by other means", undoubtedly it is admissible, at least as an administrative act "by other means". However, opinions differ as to whether it could be considered as an electronic act "in writing" so that it also meets the more formal requirements, which are stated in various statutes. While some commentators reject this

---

[4] Cf. Krahn, C., Stenner, D. & Werthmann, C.: *Kommunen und Multimedia*, Münster: 1999, p. 62; Roßnagel, A.: Die digitale Signatur in der öffentlichen Verwaltung, in: Kubicek, H. et al.: *Multimedia@Verwaltung*, Heidelberg: 1999, p. 163; Holznagel, B., Krahn, C. & Werthmann, C.: Electronic Government auf kommunaler Ebene – Die Zulässigkeit von Transaktionsdiensten im Internet, Deutsches Verwaltungsblatt (DVBl.) 1999, p. 1481; Deutscher Städtetag (ed.), Digitale Signatur auf der Basis multifunktionaler Chipkarten, Köln: 1999, p. 47f; Klein, M. & Stolz, U.: Rechtsfragen zum Internet für die Städte, der städtetag 1997, p. 390, p. 393ff.

[5] Eifert, M.: Online-Verwaltung und Schriftform im Verwaltungsrecht, in: Eifert, M. (ed.), Digitale Signaturen, Beilage 2 zu Heft 10/2000 Kommunikation und Recht (K&R), p. 11ff. An application which has been sent by computerfax meets the requirement of "Application in writing" of § 64 VwVfG also according to Obermayer-Seegmüller, § 64, Rn 15ff.

[6] Cf. Empfehlung für die Erprobungsphase des E-mail Systems (elektronische Post) und der elektronischen Informationsordner in der bremischen Verwaltung of August 11 1998, 2.1.

[7] Cf. Musterdienstanweisung des bayrischen Städtetages of 12/1999, 3.

position[8], most of them embrace it[9] if the recipient can easily print out the data.[10]

In view of these legal impediments and uncertainties and in order to gain experience regarding on-line administration in cases of formal requirements, the states of Bremen[11] and Baden-Württemberg[12] have enacted laws to allow electronic communications using a digital signature. According to the German Digital Signature Law, digital signatures can be used in listed areas and under special conditions even if state law generally requires communication in writing. However, neither specific cases, nor specific conditions have been determined at a statutory level. Instead the laws delegate power to the relevant minister to lay down the rules and regulations (Rechtsverordnung). In the light of current legislative developments (see below 3.1.3) no rule has so far been enacted and the laws will probably soon be rendered superfluous.

3.1.1 Present practice

There is neither empirical data available to determine to what extent the administration uses an electronic means of communication nor are there studies on how electronic communications are actually organised or ex-

---

[8] Cf. Knack, *Verwaltungsverfahrensgesetz*, Kommentar, 7th ed. Köln 2000, § 37, Rn. 20; Rosenbach, H.J.: Elektronische Datenverarbeitung und das Verwaltungsverfahrensgesetz, NVwBl. 1997, p. 328.

[9] Cf. Redeker, NVwZ 1986, 545, 546f; Eifert, Beilage 2 zu Heft 10/2000, 11. 19; Schmitz, H.: Moderner Staat – Modernes Verwaltungsverfahrensrecht, Neue Zeitschrift für Verwaltungsrecht (NVwZ) 2000, p. 1244; Polomski, R.: *Der automatisierte Verwaltungsakt*, Berlin 1993, p. 178ff.

[10] Kopp, F. & Ramsauer, U.: *Verwaltungsverfahrensgesetz*, 7th ed. München 2000, § 37, Rn 28; Holznagel, B., Krahn, C. & Werthmann, C.: Electronic Government auf kommunaler Ebene – Die Zulässigkeit von Transaktionsdiensten im Internet, Deutsches Verwaltungsblatt (DVBl.) 1999, p. 1477ff; Groß, T.: Öffentliche Verwaltung im Internet, Die Öffentliche Verwaltung (DÖV) 2001, p. 162; inconsistent Stelkens, Bonk & Sachs: *Verwaltungsverfahrensgesetz*, 5th ed. München 1998, § 37, Rn 51 and Rn 64.

[11] Bremisches Gesetz zur Erprobung der digitalen Signatur in der Verwaltung, Gesetzblatt der Freien Hansestadt Bremen vom 14. Juni 1999, p. 138f.

[12] Gesetz zur Erprobung elektronischer Bürgerdienste unter Verwendung der digitalen Signatur (e-Bürgerdienste-Gesetz), Gesetzblatt des Landes Baden-Württemberg vom 31. July 2000, p. 536f. (cf. also reasons in Drucksache 12/ 5240 des Landtags Baden-Württemberg v. 31.5.2000, p. 1ff).

ecuted (for internal Draft Regulations see below 3.3.5). Therefore, only a brief overview of the electronic communications services (in a broad sense) offered by public administration to date can be given. Undoubtedly, the widespread and rapid development towards Electronic Government increases the pressure on the legislator to provide legal amendments, where necessary, and fuels the legal developments described below (3.3).

All observers agree upon the fact that electronic communication methods are well used as a means to obtain information on e.g. homepages indicating agencies' office hours, lists of documents to be submitted, and downloading forms. Electronic communications are occasionally but rarely systematically used as a means of communication (e.g. e-mail inquiries)[13] and are just beginning to be more broadly used for electronic transactions (e.g. filing a suit).[14] Apart from financial restrictions, concerns about the authenticity and integrity of communication as well as privacy issues and general uncertainty about the legal situation are seen as impediments to a more widespread use.[15]

Due to the federal system (see below 3.2.1), most interactions between citizens and public administration take place at a local or regional level, making it very difficult to present an overview.[16] Nevertheless, some

---

[13] According to a representative survey (the interviewees were mayors of cities with more than 50,000 residents), which had been commissioned by the Bertelsmann Foundation, 83% of local governments have a central e-mail address for its public administration and in 75% also the individual public officials can be reached by e-mail. (Friedrichs, S. (ed.), *Virtuelle Medien als Chance für die Stadt der Zukunft*, Bonn 2000, table 1). There are no figures on the use of e-mail, however.

[14] Kubicek, H. et al.: Interaktive Rathäuser in Deutschland, Bericht Nr. X/98, Universität Bremen, Fachbereich Mathematik und Informatik, 1998; Masser, K. & Gerhards, R.: Kommunen im WEB-Test, Die innovative Verwaltung 1997, p. 24ff; Masser, K. & Gerhards, R.: Speyerer Web-Test 1998, Verwaltung und Management 1999, p. 48ff.; Bütow, S. & Floeting, H.: *Elektronische Stadt- und Wirtschaftsinformationssysteme in den deutschen Städten*, Stuttgart 1999.

[15] A survey, commissioned by the Bertelsmann Foundation, has shown that 46% of the responding mayors consider 'the problem of digital signature' a major impediment (Friedrichs, S. (ed.): *Virtuelle Medien als Chance für die Stadt der Zukunft*, Bonn 2000, p. 34); cf. also Klein, M. & Stolz, U.: Rechtsfragen zum Internet für die Städte, der städtetag 1997, p. 396; Deutscher Städtetag, Schritte auf dem Weg zum digitalen Rathaus, Köln 2000, p. 14ff.

[16] For more detailed information on action programmes cf. <http://www.bmwi-info2000.de/glob_invent_d/index_a.htm> (19 August 2001).

prominent services and agencies can be listed which are mainly involved in transaction services and which are at least attempting to use the digital signature.

At the federal level, current on-line services for citizens consist of job seeking services[17], dealing with grants for student scholarships[18], income tax forms[19], a distribution system for geographical data[20] and a statistics shop[21]. On-line services for companies include company information service for job offers[22], tax identification number requests[23], an information system for project funding[24], funding of projects in the former DDR states[25] and, last but not least, an on-line notification system for the intra-commerce statistics-w3stat[26].

At the state level, apart from typical information services and electronic communications via e-mail, at least three other developments are worth mentioning. Almost all states are about to offer and some states already do offer on-line access to Land Registers.[27] Hamburg has launched a pilot project with a first instance fiscal court, which makes it possible to file a suit electronically[28] (for problems with respect to formal requirements see below 3.2.3.). Some universities already offer various administrative services ranging from registration for written examinations to notification of a change of address.[29] Furthermore, Bremen also offers the possibility of ordering and paying on-line for personal registration certificates.[30]

---

17 Cf. <http://www.arbeitsamt.de> (19 August 2001).

18 <http://www.bva.bund.de/aufgaben/bafoeg> (19 August 2001).

19 <http://www.elsterformular.de> (19 August 2001).

20 <http://www.geodatenzentrum.de> (19 August 2001).

21 <http://www.statistik-bund.de/shop> (20 August 2001).

22 <http://www.arbeitsamt.de> (20 August 2001).

23 <http://www.bff-online.de> (20 August 2001).

24 <http://www.kp.dlr.de/profi> (20 August 2001).

25 <http://www.fhms.de> (20 August 2001).

26 <http://w3stat.statistik-bund.de> (20 August 2001).

27 E.g. <http://justiz.baden-wuerttemberg.de/Egb-web/> (20 August 2001).

28 For further information see poststelle@fg.justiz.hamburg.de.

29 Cf. <http://www.signatur.uni-bremen.de> (20 August 2001).

30 <http://www.bremer-online-service.de> (20 August 2001).

Again on a local level, one can observe a widespread tendency towards electronic government.[31] For example, there are three pilot projects supported by federal subsidies within the framework of the Media@Komm initiative.[32] At present electronic communications often include the downloading of forms etc. Several local governments have also set up some personal electronic communications even though a comprehensive approach (e.g. Karlsruhe) is still an exception.[33] The implementation of transaction services is still in the early stages. Nevertheless, there are services available ranging from ordering a rubbish bin, applying for a specific licence plate (e.g. Karlsruhe), obtaining a resident's parking permit (Nuremberg) or for requesting information about resident registrations (e.g. Karlsruhe, Hagen).[34]

3.1.2 Overview of current legislative developments

As soon as the potential of electronic communications for public administration became apparent a discussion started concerning the appropriate legal framework. This discussion focused primarily on how the numerous statutory provisions requiring communication in writing should be amended. Due to the uncertainties in dealing with inexperienced forms of electronic communications, scholars and politicians have only recently decided to set up limited experiments using digital signatures,[35] which

[31] According to a survey, commissioned by the Bertelsmann Foundation, 74% of all cities with more than 50,000 residents have already started implementing Electronic Government conceptions (Friedrichs, S. (ed.): *Virtuelle Medien als Chance für die Stadt der Zukunft*, Bonn 2000, p. 22).

[32] See Deutscher Städtetag, Schritte auf dem Weg zum digitalen Rathaus, Köln 2000, p. 14ff.; cf. for information about Media@Komm: <http://www.mediakomm.net> (20 August 2001) and a brief description in Cable&Wireless: E-Government, making the connection, The second series of studies of online government, 2000, p. 19ff. For a list of potential internet applications at the local level see Deutscher Städtetag (ed.), Digitale Signatur auf der Basis multifunktionaler Chipkarten, Köln 1999, Attachment 3; more generally Reinermann, H.: *Der öffentliche Sektor im Internet*, Speyer 2000, p. 70ff.

[33] Kubicek, H. et al.: Interaktive Rathäuser in Deutschland, Bericht Nr. X/98, Universität Bremen, Fachbereich Mathematik und Informatik, 1998, p. 165f.

[34] Cf. <http://www.karlsruhe.de/Service/Formulare/index-a-z.htm> (20 August 2001) & <http://www.verkehrsinfo.nuernberg.de/zugang_index.htm> (20 August 2001).

[35] Rat für Forschung, Technologie und Innovation, Informationsgesellschaft – Chancen, Innovationen und Herausforderungen, Bonn 1995, E 26; Roßnagel, Alexander:

have resulted in the previously mentioned (3.1.1) state-laws. Even if it must be admitted that there are uncertainties, some arrangements are required to enable a constant learning process rather than a reluctant step-by-step approach.[36] It is understandable that current legislative developments no longer pursue this approach but prefer to aim at a comprehensive adaptation of all kinds of statutes to the demands of (modern) electronic communications.

There are two major proposals for laws, one, which amends Civil Laws, and the other, which amends administrative laws through a co-ordinated effort by the federal level and the states. The proposal of an Amending Act concerning Civil Laws (Entwurf eines Gesetzes zur Anpassung der Formvorschriften des Privatrechts und anderer Vorschriften an den modernen Rechtsgeschäftsverkehr)[37] aims at introducing an "electronic form" into Civil Law, which would be an equivalent to the statutory written form unless otherwise stated (§ 126a par. 1 BGB-E). The "electronic form" would require a qualified digital signature according to the recently revised German signature law. Furthermore, it would also introduce a so-called "text form" which is not treated as an equivalent to a statutory written form and can basically suffice with an e-mail (§ 126b BGB-E). All provisions requiring a written form until now have been examined and will be amended to ban an electronic form or to allow even "text form" whenever the default equivalent "electronic form" is considered inappropriate.

The proposed amendments to administrative laws (see as a first draft Entwurf eines Gesetzes zur Anpassung des Verwaltungsverfahrensrechts

---

Die digitale Signatur in der öffentlichen Verwaltung, in: Kubicek, Herbert et al.: *Multimedia@Verwaltung*, Heidelberg 1999, p. 171; Holznagel, B., Krahn, C. & Werthmann, C.: Electronic Government auf kommunaler Ebene – Die Zulässigkeit von Transaktionsdiensten im Internet, Deutsches Verwaltungsblatt (DVBl.) 1999, p. 1486f.; Krahn, C., Stenner D. & Werthmann, C.: *Kommunen und Multimedia*, Münster 1999, p. 70f.

[36] Eifert, M. & Schreiber, L.: Elektronische Signatur und der Zugang zur Verwaltung, Multimedia und Recht (MMR) 2000, p. 340ff.

[37] <http://www.bmj.de> (20 August 2001). For a brief summary see Roßnagel, A.: Auf dem Weg zu neuen Signaturregelungen, Multimedia und Recht (MMR) 2000, p. 457ff.

an die moderne elektronische Kommunikation[38], now the Entwurf eines Dritten Gesetzes zur Änderung verwaltungsverfahrensrechtlicher Vorschriften of July 16th , 2001[39]) have been elaborated by a joint commission of federal and state officials especially with respect to the amendments of the Public Administration Acts. Its goal is to establish a number of basic rules concerning electronic communications as well as to amend the statutory written form. Further details will be explained below (section 3.3). The approach will be similar to that of civil law and is supposed to be supplemented by a revision of all other provisions in administrative law which impede the on-line services of the public administration. This work is still in progress, though, and the only presented drafts as yet concern the federal Public Administration Act (VwVfG), the similar provisions concerning social security and tax procedures (Abgabenordnung and Sozialgesetzbuch, respectively) and numerous specific tax laws. As far as formal requirements as stated in the internal Draft Regulations (Verwaltungsvorschriften) are concerned, many of them are being revised at the moment. In the area of social security regulation, for instance, the internal guideline already determines that according to the digital signature law a digital signature can be used instead of a handwritten signature (§ 41 SRVwV).[40]

---

[38] <http://www.im.nrw.de> (20 August 2001). For a summary see Rosenbach, H.-J.: Erläuterungen und Anmerkungen zum Entwurf eines Gesetzes zur Änderung des Verwaltungsverfahrensgesetzes, Deutsches Verwaltungsblatt (DVBl.) 2001, p. 332ff.; more comprehensive Roßnagel, DÖV 2001, 221ff.; cf. Also Schmitz, H.: Moderner Staat – Modernes Verwaltungsverfahrensrecht, Neue Zeitschrift für Verwaltungsrecht (NVwZ) 2000, p. 1243f.

[39] <http://www.staat-modern.de/projekte/beschreib/Daten/g_verwaltungsverfahren.pdf>.

[40] Allgemeine Verwaltungsvorschrift über das Rechnungswesen on der Sozialversicherung (SRVwV) of August 3rd , 1998 as amended; cf. Bitzer, F. & Brisch, K.M.: *Digitale Signatur*, Berlin 1999, p. 142.

3.2 Legal requirements and impediments for the electronic communications of the public administration

3.2.1 General characteristics of the administrative system

The Federal Republic of Germany, as the name already indicates, is a federal system. This system is divided into a federal level and a state level (Länder). The local level (Gemeinden, Städte) forms part of the states. However, the right of local self-government is guaranteed by the Basic Law (Art. 28 para. 2 GG).[41]

The federal system, including the right of local self-government, entails a complex setting of spheres of competences concerning legislative and administrative powers that can only be roughly outlined.[42]

Firstly, Art. 30 GG provides the basic rule according to which the states are competent in all matters unless the Basic Law states or allows a regulation to the contrary. With respect to legislative powers, however, the situation is in fact the opposite, primarily based on so-called concurrent federal legislation which presupposes a need for regulation at a federal level (Art. 72 para. 2 GG). It encompasses inter alia civil law, the law of procedure (concerning all kinds of courts) and the law of economic affairs (Art. 74 para. 1 GG). In addition, the legal framework of a number of matters, such as the registration of residents, can be determined by federal law (Art. 75 GG).

The remaining competence of the states is much stronger in the field of administration. The states, of course, implement their own laws, but the vast majority of federal laws are also implemented by the states (cf. Arts. 83-91 GG). The states, in turn, have established various levels of administrative bodies, the most important of which is the administration at the re-

[41] In addition, it is also guaranteed by most state constitutions (cf. Sachs-Nierhaus, Art. 28, Rn 29ff.). There is also a regional level, complementing the local level (Landkreise) with respect to affairs that affect several municipalities. Its right to self-government is also guaranteed, even though the state has more competence to interfere than it has with respect to the local level (Sachs-Nierhaus, Art. 28, Rn 62ff.).

[42] For a still pertinent overview of the respective Basic Law clauses in English see Lerche, P.: Principles of German Federalism, in: Kirchhof, P. & Kommers, D.P. (ed.), *Germany and Its Basic Law*, Baden-Baden 1993, p. 75ff.

gional (Landkreise) and the local (Gemeinden, Städte) level.[43] Many duties that are assigned to state administration have been delegated to the local administrative bodies for self-administration, thereby avoiding the establishment of state administration at this level and fostering citizen-oriented service delivery.[44] Therefore, local authorities are in charge of most government services and have had a major influence on the development of e-Government.

The law on administrative procedure is a particularly complex field. The procedure is partly regulated in various specific laws (Fachgesetze) or statutory rules (Rechtsverordnungen) which govern areas of regulation either by federal or by state law.[45] These laws comprise, in particular, many provisions on the formal requirements of applications or permits and participation by third parties, the general public and various administrative agencies' laws. For example, the Bundesimmissionsschutzrecht (Federal Clean Air Act) and the Bauordnungen (state laws on building projects), both require applications and permits in writing as well as the participation of various parties. If there are no specific regulations, in the vast majority of cases the provisions of the respective federal or state General Public Administration Act (VwVfG) applies.[46] These acts stipulate the general requirements of the different types of final administrative action (Handlungsformen), especially the "Verwaltungsakt" (see above 3.1.1.) and contracts governed by administrative law (öffentlich-rechtlicher Vertrag). The scope of application of these various acts depends on the respective acting authority and the function exercised by it. The federal VwVfG governs all procedures by federal authorities while most proce-

---

[43] For a description of state and local administration see Maurer, H.: *Allgemeines Verwaltungsrecht*, 11th ed. München 1997, § 21ff.; Rudolf, W.: Verwaltungsorganisation, in: Badura, P. et al., *Allgemeines Verwaltungsrecht*, 11th ed. Berlin 1998, p. 771ff., § 53.

[44] Delegated competence makes up 80% of the duties of local administration (Knemeyer, F.-L.: *Bayrisches Kommunalrecht*, 10th ed. Stuttgart 2000, Rn 161).

[45] Many provisions that are relevant to the procedure can also be found in the statutory rules of the states which govern the implementation of laws (Durchführungsverordnungen).

[46] For details on the scope of application of the APAs see Badura P.: Das Verwaltungsverfahren, in: Badura, P. et al., *Allgemeines Verwaltungsrecht*, 11th ed. Berlin 1998, § 33, Rn 12ff.; Stelkens, U., Bonk, H.J. & Sachs, M.: *Verwaltungsverfahrensgesetz*, 5th ed. München 1998, §§ 1, 2.

dures by state or local authorities are governed by the respective state VwVfG. However, due to a co-ordinated approach, there are no major differences between the various VwVfG. This text always refers to the federal VwVfG unless otherwise indicated.

3.2.2 Interplay between administrative law and civil law

For a long time the German legal system, public law and civil law have been considered separately as a matter of principle. Recently, more and more scholars hold the view that these are two parts of the legal system that are interrelated and complement each other.[47] In current laws, however, the division is still important. The VwVfGs, for instance, only apply to the public law actions of administrations (§ 1 Abs. 1 VwVfG).

In this context, two kinds of relationships between administrative and civil law seem to be of particular interest. Civil law stipulations can sometimes be applied in the framework of public law and they can influence the interpretation of public law.[48] Civil law is applicable mutatis mutandis wherever there is a gap in public law regulations that can be appropriately filled by resorting to civil law rules. This is particularly the case with respect to the law of obligations.[49] However, it is not the case regarding the formal legal requirements of "written declarations" (Schriftform).[50] I will come back to this point later. Civil law can also be "applied" to express general rules of the legal system that can also be applied in a public law context, e.g. the rule of good faith. This might be relevant under specific circumstances in communications, whether they are traditional or elec-

[47] See Hoffmann-Riem, W.: Reform des Allgemeinen Verwaltungsrechts: Vorüberlegungen, Deutsches Verwaltungsblatt (DVBl.) 1994, p. 1384; Hoffmann-Riem, W., Schmidt-Aßmann, E. (ed.): *Öffentliches Recht und Privatrecht als wechselseitige Auffangordnungen*, Baden-Baden 1996.

[48] See generally Maurer, Hartmut: *Allgemeines Verwaltungsrecht*, 11th ed. München 1997, § 3, Rn 28ff.; Ehlers, D.: Verwaltung und Verwaltungsrecht im demokratischen und sozialen Rechtsstaat, in: Badura, P. et al., *Allgemeines Verwaltungsrecht*, 11th ed. Berlin 1998, § 2 Rn 62ff.

[49] See e.g. BVerwGE 71, 85, 87ff. concerning a set-off.

[50] See Eifert, M.: Online-Verwaltung und Schriftform im Verwaltungsrecht, in: Eifert, M. (ed.), *Digitale Signaturen*, Beilage 2 zu Heft 10/2000 Kommunikation und Recht (K&R), p. 12; BVerwGE 42, 189, 192; Badura, P.: Die Form des Verwaltungsaktes, in: Festschrift Boorberg-Verlag 1977, p. 212f.

tronic. Defined by statute is the application of civil procedure law in administrative litigation. § 173 VwGO (regulation governing administrative court proceedings) stipulates that the ZPO (Code of civil procedure) is to be applied mutatis mutandis subsidiary to the VwGO unless the difference between the proceedings renders this inappropriate.

As already implied, the general division between civil and public law does not mean that public administration is necessarily governed by public law. If there are no regulations banning the use of civil law, the administration can also choose to act according to civil law (e.g. concluding a contract according to Civil Law) as long as it respects basic constitutional principles including human rights.[51] Public administration does even necessarily fall within the scope of civil law once it has chosen an organisational form according to Civil Law (e.g. a corporation with limited liability). Thus, Civil Law rules, e.g. some of the educational services (e.g. Volkshochschule), can be relevant in the field of access to facilities and subsidies.

3.2.3 **Requirements of administrative law relevant for electronic communications**

Since electronic communications differ from other forms of communication, primarily with respect to its electronic form, all administrative law requirements that implicitly or explicitly determine a formal mode of communication become problematic.[52]

---

[51] BVerwG DVBl. 1970, 735; BVerwGE 92, 56; BGHZ 91, 84, 86; Ehlers, D.: Verwaltung und Verwaltungsrecht im demokratischen und sozialen Rechtsstaat, in: Badura, P. et al., *Allgemeines Verwaltungsrecht*, 11th ed. Berlin 1998, § 2, Rn 31ff., 70ff.; Maurer, H.: *Allgemeines Verwaltungsrecht*, 11th ed. München 1997, § 3 Rn 6ff.; Stelkens, U., Bonk, H.J. & Sachs, M.: *Verwaltungsverfahrensgesetz*, 5th ed. München 1998, § 1 Rn 84f., 96ff.

[52] Cf. for different levels of formal requirements relevant for electronic communications see also Dix, A.: Digital Signaturen im Verwaltungsverfahren: Besondere Sicherheitsanforderungen erforderlich?, in: Eifert, M. (ed.), *Digitale Signaturen*, Beilage 2 zu Heft 10/2000 Kommunikation und Recht (K&R), p. 20 and some remarks in Holznagel, B. & Krahn, C. & Werthmann, C.: Electronic Government auf kommunaler Ebene – Die Zulässigkeit von Transaktionsdiensten im Internet, Deutsches Verwaltungsblatt (DVBl.) 1999, p. 1484.

The first thing to point out is that administrative procedures generally do not require a specific form (see above 3.1.1). Nonetheless, there are many cases in which the written form is required.

Many specific laws (Fachgesetze) require a written form for applications or final formal decisions, regulating individual cases in the field of administrative law (Verwaltungsakt).[53] Even if there is no specific provision concerning the form of a Verwaltungsakt so that the general provision of the respective VwVfG applies according to which a "Verwaltungsakt" can be issued "in writing, by word of mouth or by other means" (§ 37 para. 2 VwVfG), there may be an unwritten rule that implies some type of requirement. Most commentators (and many internal Draft Regulations) do demand the written form in all matters that require a precise description of the regulatory content[54], an exigency which can be derived from principles of due process.

In some formal administrative procedures (e.g. permits for major building projects, § 74 para. 4 VwVfG, an administrative decision about a formal objection concerning a "Verwaltungsakt", § 73 para. 3 VwGO) a "Verwaltungsakt" has to be delivered in a specific form (Zustellung). The laws, which implicitly govern this procedure, require a paper document to be issued.[55]

Even more restrictive are provisions that require the physical presence of the parties. This is relevant in many cases in which a certification has to be handed over (e.g. appointment as a public official, § 6 para. 2 BBG) or the identity of an applicant needs to be verified (e.g. notice of taking residence for the purpose of registration).

The provisions which require the submission of specific documents are also relevant to electronic communications. According to the general dis-

[53] The same is true for the so-called "formal procedure" according to the VwVfG (cf. §§ 64, 69 Para. 2 VwVfG), which is applicable only if a specific statute explicitly refers to it (which is seldom the case).

[54] Badura, P., Das Verwaltungsverfahren, in: Badura, P. et al., *Allgemeines Verwaltungsrecht*, 11th ed. Berlin 1998, § 38, Rn 5; Stelkens, U., Bonk, H.J. & Sachs, M.: *Verwaltungsverfahrensgesetz*, 5th ed. München 1998, § 37, Rn 35; cf. also VGH München DVBl. 1978, 181, 183.

[55] Cf. Polomski, R.M.: *Der automatisierte Verwaltungsakt*, Berlin 1993, S. 183ff.; for a brief description of the general principles of "Zustellung" see Badura, P.: Das Verwaltungsverfahren, in: Badura, P. et al., *Allgemeines Verwaltungsrecht*, 11th ed. Berlin 1998, § 38, Rn 22ff.

cretion in procedural matters (see above 3.1.1), the administration is not generally reluctant to accept scanned documents. However, if there are doubts with respect to the authenticity or integrity of the documents as well as in cases of specific significance, the administration has to require the original document.[56]

Because of the lack of any statutory regulations on electronic communications, the public administration is neither obliged to use it itself, nor to open electronic access to citizens, even though one might discuss whether the widespread use of means of communications may at some point result in a duty for the public administration to adopt new channels of communication.[57] But if the public administration uses electronic communications in an individual administrative procedure or lists an e-mail account in public indexes or on the stationery, it is bound to observe this channel in the individual procedure and in general.[58] As a general matter, in electronic communications, everyone is responsible for the proper state of electronic devices within his own sphere.[59]

3.2.4 **Problems under the present administrative law system in the light of electronic communications**

The main problems under the present administrative law system result

---

[56] Cf. Stelkens/Bonk/Sachs-Stelkens/Schmitz, § 22, Rn 32; Eifert, M.: Online-Verwaltung und Schriftform im Verwaltungsrecht, in: Eifert, M. (ed.), *Digitale Signaturen*, Beilage 2 zu Heft 10/2000 Kommunikation und Recht (K&R), p. 18.

[57] Cf. Eifert, M. & Schreiber, L.: Elektronische Signatur und der Zugang zur Verwaltung, Multimedia und Recht (MMR) 2000, p. 345; Stelkens, Bonk, Sachs-Stelkens & Kallerhof, § 24, Rn 83; rather prudent Stelkens, Bonk, Sachs-Stelkens & Schmitz, § 22, Rn. 32.

[58] Cf. Knack, *Verwaltungsverfahrensgesetz*, Kommentar, 7th ed. Köln 2000, § 22, 4.2; Eifert, M. & Schreiber, L.: Elektronische Signatur und der Zugang zur Verwaltung, Multimedia und Recht (MMR) 2000, p. 346; Rosenbach, H.J.: Verfahrensrechtliche Rahmenbedingungen für den Einsatz der elektronischen Datenverarbeitung in der Verwaltung, Nordrhein-Westfälische Verwaltungsblätter (NWVBl.) 1997, p. 122. The recently revised rules of procedure of the Federal Government stipulate that electronically received documents have to be considered as regular receipt (§ 13 GGO; cf. Zypries, B. & Peters, C.: Eine neue Geschäftsordnung für die Bundesministerien, Zeitschrift für Gesetzgebung (ZG) 2000, p. 321f.) For other internal Draft Regulations see below 3.5.

[59] Cf. BVerwG NJW 1991, 1193; VG Frankfurt, NJW 1990, 339; Stelkens, Bonk, Sachs-Stelkens-Kallerhof, § 24, Rn 64.

from the formal requirements that have been described above (3.2.3), focusing on the requirements of written communication (Schriftform). As a matter of fact, there are at least 3,800 provisions in administrative law[60], distributed amongst all levels of legislative competence with the lion's share being state legislation, that require written communication. Even though not all of them restrict communication to this form and even though – contrary to the point of view of most commentators – this formal requirement does not necessarily ban electronic communications but should be interpreted from a functional point of view as regards each provision,[61] there is at least an enormous incertitude concerning the admissibility of electronic communications in these fields.

As far as physical presence and the handing over of certificates are concerned, there are less cases that impede on-line government since a number of cases fall within an area that is not suited to on-line services anyway. At least physical presence for registration as a resident and the handing over of some "Verwaltungsakte" prevent on-line services that could be very beneficial for citizens.

There are some other areas in which electronic communication does not necessarily require statutory amendments even though legislative action is considered to be helpful by some commentators. This concerns regulations on the secure and uniform handling and archiving of electronic files (elektronische Akte) as well as additional technical and organisational precautions in order to protect privacy and official secrets.[62] With regard to the problems of the long-term archiving of digital information which also affect freedom of information, it should be possible to retain paper-based files parallel to digital files at least for files of special importance until the problems will have been appropriately

---

[60] Deutscher Städtetag (ed.), Digitale Signatur auf der Basis multifunktionaler Chipkarten, Köln 1999, p. 47f.; Bieser, W. & Kersten, H.: *Elektronisch unterschreiben*, 2nd ed. Heidelberg 1999, S. 37. The number has probably been generated by a search in the major database on German law ('juris'). It might contain some provisions of civil law, but, on the other hand, presumably misses numerous provisions of local law.

[61] For references see above 1.1.

[62] Roßnagel, A.: Die digitale Signatur in der öffentlichen Verwaltung, in: Kubicek, H. et al.: *Multimedia@Verwaltung*, Heidelberg 1999, p. 162ff.; Schreiber, L.: Verwaltung going digit@l, in: Eifert, M. (ed.), *Digitale Signaturen*, Beilage 2 zu Heft 10/2000 Kommunikation und Recht (K&R), p. 34 & p. 40ff.

solved.[63] With respect to privacy and official secrets, problems can be addressed by appropriate encryption for transmission and data storage.[64]

3.2.5 Case law relevant for the solution of the problems

In the context of this report, the most interesting case law focuses on the question whether or not a document sent by means of telecommunication meets the requirement of "written communication". It always refers to provisions which govern communication with courts, especially those that require the filing of a suit or an appeal "in writing". Whereas these precedents can hardly be applied to corresponding formal requirements in civil law (e.g. concluding specific contracts) since § 126 Civil Code (BGB) explicitly requires a handwritten signature and arguably a paper document (Urkunde) as well, they are highly relevant in administrative law. This is because with respect to applications "in writing" according to the VwVfG, all commentators, after mentioning § 126 BGB just as an example, also refer to the line of cases in this area.[65] The same is true, for example, with respect to the formal requirement for a formal objection concerning a "Verwaltungsakt" (§ 70 para. 1 VwGO).[66] Incidentally, it is precisely for this reason that it is difficult to understand why so many scholars are in favour of prohibiting on-line communication in these cases

---

[63] Cf. Dix, A.: Digital Signaturen im Verwaltungsverfahren: Besondere Sicherheitsanforderungen erforderlich?, in: Eifert, M. (ed.), *Digitale Signaturen*, Beilage 2 zu Heft 10/2000 Kommunikation und Recht (K&R), p. 34, 20 & 22; Groß, T.: Öffentliche Verwaltung im Internet, Die Öffentliche Verwaltung (DÖV) 2001, p. 163f.

[64] Cf. Dix, A.: Verwaltung und Internet aus der Sicht des Datenschutzes, in: Kubicek, H. et al.: *Multimedia@Verwaltung*, Heidelberg 1999, p. 182f.; Groß, T.: Öffentliche Verwaltung im Internet, Die Öffentliche Verwaltung (DÖV) 2001, p. 164; Deutscher Städtetag, Schritte auf dem Weg zum digitalen Rathaus, Köln 2000, p. 19ff.; Reinermann, H.: *Der öffentliche Sektor im Internet*, Speyer 2000, p. 37f.; Traunmüller, R.: Systeme der IT-Unterstützung, in: Lenk, K. & Traunmüller, R.: *Öffentliche Verwaltung und Informationstechnik*, Heidelberg 1999, p. 89f.

[65] Cf. Kopp, F. & Ramsauer, U.: *Verwaltungsverfahrensgesetz*, 7th ed. München 2000, § 22, Rn 32f., § 64, Rn 10f.; Stelkens/Bonk/Sachs-Stelkens-Schmitz, § 22, Rn 31ff. Obermayer-Seegmüller, § 64, Rn 15ff; Knack, *Verwaltungsverfahrensgesetz*, Kommentar, 7th ed. Köln 2000, § 64, Rn 7.

[66] Cf. Badura, P.: Die Form des Verwaltungsaktes, in: Festschrift Boorberg-Verlag, 1977, p. 213.

(see above 1.1). As has been pointed out by some courts[67], whether or not electronic communication meets the formal criteria first of all depends on the security standard of the transmission channel. At least e-mail communication using the advanced electronic signature according to the EU Electronic signature directive provides a complete equivalent to telefax transmission in this regard.[68]

Turning to the mentioned precedents, there have been different interpretations by different courts concerning the question at stake. Whereas the highest administrative court (Bundesverwaltungsgericht)[69] and the highest social security court (Bundessozialgericht)[70] had decided that an appeal which is filed by an e-mail-like service (Btx, now t-online)[71] meets the requirement of communication "in writing", the highest civil court (Bundesgerichtshof) did not even want to accept a Fax directly sent from a computer (Computerfax), including merely a scanned signature[72] and demanded a decision from the common division of all the highest federal courts (Gemeinsamer Senat der obersten Gerichtshöfe des Bundes) according to § 2 RspEinhG.[73] This division did not share the restrictive point of view of the Bundesgerichtshof and ruled that a computerfax, including a scanned signature, meets the formal criteria provided that the sender is unambiguous.[74] It referred to the established case law according to which a telegram and a regular telefax is also sufficient[75] and stated

---

[67] Cf. OLG Düsseldorf, NJW 1995, 2177; see also Polomski, R.M.: *Der automatisierte Verwaltungsakt*, Berlin 1993, p. 180; Redeker, NVwZ 1986, 545, 548.

[68] For further details on the legal point of view see Eifert, M.: Online-Verwaltung und Schriftform im Verwaltungsrecht, in: Eifert, M. (ed.), *Digitale Signaturen*, Beilage 2 zu Heft 10/2000 Kommunikation und Recht (K&R), p. 14f.; for an opinion on the security standard of digital signatures see Bieser, W. & Kersten, H.: *Elektronisch unterschreiben*, 2nd ed. Heidelberg 1999, p. 35.

[69] BVerwG NJW 1995, 2121.

[70] BSG NJW 1997, 1254.

[71] Btx, contrary to most e-mail communications, is not an open network service.

[72] Contrary to the opinion of the Bundesgerichtshof, this had been accepted by the highest tax court (Bundesfinanzgericht) in an earlier decision, BFH, BFH/NV 1998, 604.

[73] BGH NJW 1998, 3649.

[74] GmS-OGB NJW 2000, 2340.

[75] Cf. inter alia BGH NJW 1957, 1275; BGH NJW 1981, 1618; BVerwG NJW 1955, 1454; BFHE 136, 38. For a discussion of these questions see inter alia Melullis, K.: Zum Regelungsbedarf bei der elektronischen Willenserklärung, Monatsschrift für Deutsches Recht (MDR) 1995, p. 109ff.; Heun, S.: Elektronisch erstellte oder übermittelte Dokumente und Schriftform, Computer und Recht (CR) 1995, p. 2ff.

that this decision would be in line with this tendency to accept technical progress.[76] However, the decision on the other hand stressed that this matter was just an exception.[77] In sum, it supports the opinion that electronic communication fits in with the legal system but it does not render legal amendments superfluous.

3.2.6 Influence of other legal domains, especially civil law on problemsolving in administrative law

The influence of other legal domains on administrative law can be exercised in different ways. With respect to the interpretation of formal requirements, it has already been pointed out that at least some case law on other provisions has a remarkable influence on administrative law, even though many scholars only draw limited conclusions with respect to electronic government. Civil law, however, is governed by far more restrictive standards with respect to "written communication" than administrative law.

Concerning the legislative developments, however, the amendments to the Civil Law, which are expected to be enacted before the amendments to the administrative law, will not affect the formal requirements of administrative law.[78] By changing the way in which legally binding communication is traditionally bound to paper documents in the area of civil law, it will without doubt heighten the political pressure on corresponding amendments in administrative law.[79]

---

[76] A similar argument was also used concerning formal requirements in administrative law long before this dispute emerged, cf. Lazaratos, P.: *Rechtliche Auswirkungen der Verwaltungsautomation auf das Verwaltungsverfahren*, Berlin 1990, p. 94ff.

[77] For comments on this decision see Römermann, V. & van der Moolen, M.: Schriftsätze per Computerfax: Willkommen im 21. Jahrhundert, Betriebsberater (BB) 2000, p. 1640ff.; Düwell, F. J.: Computerfax richterrechtlich zugelassen, Neue Juristische Wochenschrift (NJW) 2000, p. 3334.

[78] Eifert, M. & Schreiber, L.: Elektronische Signatur und der Zugang zur Verwaltung, Multimedia und Recht (MMR) 2000, p. 342f.; Schmitz, H.: Moderner Staat – Modernes Verwaltungsverfahrensrecht, Neue Zeitschrift für Verwaltungsrecht (NVwZ) 2000, p. 1243; for a different point of view see Rosenbach, H.-J.: Zur geplanten Änderung der BGB-Regelungen betreffend die Schriftform und deren Auswirkungen auf das Verwaltungshandeln, Nordrhein-Westfälische Verwaltungsblätter (NWVBl.) 2000, p. 162ff.

[79] Schmitz, H.: Moderner Staat – Modernes Verwaltungsverfahrensrecht, Neue Zeitschrift für Verwaltungsrecht (NVwZ) 2000, p. 1238, Rosenbach, H.-J.: Zur geplanten

3.2.7 Conclusion

There are many areas in which it is already at the discretion of the public administration to use electronic communications. Due to concerns about privacy and security (the authenticity and integrity of data), it is not yet a widespread means of communication with citizens, though. But there are also many formal requirements in administrative law, which result in uncertainty concerning the admissibility or even in a prohibition of electronic communications falling within these provisions. Therefore, legal amendments are necessary; some have already been elaborated to a certain extent and are expected to be enacted soon. Amendments in civil law, which will probably be the first to be enacted, do not facilitate electronic communications in the fields of administrative law.

3.3 Amending administrative procedure law

3.3.1 General considerations

The federal system (see above 3.2.1, 3.2.4) and the widespread distribution of procedural and especially formal requirements makes a joint effort at all administrative levels and an efficient coordination of all legislative activities crucial to fostering electronic communications between citizens and public administrations.[80] At least federal and state levels have started to co-operate intensely in a joint working group on amendments to administrative procedure law. Even though at the time being there is only a proposal on amendments to some statutes (see sections 3.1.3 and 3.3.2), it is said that a comprehensive revision of all administrative law provisions relevant to electronic communication will be completed in the near future so that the VwVfG and all other relevant laws can be amended at the same time by an omnibus act (*Artikelgesetz*). This is supposed to be done

---

Änderung der BGB-Regelungen betreffend die Schriftform und deren Auswirkungen auf das Verwaltungshandeln, Nordrhein-Westfälische Verwaltungsblätter (NWVBl.) 2000, p. 162ff.

[80] Eifert, Martin: Electronic Government als gesamtstaatliche Organisationsaufgabe, Zeitschrift für Gesetzgebung (ZG) 1/2001.

by the federal and all state parliaments within a short period of time. It remains to be seen, however, whether this ambitious approach can soon be realised.

To a certain extent, the proposed amendments of formal requirements can and need to refer to defined levels of electronic signatures in order to ensure an appropriate level of confidential and secure communication and transaction. Since the law on electronic signatures, which had been enacted as early as 1997, has recently been adapted to the requirements of the European Directive on a Community framework for electronic signatures, all other provisions in administrative law can refer to it. It has already become evident that the electronic signature will be a key to the formal requirements concerning electronic communications and that a great deal of applications are going to rely on it.[81]

3.3.2 General stipulation versus specific (detailed) stipulations

Whether amendments are made by means of a general stipulation, affecting all specific stipulations in administrative law or by a revision of all pertinent specific stipulations first of all depends on how the traditional administrative law system looks like. As described above (3.2.1), in German administrative law, general requirements are laid down in the VwVfG, being complemented or modified by numerous requirements in specific laws. As far as electronic communication affects a general type of administrative decision such as the "Verwaltungsakt" which has traditionally been defined and regulated in the general VwVfG, there is hardly an alternative to amending these general laws in the long run (in the short term, there can also be specific amendments, limited to certain areas as an experiment (see above 3.1.1)). As far as unprecedented general questions of electronic communications are concerned, for reasons of systematical consistency, they are to be regulated at this level as well.

As far as the requirements of specific laws are concerned, there are two different cases. Requirements which are basically identical even though they are laid down in specific laws, such as the requirement of communi-

[81] According to a comprehensive survey which has recently been conducted by the Deutsche Institut für Urbanistik (difu) and which will soon be published, about 72% of local governments implementing on-line services plan to use electronic signatures

cation "in writing", can be amended either by means of a general stipulation[82], or on a case by case. Requirements which are different in the respective specific laws, by their very nature can only be amended specifically. Thus, the question of general versus specific stipulations comes down to whether there should be a general stipulation, amending specific, but at least very similar requirements that can be found in specific laws.

Case-by-case amendments have the advantage that experience can be gained in advance of the amendments. Obviously, this also has the disadvantage that it takes far more time and presents a risk of ignoring some provisions unintentionally. The opposite is true for the advantages and disadvantages of general amendments, whereas the risk of ignoring something important could have unintended effects on specific stipulations.

While at the outset, most comments favoured a step-by-step approach (see above 3.3.2), federal and state ministers have decided to amend all laws at the same time, enabling the amendment of the identical requirements in specific laws by means of a general provision as a default solution taking into consideration the specific needs of individual specific laws by amending them at the same time. Thus far, however, only the amendments to the (general) federal Public Administration Act (VwVfG-E), to the similar provisions of the social security and tax procedure Acts, respectively, and to numerous specific tax laws seem to have been spelled out (see above 3.1.3). Besides, there has not yet been a general decision as to which procedures will not be suitable for electronic communication. Some of the specific amendments in tax laws do already prohibit electronic communication, however.[83]

3.3.3 Issues regulated at a general level

At the general level of the VwVfG, the joint working group of federal and state officials proposes in particular regulations on access, electronic communications substituting the formal requirement of being "in writing", the handling of electronic documents which are not readable for technical rea-

---

[82] This stipulation can in turn provide for a set of requirements between which the specific stipulation can choose by refererence, or it can provide for just one solution.

[83] E.g. § 19 sub. 1 Mineralölsteuer-Durchführungsverordnung; § 18 sub. 1 Grunderwerbsteuergesetz. The reasons given in the draft do not reveal the considerations.

sons and the issuing of an electronic "Verwaltungsakt" which will be described below. Apart from these regulations, of course, all other provisions of the VwVfG have also been revised in order to adapt them to the needs of electronic communications if necessary.

The pivotal provision governing general questions of electronic communications and affecting many specific stipulations is § 3a VwVfG-E ("E" stands for proposal). It stipulates that the transmission of electronic documents in administrative procedures is permitted and to the extent that access has been provided (para. 1). This is true for the public administration as well as for citizens. The provision of access should be interpreted so as to include the expression of a will to accept electronic communication. This ensures that neither a citizen nor the public administration is forced to accept electronic documents unless it has decided to do so and has installed the technical infrastructure for this purpose.[84] Of course, it also implies that the public administration is not obliged to provide access at all.

The provision also lays down that an electronic document, signed with a qualified electronic signature according to the German Electronic Signature Act as amended (which corresponds to an advanced electronic signature based on a qualified certificate and created by a secure signature creation device according to EU Electronic Signature Directive), is a substitute for statutorily required communication "in writing", unless otherwise stated (para. 2).

Finally, the proposed stipulation requires the public administration to notify the sender if an electronically transmitted document cannot be handled. It has to specify the valid technical requirements in this notifica-

---

[84] Since access must be provided for every citizen addressed by the public administration, any communication that is to be communicated to many citizens can only be provided electronically to the extent that the respective citizens have accepted this means of communication. As far as the agency chooses the way of public communication (Öffentliche Bekanntmachung), there are no rules on electronic publication in the Public Administration Act amendments. Thus, according to general VwVfG-E rules, the traditional means (newspaper etc.) cannot be replaced by electronic means. However, with respect to access to information, § 5 Sub. 6 of the Informationsfreiheitsgesetz Schleswig-Holstein (Freedom of Information Act, Schleswig-Holstein) states that (within the field of application of this act) the agency is allowed to refer to a publication on the Internet.

tion (subs. 3).[85] This implies that the public administration may determine technical requirements which have to be fulfilled for the valid submission of electronic documents. Correspondingly, if a recipient notifies the public administration that an electronically transmitted document cannot be handled, the public administration is obliged to send the document either in an electronic form suitable for him or as a paper document (sub. 3).[86]

As far as the "Verwaltungsakt" is concerned, § 37 sub. 2 VwVfG-E will explicitly mention that a "Verwaltungsakt" can also be issued electronically ("... in writing, electronically, by word of mouth or by other means ..."). There has been some debate, however, concerning under which conditions a "Verwaltungsakt" could be issued electronically even though a specific law requires communication "in writing". According to the first draft, § 37 sub. 3a VwVfG-E specified these conditions. Only an electronic document that had been signed with a durably checkable electronic signature according to the German Electronic Signature Act as amended could be a substitute for statutorily required communication "in writing". However, the stipulation had become unclear due to the changes in the drafted Amendments of the German Electronic Signature Act. At the time when the first draft of the VwVfG-E had been agreed upon, a "durably checkable electronic signature according to the German Electronic Signature Act" was well defined. The formerly proposed amendments to the Electronic Signature Act stated that should a trust-centre exit, only those trust-centre documents have to be adopted by the agency responsible for the trust-centre supervision (RegTP)[87] which stem from

[85] There are no regulations on how the technical requirements are to be specified. Presumably, in most cases this will be done in internal Draft Regulations. Although there is no obligation to do so, they will presumably be published. Apart from these technical reasons and, of course, the lack of legally required form (e.g. qualified electronic signature), the public administration cannot refuse to accept electronic documents once it has provided access.

[86] Since the public administration can either meet the technical standards spelled out by the citizen or return to paper-based communication, this provosion, as well as sub. 1, does not contain an obligation for the public administration to provide for externally defined technical standards. There is no stipulation on the case when an electronic document differs from its paper-based version. This will become a question to be resolved on a case-by-case basis, weighing the evidence according to the specific circumstances.

[87] The full name is "Regulierungsbehördc für Post und Telekommunikation". It regulates telecommunication and postal services.

trust-centres that are voluntarily accredited with the RegTP. Therefore, if no other trust-centre has adopted the documents, the signatures of non-accredited trust-centres cannot be checked after the market exit. An accreditation, in turn, required an ex-ante examination and following periodic examinations of the security concept of the trust-centre by an accredited certification authority and arguably also a security standard slightly higher than the one applicable to qualified signatures. Therefore, making use of Art. 3 sub. 7 of the EU Electronic Signature Directive, "durably checkable" ultimately referred to this type of signature, which was equivalent to the electronic signature according to the German signature law before it had been amended. However, the German Electronic Signature Act has finally been amended somewhat differently. It still contains the requirements on the signatures of trust-centres voluntarily accredited with the RegTP (§§ 15, 16 SigG). According to the law, under certain conditions the RegTP also has to take charge of the documentation of trust-centres offering qualified signatures (§ 13 para. 2 SigG). Apart from these problems it was also questionable whether the intended rather general limitation to signatures of voluntarily accredited trust-centres would have fallen within the provision of Art. 3 sub. 7 of the EU Directive.[88] Even though it only regulates the security infrastructure for electronic signatures as a matter of principle, the German Electronic Signature Act as amended also repeats the wording of Art. 3 sub. 7 of the EU Directive with respect to the requirements concerning administrative operations governed by administrative law (§ 1 sub. 3 SigG). Thus, a reference to voluntarily accredited trust-centres would have also raised concerns with respect to this provision of German law.

However, the most recent draft of federal VwVfG amendments has changed the approach. It refrains from imposing additional requirements in general for all electronic "Verwaltungsakte" that substitute "Verwaltungsakte" in writing. Consequently, the general rule of § 3 a VwVfG-E will apply and a qualified electronic signature will substitute a statutorily required "Verwaltungsakt" in writing. § 37a VwVfG-E of the most recent draft, however, explicitly allows for additional specific requirements for

[88] Cf. Eifert, M.: Rechtsentwicklung – Bremsklotz oder Beschleuniger für das virtuelle Rathaus?, in: Bundesministerium für Wirtschaft und Technologie (ed.): *Virtuelles Rathaus*, Berlin 2001.

electronic signatures and their certificates in specific laws or regulations with respect to both, the durable checkability and the technical and administrative security. The Ministry of the Interior is empowered to regulate the details of those requirements by rule-making (Rechtsverordnung).

In addition, there is another difficult question with regard to the electronic "Verwaltungsakt". § 37 sub. 3a VwVfG-E also stipulates that the certificate, belonging to the signature, displays the agency ("Behörde") which issued the "Verwaltungsakt". Since the German Electronic Signature Act only admits the electronic signatures of individuals, this requires that the certificate of the acting official contains information on his professional character as an employee with this agency. Even though it is possible to make the official character of a message transparent and to prohibit abuse by including information on the official character in the certificate, the stipulation still seems to be too restrictive. The first draft of the proposed stipulation[89] impeded the private use of signatures by necessarily revealing the profession of the sender in the main certificate, thereby hampering the diffusion of electronic signatures since potential users are missing for commercial applications. As the certificate becomes false as soon as the official changes the agency and needs to be irreversibly suspended (rendering the signature invalid) as a whole in case he or she is not allowed to act as an official even for a limited time, it also restricted flexibility especially for state administrations.[90] But the balance of desired transparency could on the one hand be better struck and has partly been done so by merely slightly modifying the provision. The German Electronic Signature Act also provides for certificates which are attributed and refer to the "main certificate" of a digital signature which can, but does not need to be, also attached to the signature.

According to the most recent version of the draft,[91] information on the capacity in which officials sign need not be included in the main certificate but could also be included in these "attributed" certificates, which would only be attached in case of official use and could be individually suspended without effecting the validity of the signature. However, con-

---

[89] § 37 sub. 3a according to the "Magdeburger Fassung".

[90] The problem is less important for local governments since the acting agancy at the local level is the "Oberbürgermeister", comprising all branches of local administration.

[91] VwVfG-E (16 July 2001).

trary to the proposal, it appears to be sufficient to inform the recipient about the legal entity in the capacity of which the official is admitted to act (e.g. "state (name)") instead of the precise agency. This would allow for a higher degree of flexibility for human resource management and would make the key management of administrations cheaper.[92]

As far as additional statutory regulations on privacy, file handling or archiving are considered necessary, they may and should also be regulated at a general level.

Apart from these issues which are regulated at a general level by statute, there are also general regulations which are contained in internal Draft Regulations. They mainly concern rules on careful electronic communications and are described in section 3.3.5.

3.3.4 **Issues regulated at a specific level**

As previously mentioned, there are still no proposals for amendments to specific administrative law. The issues to be addressed at this level basically consist of all the problems described in 3.2.4 which will not be regulated at a general level.

First of all, corresponding to the proposed amendments to civil law, every case in which the default regulation of § 3a sub. 2 VwVfG (which deals with a qualified electronic signature equivalent to a statutory written form) is not considered appropriate needs to be specifically amended. If there is no need for a high standard of security (e.g. many applications), electronic communications not including a high-level electronic signature (e.g. e-mail) could be admitted. However, if there are specific needs which are not adequately met by a qualified signature, specific additional requirements are to be stated, taking into consideration the limitations drawn by Art. 3 para. 7 EU Electronic Signature Directive and § 1 sub. 3 German Electronic Signature Act. Those specific requirements may be aimed at durable checkability as well as at an enhanced level of technical

[92] The problem is not being sufficiently discussed at the moment. One reason might be that most administrations do not as yet seem to have thought about key management for this. According to a comprehensive survey which has recently been conducted by the Deutsche Institut für Urbanistik (difu) and which will soon be published, more than 90% of local governments implementing e-government have not yet developed a key-management concept.

security. They should also ensure that a citizen is warned before performing a legally binding transaction since this is not necessarily understood when signing electronically due to its lack of cultural connotations.[93]

Besides these questions of the equivalence of written and electronic communications, amendments to regulations on physical presence or the handing over of certificates also need to be regulated at a specific level since their ratio may differ significantly.

3.3.5 Rules on careful electronic communications

In addition to the notification requirement with respect to electronic documents not manageable by the public administration (see 3.3.3), rules on careful electronic communications are regulated in internal, but nonetheless legally binding Draft Regulations ("Dienstanweisungen", "Verwaltungsvorschriften").[94] Typically, they contain rules on the competent authorities for technical and organisational matters, the establishment and use of mailboxes, the field of application of e-mail communications, formal requirements in e-mail communications, cases in which encryption is required, archiving and documentation as a printout and, last but not least, general references to matters of network security such as dealing with suspicious mails, the danger of viruses etc. Furthermore, they regularly announce general rules on paper-based communications which are applicable mutatis mutandis.

Generally speaking, these Draft Regulations prescribe the establishment of a central e-mail mailbox for every agency as well as the establishment of individual mailboxes for every employee and stipulate that the mailboxes are to be checked at least once a day. The time of receipt of incoming mail has to be registered. Misguided e-mails are to be forwarded to the proper receiver. E-mails should be deleted as soon as possible unless they are to be archived or are of permanent relevance. For reasons of legal uncertainty, external e-mail communication is not usually

[93] Cf. Eifert, M.: Online-Verwaltung und Schriftform im Verwaltungsrecht, in: Eifert, M. (ed.), *Digitale Signaturen*, Beilage 2 zu Heft 10/2000 Kommunikation und Recht (K&R), p. 14f.

[94] For examples and a sample see <http://www.staedtetag.de/mitgliederservice/dez8/umfrage_email/> (22 August 2001); Abel, H.: Praxishandbuch Datenschutz, Augsburg, Loseblattsammlung.

admitted or at least not fostered as far as matters of legal significance are concerned. However, it is frequently indicated that this will change as soon as the electronic signature is available. It can also be assumed that these internal rules, which focus very much on e-mail communication, will also be extended to other means of electronic communication as soon as they become more widespread.[95]

As far as electronic communications are relevant to an administrative procedure or any other procedure documented in a paper-based file, usually a printout for the paper-based file is required. All communications containing information which is subject to the rules on privacy (mainly data related to an individual) must be encrypted. Notification from the sender, confirming the receipt of the document from the public administration is only referred to as communication which lacks formal requirements (e.g. communication required "in writing"). However, a lower administrative court has also required notification when it was evident to the agency that the intended content of the message was missing [96] and it is also sometimes discussed by commentators for similar cases.[97]

As a general rule, electronic communications are received as soon as they are actually received or retrievable.[98] With respect to an electronically transmitted "Verwaltungsakt", the proposed amendments to the VwVfG (§ 41 sub. 2) stipulate that it is deemed to have been received the day after it was transmitted (as opposed to the third day after handing it over to the mail service with respect to written communications).[99] However, for traditional as well as for electronic communication this is not valid if the "Verwaltungsakt" has been received later or has not been received at all. In the case of doubt, public administration bears the burden of proof concerning reception. All other regulations containing legal fictions of reception implicitly demand paper-based communication, but

---

[95] Questions of direct access to databases, however, are usually regulated in the specific law that governs the database and in data protection laws, respectively.

[96] VG Saarlouis, MMR 1999, p. 247f.

[97] Cf. Dix, Beilage 2 zu Heft 10/2000 K&R, p. 22.

[98] Stelkens, Bonk, Sachs-Stelkens & Kallerhoff, § 24, Rn 84; OLG Köln NJW 1990, 1608.

[99] Concerning electronic communication there is no specification as to the moment when a document is sent. "Transfer" always implies reception within the sphere of the receiver.

they will be modified along with the comprehensive administrative law amendments (see above 3.1.3).

3.3.6 Specific issues concerning electronic signatures

All relevant issues concerning electronic signatures have already been dealt with in the context of regulations at a general or specific level (see above 3.3.3, 3.3.4). It is worth repeating, however, that the only specific requirement for electronic signatures in electronic communications which has been proposed thus far is the requirement of durable checkability.

3.3.7 Competent bodies for the specification of the requirements relevant for careful electronic communications

In as far as there are no statutory requirements concerning careful electronic communications, such rules are part of the general power of the head of the respective public administration to determine organisational matters. This is often delegated to internal units.

3.3.8 Conclusion

The main focus of the present legislative amendments is on formal requirements in order to enable the public administration to use electronic communications in cases where traditional communication "in writing" is required. A differentiated approach is emerging, admitting simple e-mail communication where possible and requiring a qualified electronic signature and sometimes even additional features where necessary. These amendments are supplemented by a simultaneous comprehensive revision of administrative law in the light of the new opportunities involving electronic communications in general and the digital signature in particular. An evaluation of the whole set of amendments cannot yet be made because, up to now, there has only been a proposal concerning the regulations at a general level. The approach as a whole is convincing even though some individual provisions should be modified. The rules on careful communication which mainly consist of internal Draft Regulations need to be and certainly will be revised as soon as the legal framework has become clear.

3.4 Electronic communication versus traditional communication

3.4.1 Remaining differences between traditional and electronic communications

As the revision of administrative laws is not yet complete, it is difficult to assess what the differences are between traditional and electronic communications from a legal point of view. It has become obvious, however, that most politicians embrace the broad movement towards Electronic Government so that traditional communications will certainly be minimised. There will still be certain cases where an individual's physical presence or the handing over of a certificate will be required for an absolutely reliable identification or symbolic meaning. In addition, paper-based communication will be necessary as a universal service at least for a longer transmission period and at least with respect to the general public. However, this is already shifting the focus to questions of access.

3.4.2 Discrimination of access

The discussion on whether or not there is, and to what extent, discrimination of access to public administration or to information provided by public administration has just begun. Primarily, it should be stated that discrimination may occur at different levels. It could be introduced at the basic technological level as well as at the secondary level of fees. In the first case, access to a service is more or less exclusively linked to the use of specific technology, e.g. a smart card with an electronic signature, Internet technology. In the second case, various channels of distribution provide a service but different fees make the use of a certain channel cheaper than another. Generally speaking, German law is very restrictive with regard to exclusive access to the services of the public administration but only provides a framework with respect to "pricing", leaving ample discretion to the public administration.

As for discrimination at the technological level, the proposed § 3a sub. 3 VwVfG-E stipulates that the public administration is obliged to send the document either in an electronic form suitable for the recipient or as a paper-document in case the recipient asserts that an electronic document is not suitable. This corresponds to the tradition of ensuring access to public administration to everybody. Formal applications, for instance, can not only be made by a written statement but also by dictating it to a public official so that citizens who are illiterate are not discriminated against (cf. §§ 24, 64 VwVfG). Even with respect to tenders that are only relevant to enterprises, Germany neither favours nor has legally introduced the possibility of exclusive electronic communications although this opportunity has been created by EU law.[100] As far as there are any comments on this issue by scholars, at least exclusive access to public administration is considered unconstitutional, violating the principle of equality laid down in Art. 3 Basic Law[101] as well as the due process clause, and principles of the democratic and social welfare state, embodied in Art. 20 Basic Law.[102] A "public access infrastructure"[103], consisting e.g. of easily accessible public terminals as are currently planned by many local governments[104], could be a remedy for undue discrimination. At present, access does not only presuppose technical access but also sufficient media competence on the part of the users[105], and there is therefore an argument in

---

[100] Cf. Proposal for a Directive of the European Parliament and of the Council on the coordination of procedures for the award of public supply contracts, public service contracts and public works contracts, COM(2000) 275def v. 10.5.2000.

[101] Schmidt-Aßmann, E.: Verwaltungsrecht in der Informationsgesellschaft: Perspektiven der Systembildung, in: Hoffmann-Riem, W. & Schmidt-Aßmann, E. (ed.), *Verwaltungsrecht in der Informationsgesellschaft*, Baden-Baden 2000, p. 422.

[102] Roßnagel, A.: Möglichkeiten für Transparenz und Öffentlichkeit im Verwaltungshandeln – unter besonderer Berücksichtigung des Internet als Instrument der Staatskommunikation, in: Hoffmann-Riem, W. & Schmidt-Aßmann, E. (ed.), *Verwaltungsrecht in der Informationsgesellschaft*, Baden-Baden 2000, p. 312.

[103] Trute, H.: Öffentlich-rechtliche Rahmenbedingungen einer Informationsordnung, Veröffentlichungen der Vereinigung der Deutschen Staatsrechtslehrer (VVDStRL) Vol. 57 (1998), p. 254f.

[104] Cf. the short versions of the Media@Komm applications on the CD-ROM supplement of Kubicek, H. et al.: *Multimedia@Verwaltung*, Jahrbuch Telekommunikation und Gesellschaft 1999, Heidelberg 1999.

[105] Kubicek, H.: Was versteht man unter allgemeinem Zugang und worauf kommt es an?, in: Kubicek, H. et al.: *Multimedia@Verwaltung*, Heidelberg 1999, p. 332ff.; Schoch, F.: Öffentlich-rechtliche Rahmenbedingungen einer Informationsordnung, Veröffentlichungen der Vereinigung der Deutschen Staatsrechtslehrer (VVDStRL) Vol. 57 (1998), p. 178. Administrations also consider support and advice to be a necessity, as this is crucial to the development of Electronic Government (cf. Friedrichs, S. (ed.): *Virtuelle Medien als Chance für die Stadt der Zukunft*, Bonn 2000, p. 41).

favour of supplementary obligations for public administrations to provide for appropriate advice and support.[106]

With regard to discrimination on the "pricing" level, there have not as yet been any specific regulations, nor have there been any practical cases. Since electronic services which are subject to a fee have only been launched quite recently, it cannot be concluded that this issue will not become relevant. In any event, a closer examination of the administrative law governing the determination of fees by public administration has shown that there is ample discretion for public administrations to price electronic and paper-based access differently.[107]

3.4.3 **Conclusion**

Since the development towards Electronic Government has recently resulted in the implementation of interactive services, it is still too early to assume what the differences between different media and communication channels will be in the future.[108] Nevertheless, is already apparent that questions of access are particularly very important and have to be analysed and treated carefully.

3.5 Conclusion of the main findings

There is a broad development towards Electronic Government at all levels of administration (federal, state and local level) in Germany. Presently, electronic communications are not specifically regulated. Even though administrative procedure is not subject to formal requirements as a matter of

[106] Hoffmann-Riem, W.: Verwaltungsrecht in der Informationsgesellschaft – Problemskizze, in: Hoffmann-Riem, W. & Schmidt-Aßmann, E. (ed.), *Verwaltungsrecht in der Informationsgesellschaft*, Baden-Baden 2000, p. 49f.

[107] Cf. Schreiber, Lutz: Elektronische Verwaltungsverfahren, script (to be published at the end of 2001).

[108] Lenk has already pointed out that communication with the public administration and the question of appropriate access is more complex than just choosing between electronic or paper-based communication. (Cf. Lenk, K.: Bürger, Demokratie und Verwaltung: neue Möglichkeiten und Entwicklungen, in: Lenk, K. & Traunmüller, R.: *Öffentliche Verwaltung und Informationstechnik*, Heidelberg 1999, p. 260ff.).

principle, many formal requirements of various statutes impede electronic communications or at least induce considerable uncertainty about the admissibility of electronic communications. Both the federal government and state governments are responsible for the vast majority of legislation which is relevant to electronic communications and have started a comprehensive revision of civil law and administrative law. Amendments to numerous civil law statutes as well as of those administrative laws comprising general regulations on administrative procedure and formal requirements of crucial types of administrative actions, have already been made and published. Proposals concerning specific administrative laws are planned to follow soon. In the field of administrative law, the federal government and state governments face the challenge of efficient co-ordination and co-operation and have therefore established numerous joint-working groups. According to their plans, all amendments are to be enacted in the near future. This will lead to at least three levels of electronic communications. Some communications will only require an e-mail, some will demand a (qualified) electronic signature according to the German Electronic Signature Act as amended pursuant to the European Electronic Signature Directive. It is not yet clear to what extent and in which cases further requirements besides a qualified electronic signature will be required. But in all likelihood there will be a requirement of durable checkability and/or of specific technical or organizational perequisites of the electronic signature used by the public administration. Most of the questions concerning electronic communications will be regulated at a general level. Specific laws will contain differing requirements in cases in which the "default" regulation is considered not appropriate and regulations on questions that are specific to the field which is regulated in the respective law. Rules on careful electronic communications will primarily be embodied in internal Draft Regulations, enacted by the head of the respective administrative body. Of course, there will also be rulings by the courts. One of the upcoming problems is how to regulate access in the case of a multi-channel administration.

Chapter 4
NORWAY

Chapter 4
NORWAY

4.1 INTRODUCTION

Government agencies in Norway are increasingly using the Internet for their communications with citizens and private companies. This chapter deals with the legal framework involved in such electronic communication. First, a brief introduction is given to the daily use of the Internet by government agencies. Section 4.2 outlines the current legislative developments in administrative law which are aimed at removing legal obstacles in electronic communication.

4.1.1 **Present practice**[1]

There are no empirical studies available on the present use by government agencies of the Internet and any other means of electronic communication. However, according to the observers we interviewed, both central and local goverments use the Internet for two purposes on a large scale. First, to provide citizens and private companies with government information[2], and thus to contribute to ensuring equal treatment and emphasizing openness. Second, to deliver electronic services to citzens and private companies.[3] Making information user-friendly is an important aspect in this respect.

[1] This paragraph is based on interviews with Mr. H.F. Berg, Statskonsult, Oslo, and Professor D.W. Schartum, University of Oslo, Section for Technology and Administrative Systems.

[2] See e.g. the websites of the municipalities of Levanger and Hole: <http://www.levanger.kommune.no>, <http://www.hole.kommune.no>, and the website of the central government: <http://odin.dep.no/odin/global/language-no/index-b-n-a.html>.

[3] See the website developed in collaboration with the National Privacy Authority where citizens can refuse direct marketing, according to article 26 of the Data Protection Act. See: <http://www.brreg.no/reservasjon>.

The use of the Internet by government agencies is stimulated by the Electronic Government Action Plan 1999-2001.[4] However, the development to electronic service delivery by government agencies is hindered by legal obstacles for electronic communication in the Public Administration Act, and by concerns about the authenticiy, integrity and confidentiality of electronic communication. At present, preparations are being made to amend the Public Administration Act, and to develop Draft Regulations for the use of electronic signatures and encryption in the public sector, so as to remove these legal obstacles and uncertainties.

4.2 Norwegian administrative law

4.2.1 Current legislative developments

The proposal for amendments to the Public Administration Act is part of a wider legislation project which is aimed at removing legal obstacles for electronic communication in all areas of the law (for example contract law, transport law, etc). This legislation project, called *eRegelprosjektet*, is coordinated by the Ministry of Justice and the Ministry of Trade and Industry. The proposal for amendments to various areas of law, including the Public Administration Act, was submitted to Parliament on 31 August 2001. Thus, the proposed amendments to the Public Administration Act will be debated in Parliament together with the proposals for amendments in the other areas of the law.

4.2.2 Amendments to the Public Administration Act

On 15 January 2001, the Ministry of Justice published a Draft Bill for Amendments to the Public Administration Act[5] which is aimed at removing the legal obstacles to electronic communication between government

---

[4] Handlingsplan 1999-2001, Elektronisk Forvaltning, p. 4-9: <http://www.odin.dep.no/aad/norsk/publ/rapporter/002005-990168/index-dok000-b-n-a.html>.

[5] Act of 10 February 1967 relating to procedure in cases concerning the public administration.

agencies and citizens.[6] A 'public hearing' took place from 15 January until 1 March 2001 in which citizens could react to the draft proposals via e-mail, mail or at public meetings. On 31 August 2001, the Government sent a Bill to Parliament with the proposed amendments.[7] This Bill is to be re-submitted to the new Parliament, to be elected in September 2001. The re-submission was expected to take place some time in October or November 2001.

In the Explanatory Memorandum to the Bill for Amendments (hereafter: the Bill) the following terms and expressions are addressed in the Public Administration Act as possible obstacles to electronic communication between government agencies and citizens:

- Document [dokument]: § 13 c, 17-21, 25, 27, 33 of the Public Administration Act;
- Copy [kopi]: § 20, 25, 33 of the Public Administration Act;
- In writing [skriftlig]: § 12, 13c, 16, 23, 27, 32, 37 of the Public Administration Act;
- To be put down in writing [nedtegne/protokollere]: § 11 d, 15 of the Public Administration Act;
- Orally [muntlig]: § 11 d, 15 of the Public Administration Act;
- Signed [undertegne]: § 32 of the Public Administration Act;
- To lodge an appeal [avgitt]: § 30 of the Public Administration Act;
- Having reached the party [kommet fram]: § 29, 35, 36 of the Public Administration Act;
- Notification [varsling/unterretning]: § 16, 27, 33, 37 of the Public Administration Act;
- Public announcement [kunnjøring]: § 29, 35, 36 of the Public Administration Act.

Having analysed which terms and expressions could lead to possible obstacles to electronic communication, the drafters of the Bill then examined whether amendments were necessary and, if so, which amendments

---

[6] ERegelprosjektet om tilrettelegging for elektronisk kommunikasjon i lovverket: <http://odin.dep.no/nhd/norsk/publ/rapporter/024011-220007/index-dok000-b-n-a.html>.

[7] Ot.prp. nr. 108 (2000-2001) Om lov om endringer I diverse lover for å fjerne hindringer for elektronisk kommunikasjon: <http://www.dep.no/nhd/norsk/publ/otprp/index-b-n-a.html>.

should be made. An overview is given below of the approaches that were chosen with regard to each of the possible obstacles.[8]

Document

The Bill inserts in paragraph 2 (list of definitions) a new definition of a document: "Document: a logically defined amount of information which is stored on a medium for later reading, listening, showing or transmission". Thus, the Bill follows a recent amendment to the Freedom of Information Act, which defines 'document' in that Act in a similar way.

Copy

The drafters of the Bill considered that, in the digital environment, it is not possible to distinguish an 'original' from a 'copy', because a 'copy' and an 'original' always contain the same amount of information.[9] However, according to the drafters of the Act, this does not mean that the term 'copy' does not fulfil its function when the Act is applied in an electronic environment. In the present text of the Public Administration Act, the term 'copy' can be interpreted as 'an electronic copy'. For example, paragraph 33 of the Act requires that a copy of the appeal must be attached if the respondent to an appeal case is notified by letter. In this case, the term 'copy' can be interpreted as 'an electronic copy'. Therefore, it was not considered necessary to amend the Act.

In writing

The Bill inserts a new definition in paragraph 2 (list of definitions): "In writing also constitutes an electronic message if the information contained in the data message is accessible so as to be usable for subsequent reference." Thus, the Bill follows the functional approach towards the requirement of 'in writing' as given in the UNCITRAL Model law on Electronic Commerce with Guide to Enactment.[10]

---

[8] ERegelprosjektet om tilrettelegging for elektronisk kommunikasjon i lovverket, p. 16-36. Additional information was provided in an interview by Mr. O. Røhnebæk, Ministry of Justice, 15 February 2001.

[9] Interview with Mr. O. Røhnebæk, Ministry of Justice, 15 February 2001.

[10] United Nations Commission on International Trade Law (UNCITRAL), *UNCITRAL Model Law on Electronic Commerce with Guide to Enactment* (article 6), 1996: <http://www.uncitral.org/english/texts/electcom/ml-ecomm.htm>.

To be put down in writing

The Bill inserts a new definition of 'to be put in writing' in paragraph 2 (list of definitions): "To be put down in writing or recorded" also to be put down in writing electronically, if this fulfills the reasons underlying the requirement of 'to be put down in writing' as much as 'to be put down in writing on paper'. The drafters of the Bill indicated in an interview that the reasons for this are: 1) to secure evidence of what happened during the proceedings, and 2) to reconstruct a case later on.[11]

Signed

The phrase 'signed' appears only once in the Public Administration Act. According to Paragraph 32, the notice of appeal against an individual decision must be 'signed by the appellant or his agent'. The Bill proposes an addendum, stating that electronic authentication in accordance with technical regulations given on the basis of Paragraph 15a, will suffice as 'signed'. Furthermore, the Bill proposes to add a new provision (Paragraph 32, subsection 4), stating "that a notice of appeal may be lodged by electronic means, if the administrative agency has made arrangements to receive an appeal in an electronic form".

Orally

As this expression retains its traditional meaning – communication by voice – in the digital era, no amendment is proposed here.

To lodge an appeal

Paragraph 32, under b, provides "that the notice of appeal shall be signed by the applicant or his agent". The Bill proposes to add a new provision (Paragraph 32, subsection 4), providing: "that a notice of appeal may be lodged by electronic means, if the administrative agency has made arrangements to receive an appeal in an electronic form". See also, under "Signed".

Having reached the party

With regard to this expression the Explanatory Memorandum to the Bill states that, when a decision is sent electronically, the decision is regarded

[11] Interview with Mr. O. Røhnebæk, Ministry of Justice, 15 February 2001.

as having reached the party at the time when the message *has been opened.* This implies an information system whereby the sender of the message (i.e. the administrative agency) can time the moment when the message is opened by the receiver (in this case the citizen). The Explanatory Memorandum to the Bill further states that, when a decision is also made public in another way (for example on a website on the Internet), the decision is regarded as having reached the party when the individual was first informed of the decision.

Notification (of the decision)
Paragraph 27 of the present text of the Public Administration Act provides that "the administrative agency which has made the decision shall ensure that the parties are notified of the decision as soon as possible. Normally the notification shall be in writing. Should it be particularly burdensome for the administrative agency to give written notification, or if the matter is urgent, notification may be given orally or by other means". The Bill inserts a new sentence in this parapraph, after the words 'in writing': "The written notification may be given electronically, if the receiver has expressively accepted this". In an interview the drafters of the Bill indicated that secondary legislation is being prepared (see paragraph 4.2.3). However, this secondary legislation contains no further details on the interpretation of the term "expressively". This could come in comments to the regulation, but at the time when this study was finalized, no such comments had been suggested.[12]

Public announcement (of a decision)
Paragraph 29 of the present text of the Public Administration Act provides that: "if notification of the decision is made by public announcement, the time limit of appeal shall run from the date on which the decision was first published." According to the Explanatory Memorandum to the Bill, the expression "by public announcement" does not constitute an obstacle to electronic communication, as this expression can also be interpreted as 'by public announcement in an electronic way', for example on the website of the administrative agency. Therefore, the drafters of the Bill consider it to be unnecessary to amend this provision.

[12] Comment by Mr. R. Riisnæs, of the University of Oslo.

4.2.3 Draft Regulations on electronic communication with and within the Public Administration[13]

In addition to the amendments to the Public Administration Act which were discussed in the previous sections of this chapter, secondary legislation is being prepared which will provide procedural rules for electronic communication with and within the public sector. These rules are laid down in *The Draft Regulations on electronic communication with and within the Public Administration* (hereinafter: Draft Regulations). At the time when this report was finalized, the rules were still under discussion in the Ministry and were expected to be published in October or November 2001.

To ensure that the Draft Regulations have binding effect, the Bill proposes a new Paragraph 15a in the Public Administration Act. It reads:

> "Paragraph 15a (Electronic Communication)
> The King may prescribe regulations regarding electronic communication between administrative agencies and the public, electronic handling of cases and communication inside the administrative agencies, inter alia regarding:
> a) which electronic address or information service to use;
> b) signing, authentication, the securing of integrity and confidentiality;
> c) receipt of the submission of an electronic message;
> d) technical requirements for the products, services and standards which may be used;
> e) the right of administrative agencies to block a user who misuses data designated for signing, authentication, the securing of integrity and confidentiality, and on what constitutes misuse."

The question of whether or not electronic communication will be allowed in administrative law proceedings is not subject to the Draft Regulations but to the Public Administration Act, as amended in the law reform currently taking place ("eRegelprosjektet").[14]

---

[13] At the time of writing this chapter, the Draft Regulations had not yet been published. This paragraph was written on the basis of an interview with Mr. R. Riisnæs, of the University of Oslo, who is one of the drafters of the Draft Regulations.

[14] ERegelprosjektet om tilrettelegging for elektronisk kommunikasjon i lovverket: <http://odin.dep.no/nhd/norsk/publ/rapporter/024011-220007/index-dok000-b-n-a.html>. See above in section 4.2.2 of this chapter.

The basic rules provided by the Draft Regulations can be listed as follows:

- Electronic signatures and related services should be provided by the market and not by the administration.
- A permanent committee will be established to evaluate systems and to co-ordinate the use of electronic signatures in the public sector (Section 12 of the Draft Regulations).
- There are no general requirements for security services. The level of security services will be determined by the administration depending on other legal requirements and the nature of the transaction or procedure in question. A choice may be made for a certain type of procedure/transaction when this is considered to be necessary (Section 3 of the Draft Regulations).
- If the user does not meet the above requirements, the administration shall notify the sender of the error and give advise as to how it could be rectified (Section 5 of the Draft Regulations).

The Draft Regulations include provisions on the communication of electronic decisions made by the administration:

- Decisions can be communicated electronically, subject to the consent of the individual (Section 6 of the Draft Regulations).
- Such communication should be made by sending a message to the individual, informing him that the electronic decision is available from a certain information system and advising him how to access it.
- If the electronic decision has not been opened by the individual within seven days, a paper copy will be sent.

Notices of appeal may be filed electronically if the administrative agency decides to do so (Section 7 of the Draft Regulations).[15]

Access to files/information may be requested and, if technically possible, opened by electronic means provided that sufficient authentication and confidentiality is assured (Section 8 of the Draft Regulations).

Electronic messages, signed with electronic signatures, or authenticated by other means, should be archived together with such information as is

[15] See also Paragraph 32 of the Public Administration Act.

necessary to guarantee the reliability of the message for the relevant period of time (Section 10 of the Draft Regulations).

The Draft Regulations also provide rules on how to obtain electronic signatures and requirements for loyal and secure use of the keys and certificates, notification of security breaches, and secure system configuration. The administration may restrict the use of a certificate if it is misused (Sections 14-22 of the Draft Regulations).

If individuals use electronic communication to correspond with an administrative agency, the administrative agency shall ensure that encryption services or other security services are available, if necessary, to ensure privacy or confidentiality (Sections 23-26 of the Draft Regulations). Information to a government agency should be encrypted using the key of the government agency (not of an individual employee), unless otherwise decided by this agency. Information, received by any administrative agency, should be decrypted immediately. If decryption is impossible, the message should be rejected. Spare copies of government agency encryption keys should be escrowed or backed up unless otherwise decided for certain areas.

4.3 Case law

During this research project no case law relating to electronic communication in administrative law was found.

4.4 Interaction between administrative and civil law

One of the characteristics of Norwegian law is that administrative law and civil law are two separate legal systems. If the written Public Administration Act and other written legislation in the field of administrative law do not regulate a certain issue in the public sector, this issue will be addressed by applying the general principles of administrative law, and not by applying the rules of civil law.

4.5 Conclusions and main findings

Government agencies in Norway are making increasing use of the Internet to communicate with citizens and private companies to provide them with government information and to deliver electronic services. However, the development of "electronic government" in Norway is hindered by legal obstacles in the Public Administration Act, as well as uncertaincies with regard to the authenticity, integrity and confidentiality of electronic communication. At present legislation is being prepared to remove these obstacles and uncertainties. A Bill of Amendments to the Public Administration Act was presented to the Norwegian Parliament on 31 August 2001. In conjunction with this Bill of Amendments, secondary legislation is being prepared which will provide procedural rules for electronic communication with and within the public sector.

Chapter 5
THE UNITED STATES

Chapter 5
THE UNITED STATES

5.1 INTRODUCTION

Federal administrative law in the United States differs quite substantially from the administrative law we know in the civil law systems of Europe. This makes it complicated to undertake a comparative survey on how US federal government agencies and departments use electronic forms of communication. In order not to get entangled in the details concerning the differences between the US administrative law and most of the European administrative law systems, the present survey will be limited to comparing the way some important federal government agencies do or do not use information and communication technologies and concepts (ICT) to improve their services. Two major federal government agencies were studied: the Internal Revenue Service (IRS), and the United States Patent and Trade Mark Office. These agencies will serve as illustrations of the attitudes towards and the policies and realities of 'e-government' at the federal level in the United States. They will also provide a good insight into the structure and functioning of federal administrative law and the most recent developments, for example e-filing and electronic signatures.

5.2 PRESENT PRACTICE

5.2.1 Approaches and policies related to e-government

Ever since information and communication technologies became available, federal agencies have used them for different purposes. The federal government agencies' and departments' most important motives for using ICT were to facilitate their own working processes by making them more effective and cost-efficient and consequently, to enable them to improve their services to the public. The federal government agencies and departments are the most important actors in the field of federal administrative law. Up until the 1990s, the main focus was on the internal organization of the agencies; ICT was predominantly used to improve the internal working processes of agencies and departments. The advent of more sophisticated communication technologies and the growth of the Internet prompted a more client-oriented, external attitude. The concept of 'e-Government'[1] which emerged, uses ICTs not only for static information dissemination, but as a basis for the development of interactive and integrated digital services such as, electronic filing, on-line applications for permits and licenses, paperless acquisitions of electronic government services and the tailoring of information to the public. The National Performance Review report of September 1993 on *Reengineering Through Information Technology*, Accompanying Report of the National Performance Review, contained the requirement to implement electronic government. Al Gore's 1997 report *Access America* contained the initiatives to accomplish this requirement. The electronic government idea in the United States is based on the concept of integrated service delivery (ISD) which, in a broad sense, denotes the convergence of government services under *one* interface which is accessible to citizens.[2] In the US a characteristic of this ISD concept is the citizen-focused view

[1] According to the definition given in the Deloitte Research report, *At the Dawn of e-Government; the Citizen as Customer*, <http://www.dttus.com/pub/ggovt/gegovt.htm> (15 May 2001), e-government means: "the use of technology to enhance the access to and delivery of government services to benefit citizens, business partners and employees", p. 1, New York, 2000. See also Jeff Breen, At the Dawn of e-Government; the Citizen as Customer, *Government Finance Review*, October 2000, p. 15 ff. This is a distinctly different definition than the one Jörn von Lucke gives in his contribution 'Electronic Government in der Welt' in: Heinrich Reinermann (Hrsg.), *Regieren und Verwalten in Informationzeitsalter*, Heidelberg 2000, p. 186. Von Lucke sees e-Government as (in a free translation from German) the integrated management and redress of societal processes, problems and issues using IT. His definition is somewhat more government-oriented.

[2] See the Report of the Intergovernmental Advisory Board and the Federation of Government Information Processing Councils in cooperation with the Office of Intergovernmental Solutions, Office of Government-wide Policy U.S. General Services Administration, *Integrated Service Delivery*; Governments Using Technology to Serve the Citizen, August 1999, p. 5. Published at <http://www.gsa.gov/attachments/ GSA_PUBLICATIONS> extpub (20 July 2001).

of technology and the desire to provide government services on the citizen's terms bypassing bureaucracy and the red tape plaguing government at all levels. Most US government agencies and departments are a long way from achieving truly citizen-oriented government services. The 1999 Report *Integrated Service Delivery* (Governments Using Technology to Serve the Citizen) of the Intergovernmental Advisory Board and the Federation of Government Information Processing Councils concludes that US agencies and departments use a wide variety of approaches to benefit from state-of-the-art ICTs. However, integrating electronic interactive services under one interface is still in progress. One of the emerging trends in the US is that ISD is being targeted towards specific citizens' groups like seniors and students. Another trend is a definite increase in electronic government services on-line.[3] The US government was definitely not a clear leader in the early stages of e-government as an editorial review in the Government Finance Review put it.[4] The highly decentralized and varied operational practices of the different governmental agencies and departments are key factors for this leeway.

5.2.2 IRS present practice in electronic communication[5]

The IRS (the US tax authority) is a government agency that in comparison with other US government agencies or departments, very actively employs ICT and new forms of electronic communication to improve its services to the public. The continuing introduction and integration of ever more state-of-the-art computer technology have proven to be extremely useful to tax planners and preparers.[6] Especially the practice of electronic filing (e-filing) and electronic payment of taxes via electronic funds trans-

[3] See the *Integrated Service Delivery*-report, p. 3.

[4] Digital Government on the Internet; Rating e-Gov Websites, *Government Finance Review*, October 2000, p. 54.

[5] The following paragraphs are based on interviews with the IRS (Mr. M. Mundaca, legal counselor IRS, April 12, 2001) and the USPTO (Ms. K. Byars and L. Beressord, April 13, 2001).

[6] See Mehmet C. Kocakulah and Galen M. Gower, Modernizing the Bureaucracy: Government Information Systems and Technology, *National Public Accountant*, 1999, p. 24-41.

fer (EFT)[7] have made the entire tax process much more dependent on improving the level of information technology to meet the increasing needs and complexity of the tax environment. One of the main missions of the IRS is to increase e-filing to 80% of the total tax returns. These missions were imposed upon the IRS by the IRS Restructuring and Reform Act of 1998 (IRSRRA '98). This Act obliges the IRS to:

1. Make paperless filing the preferred and most convenient means of filing Federal tax and information returns;
2. Achieve the goal of electronically filing at least 80% of all such returns by 2007; and
3. Encourage the private sector through cooperation to increase the e-filing of such returns.

The IRSRRA '98 also created the Electronic Tax Administration Advisory Committee (ETAAC), which anually reports the progress of the IRSRRA '98 goals to Congress. The IRS' plans are truly ambitious, especially considering the fact that in 1998 only 10% of all the tax returns were filed electronically. A major obstacle for smooth and expedient e-filing was overcome this year. Taxpayers who filed electronically were obliged to send an (additional) paper copy of a form verifying their identity.[8] This year the IRS will now allow a self-selected, five-digit personal identification number (PIN), together with two 'shared secrets' (tax liability and prior year adjusted gross income) and the taxpayer's name and Social Security number.[9] This will together constitute a valid signature.[10] This kind of electronic communication however, only applies to the first part of the IRS' communication with the taxpayers, i.e. the filing of the initial tax return-file. All other forms of communication between the IRS and its clients are paper-based. At present, strict rules and policies on confidentiality and privacy leave no other options. The IRS is looking into the possibility of using 'waivers' whereby clients will forfeit some of their

[7] The electronic payment of taxes was given a new incentive in 1996 when a new Electronic Federal Tax Payment System (EFPTS) was set up.

[8] Up until 2001 taxpayers had to file a paper copy of Form 8453, U.S. Individual Income Tax Declaration for Electronic Filing.

[9] See Stuart Kahan, Sign in, Please!, *Practical Accountant*, October 2000, p. 64-66.

[10] See Lesli S. Laffie, News Notes, The Tax Adviser, August 2000, p. 532.

privacy and confidentiality rights in order to enable the IRS to communicate with them electronically.

A specific type of electronic communication is available from the IRS website.[11] Different forms for e-filing together with all kinds of information may be downloaded from the IRS website.

5.2.3 USPTO present practice in electronic communication

The primary services of the USPTO include processing patents and trade marks and disseminating patent and trade mark information. Through the issuance of patents, the USPTO encourages technological advancement by providing incentives to invent, invest in, and disclose new technology worldwide. Through the registration of trade marks, the USPTO assists businesses in protecting their investments, promoting goods and services, and safeguarding consumers against confusion and deception in the marketplace. The USPTO also uses ICT very actively to promote and improve its services. First of all, the USPTO uses ICT to enable clients to file applications for patents and to register trade marks electronically. USPTO initiated the full production of its electronic patent application filing system (EFS) in October 2000. Patent applications are confidential by statute. Thus, the agency also offers filers a customer number and digital certificate to sign the application, and uses a digital certificate to ensure that EFS transmissions are encrypted from the applicant's computer all the way to USPTO's electronic mailroom. The agency uses the latest public key infrastructure (PKI) technology to guarantee the security of electronic applications. EFS has a built-in validation function to help applicants adhere to USPTO rules and to avoid mistakes of form that can cause delays. EFS is – according to the USPTO – a major step toward fully automating and improving the quality of patent application processing.[12]

A similar e-filing system already existed for the filing of trade mark registering requests: the Web-based Trademark Electronic Application System (TEAS). TEAS allows trade mark filers to fill out an application

---

[11] Located at <http://www.irs.ustreas.gov/> (10 April 2001).

[12] See the press release of October 27 2000 Doors Open to Electronic Patent Filing; USPTO will accept patent applications for inventions over the Internet, published on the USPTO website at <http://www.uspto.gov/web/offices/com/speeches> (25 July 2001).

form and check it for completeness over the Internet. More than 23,000 applicants have used TEAS successfully to file their trade mark applications since this service went on-line in October 1998. E-TEAS has two components. Using e-TEAS, a customer can submit an application directly to the trade mark examining operation over the Internet, paying by credit card or through an existing PTO deposit account. The applicant can also use PrinTEAS to print out a completed application for mailing to the PTO, paying by cheque, money order or through a deposit account.[13]

Another important digital communication USPTO service is the Trademark Electronic Search System (TESS). TESS allows the public to search and retrieve, via an Internet browser, the 2.6 million plus pending, registered, abandoned, cancelled or expired trade mark records found in PTOs' X-Search system. PTOs' X-Search is the same database and search system used by PTOs' examining attorneys for examining trade mark applications. TESS replaces the on-line trade mark search database that PTO made available to the public in August 1998.[14]

USPTO manages to deliver almost all of its services electronically. Not only can applicants use electronic application forms, but all other interested parties may search and visit the public records of the USPTO. In 1999 § 2.33 section d of the (37 CFR, part II) Trademark Law Treaty Implementation Act was amended in order to make electronic signatures of electronic trade mark and patent files possible. The USPTO was quite successful in digitalizing its services. The 2000 annual report shows that e-filing is very popular and exceeds expectations.[15]

5.3 Legislative action and initiatives for electronic communication

At present there are only few federal provisions on electronic communication. The concept of an electronic decision does not appear in federal leg-

[13] URL for the e-TEAS system: <http://www.uspto.gov/teas/index.html> (9 April 2001).

[14] See the press release of February 29 2000 PTO Introduces New Trademark Electronic Search System, published on the USPTO website at <http://www.uspto.gov/web/offices/com/speeches> (25 July 2001).

[15] See the annual report for 2000 at <http://www.uspto.gov/web/offices/com/annual/2000> (25 July 2001).

islation. However, this does not mean that electronic decision-making does not exist. The IRS, for instance, handles a great deal of tax returns using ICTs. Legislation of a general nature regarding electronic communication is only found in the Electronic Signatures in Global and National Commerce Act (ESIGN), enacted by Congress on June 30, 2000. ESIGN facilitates the use of electronic records and signatures in interstate or foreign commerce and can be used to remove uncertainty about the validity of contracts entered into electronically. Under the Act, businesses that are required to provide or make available information to consumers in writing may provide consumers with that information using electronic records only if the consumer affirmatively consents, in a manner that reasonably demonstrates the consumer's ability to access the electronic record. ESIGN is not only applicable in the private sector but also has a bearing on relations in the public sector. In the foregoing paragraph we already signalled the IRSs' and USPTOs' initiatives to acknowledge and validate electronic signatures. This led to legislative action only in the case of the Trademark Law. The IRS' acceptance of e-signatures was not a matter of law, but a matter of fact.

Another important federal legislative project related to electronic communication is the Paperwork Reduction Act of 1995.[16] The goals of this Act are to, amongst other things, a) minimize the paperwork burden for persons and companies resulting from the collection of information by or for the Federal Government, b) ensure the greatest possible public benefit from and maximize the utility of information created, collected, maintained, used, shared and disseminated by or for the Federal Government; c) coordinate, integrate, and to the extent practicable and appropriate, make uniform Federal information resources management policies and practices as a means to improve the productivity, efficiency, and effectiveness of Government programs, including the reduction of information collection burdens on the public and the improvement of service delivery to the public; d) provide for the dissemination of public information on a timely basis, on equitable terms, and in a manner that promotes the utility of the information to the public and makes effective use of information technology; e) ensure the integrity, quality, and utility of the Federal statistical system; and f) ensure that information technology is acquired,

[16] 44 U.S.C. 3501 et seq.

used, and managed to improve performance of agency missions, including the reduction of information collection burdens on the public. One of the practical implications of this 1995 Act is the promotion of e-filing. The aforementioned IRS Restructuring and Reform Act of 1998 (IRSRRA '98) applies the paper reduction principles from the 1995 Act to the functioning of the IRS.

Other important legislative developments as regards the issue of electronic communication are the Electronic Freedom of Information Act Amendments of 1996 which amends the Freedom of Information Act.[17] These amendments stipulate that for records created on, or after November 1, 1996, within one year after such date, each agency must make such records available, including by computer telecommunications or, if computer telecommunication means have not been established by the agency, by other electronic means. Other records had to be digitalized by the end of 1999.

5.4 Administrative law in the United States

5.4.1 General characteristics of the administrative system

Federal administrative law is very diverse in the US. Administrative law at the federal level includes an entire range of actions by government with respect to the citizen or by the citizen with respect to the government, except for those matters dealt with by the criminal law and those left to private civil litigation where the government's participation is in furnishing an impartial tribunal with the power of enforcement.[18] Quite simply, administrative law concerns the limitations of the powers and actions of administrative agencies.[19] Ever since the beginning of the 20th century a great deal of new agencies[20] have been established and vested with pow-

[17] 5 U.S.C. § 552, as Amended By Pub. L. 104-231, 110 Stat. 2422.

[18] A. Friendly, New Trends in Administrative Law, 6 Md., *Bar J.*, No. 3, 1974, p. 9.

[19] See Ernest Gellhorn and Ronald M. Levin, *Administrative Law and Process*, third ed., St. Paul Mn. 1990, p. 8.

[20] The concept of an agency is however much older. The first one was established by the Act of July 31, 1789, to estimate the duties payable on imports and to perform other related duties.

ers emanating from different Acts. This empowerment of agencies by Statute Acts is called 'delegation'. Throughout the modern era of administrative regulation, agencies have been delegated varying powers. Some of these powers are assigned on an industry-wide basis, as with the Interstate Commerce Commission, or the Nuclear Regulatory Commission, other agencies are charged with enforcing certain norms of conduct throughout the economy, as is the case with the Federal Trade Commission. The specific Act that empowers an agency is called an agency organic Act.[21] Delegations may involve different powers. Many agencies, for instance, operate under statutes that give them *legislative power* to issue rules which control private behaviour (including criminal or civil penalties in case of violations). Statutes may also delegate *executive* power to an agency, for instance, to investigate potential violations, issue licences,[22] etc. Even judicial powers to *adjucate*[23] particular disputes over whether an individual or company has failed to comply with the governing standards may be granted by an agency organic Act.

Agencies are typically governed by a specific agency organic Act which lays down the bulk of the substantive law applicable to the functioning of the agency. Apart from these specific substantive norms, general administrative rules also apply. Most of them are to be found in the Public Administration Act (APA) enacted in 1946. The APA sets a uniform standard for administrative procedure in much of the national government's bureaucracy.

The point of reference for the judicial review of administrative acts by agencies in the administrative law system of the USA is not, as is the case in many continental law systems, the administrative decision, rule or order, but the agency and the way it has (ab)used its powers. The central concepts in the APA are therefore 'agency' which is defined in § 551 of the APA and 'judicial review' in Chapter 7 of the APA. § 706 of the APA defines the scope of review as follows:

---

[21] See Kenneth Culp Davis and Richard J. Pierce jr., *Administrative Law Treatise*, third ed., Boston/New York, Toronto/London 1994, p. 2.

[22] See § 551, S8 of the Public Administration Act (APA).

[23] See § 554 APA.

Sec. 706. Scope of review

To the extent necessary to reach a decision and when presented, the reviewing court shall decide all relevant questions of law, interpret constitutional and statutory provisions, and determine the meaning or applicability of the terms of an agency action. The reviewing court shall:

1. compel agency action unlawfully withheld or unreasonably delayed; and
2. hold unlawful and set aside agency action, findings, and conclusions found to be:
   a) arbitrary, capricious, an abuse of discretion, or otherwise not in accordance with law;
   b) contrary to constitutional right, power, privilege, or immunity;
   c) in excess of statutory jurisdiction, authority, or limitations, or short of statutory right;
   d) without observance of procedure required by law;
   e) unsupported by substantial evidence in a case subject to sections 556 and 557 of this title or otherwise reviewed on the record of an agency hearing provided by statute; or
   f) unwarranted by the facts to the extent that the facts are subject to trial de novo by the reviewing court. In making the foregoing determinations, the court shall review the whole record or those parts of it cited by a party, and due account shall be taken of the rule of prejudicial error.

The judicial review of agency action is exercised by the ordinary courts. They can – in ordinary cases – be addressed when all administrative remedies (such as hearings, etc.) or avenues have been exhausted and when the litigant has sufficient standing, i.e. sufficient interest in an issue to bring suit.

5.4.2 Interaction between civil law and administrative law

The interaction between civil law and administrative law in the US is very intense. The US administrative law system developed on the basis of US civil law and has strong roots in the common law tradition. Over the last decades however, administrative law in the US has specialized dramatically. Administrative law now has its own standing and is treated more and more like 'public law' is in (European) continental law systems.[24] Most administrative litigation, however, is – ultimately – handled by the ordinary courts and a great deal of applicable principles and legislation stem from civil law origins. The scope of this survey does not allow one to go into this myriad of principles and provisions in any detail. The scope of review of Chapter 7 of the APA. § 706 of the APA provides an accurate insight into the 'administrative principles' applicable to administrative actions.

5.5 Requirements of the system relevant to electronic communication: IRS and USPTO and administrative law

Both the IRS and the USPTO are federal agencies that exercise powers under organic agency acts. The Internal Revenue Code[25] of 1986 (IRC) is one of the most important codes within the IRS. The IRC grants various powers to the IRS ranging from the authority to assess tax returns (Chapter 63) to arranging hearings before levies,[26] giving licenses[27], etc. The most important Act for the USPTO is the Patent Code[28] that gives the USPTO different responsibilities in the process leading up to the (refusal to) issue of patents and the registration of trade marks.[29]

The APA does not have any specific provisions regarding electronic communication between agencies and their clients. Most of the law re-

[24] See Richard J. Pierce, Syney A. Shapiro and Paul R. Verkuil, *Administrative Law and Process*, third ed., New York 1999, p. 6-9.

[25] US Code Title 26.

[26] Sec. 6330. Notice and opportunity for hearing before levy.

[27] Sec. 7001. Collection of foreign items.

[28] US Code Title 35 contains the basic authorities for the administration of patent laws, derived from the Act of July 19, 1952, and subsequent enactment.

[29] There are however more codes and statutes relevant to the work of the USPTO, for instance 15 U.S.C. 1051-1127 that contains provisions of the Trademark Act of 1946 that govern the administration of the trade mark registration system of the Patent and Trade Mark Office, 15 U.S.C. 1511 that states that the Patent and Trade Mark Office is under the jurisdiction and supervision of the Department of Commerce, and 44 U.S.C. 1337-1338 that contains authority to print patents, trade marks, and other matters relating to the business of the Office.

garding electronic communication is to be found in the specific Acts (e.g. the IRSRRA '98 or the Trademark Law Treaty Implementation Act that were dealt with in the former paragraphs). Federal Acts of a general nature relating to electronic communication are the Freedom of Information Act as amended in 1996 (obliging federal agencies to supply most of their records, accessible under the Act, in an electronic format) and the Privacy Act.[30] The Privacy Act of 1974 contains provisions that forbid agencies from disclosing any information which is contained in a system of records to any person, or to another agency, except pursuant to a written request by, or with the prior written consent of, the individual to whom the record pertains.[31] Furthermore, it obliges them to keep track of disclosures of records, to amend personal records at the request of the individuals to whom the record pertains, to maintain all records which are used with such accuracy, relevance, timeliness, and completeness as is reasonably necessary to assure fairness to the individual in the determination, etc.[32] These provisions, of course, also have a bearing on the electronic forms of communication, for instance in the case of e-filing. The Privacy Act of 1974 is not especially aimed at regulating electronic communication. At the federal level the Electronic Communications Privacy Act (ECPA) is an Act that is especially geared to electronic communication. It was adopted in 1986 to address the legal privacy issues that were evolving with the growing use of computers and other new innovations in electronic communications. The impact of the ECPA on electronic communication between agencies on the one hand, and citizens on the other, is however marginal. Most of the ECPA's provisions are on surveillance. The ECPA clarifies what constitutes invasion of privacy when electronic surveillance is involved. The ECPA extends privacy protection outlined in the earlier legislation to radio paging devices, electronic mail, cellular telephones, private communication carriers, and computer transmissions. The privacy between the IRS and taxpayers is safeguarded by the principle of confidentiality protected by section 6103(a) of the Internal Rev-

---

[30] 5 U.S.C. 552a.
[31] See § 552a section b.
[32] See § 552a sections c, d, e, f and following.

enue Code. This section prohibits the disclosure of taxpayer returns and return information (subject to certain limited exceptions).[33]

5.6 Problems under the present administrative system in the light of electronic communication

One of the problems under the present administrative system seems to be the status of e-mail communication. Both in the case of the IRS and the USPTO not all of the legal details seem to have been elaborated. Legal problems do not directly occur when a first application or tax return (first e-file moment) is submitted but when the agency needs to reply (by confirming the receipt of the e-file) or the citizen is informed of the agency's decision. The IRS admits that it would like to send more documents by e-mail than it is able to at the moment, but privacy and confidentiality requirments prohibit the extended use of e-mail communication in this respect. The IRS is currently investigating the possibilities of 'waivers' whereby taxpayers waive a number of privacy and confidentiality rights in exchange for expedient e-mail communication with the tax authorities. The spokesperson in the interview however, did have a strong reticence towards 'waivers'. It is, in his view, a sign of weakness on behalf of the IRS not to be able to safeguard all privacy and confidentiality demands in e-mail communications. A real solution would be preferable. The USPTO encounters similar problems. They do send electronic filing receipts and send final decisions by electronic mail. The electronic filing receipts do not have any legal standing. Final decisions are sent by ordinary or electronic mail, depending on the recipient's desire. This does not give rise to many problems. Time-limits and deadlines for lodging objections begin to run at the moment the final decision – or any other message – is sent by the USPTO, not at the moment when the addressee receives the message.

[33] Section 6103 does contain certain limited exceptions to its bar on the disclosure of confidential information. For example, sections 6103(h)(4)(B) and 6103(h)(4)(C) provide that third-party taxpayer information can be provided in situations where the treatment of an item reflected on the taxpayer's return is *directly related* to the resolution of an issue in the proceeding in which the information is sought or where there is a *direct transactional relationship* between the party seeking the information and the taxpayer and that relationship *directly affects* the resolution of the issue.

The USPTO informed the interviewer for this survey that US Courts still – as a rule – do not accept briefs or documents in electronic format or by e-mail. This is considered to be a failed opportunity. Some experiments however are underway to also imply Courts in the e-government plans.[34]

5.6.1 **Case law**

No case law on the admissibility of e-filing or case law relating to electronic communication by the USPTO or IRS was found during this research project.

5.7 Amending administrative procedure law

In the former paragraphs, notably in section 5.3, the legislator's approach to new forms of communication was outlined. The following trends and developments could be concluded for both the IRS and the USPTO:

a) The general Public Administration Act (APA) does not touch upon the subject of electronic communication. Regulatory provisions relating to electronic communication even in substantive administrative law can hardly be found. The legislative attitude to the advent of the electronic age in administrative law seems to be a predominantly practical one. Both the IRS and the USPTO have managed to upgrade their services by using different forms of electronic communications without substantial changes to the law. The IRS Restructuring and Reform Act of 1998 (IRSRRA '98) does not really constitute an exception to this practical approach.
b) Especially for the IRS the privacy and confidentiality rules are very strict and do, to some extent, obstruct expedient and smooth electronic communication. The general privacy regime for both the IRS and the USPTO can be found in the Privacy Act of 1974 (see § 2.3 of this survey). Privacy in the relations between the IRS and taxpayers is safeguarded by the principle of confidentiality protected by section 6103(a) of the Internal Revenue Code. In this survey no distinct set

[34] See Anthony Aarons, California leads the way in electronic filing of court docs., *California Lawyer*, January 1999, p. 24.

of unwritten principles on careful communication was encountered in the case studies into the IRS and the USPTO.

c) The problem of (electronic) identification of e-filers did, in the case of the USPTO, result in limited secondary legislative action. As we noticed earlier on in this survey in 1999 § 2.33 section d of the (37 CFR, part II) Trademark Law Treaty Implementation Act was amended in order to make electronic signatures of electronic trade mark and patent files possible. In the case of the IRS the problem of electronic signatures was resolved technically by accepting electronic tax returns that bear an electronic signature consisting of a pin-code and two 'shared secrets'.

The conclusion which can be drawn from this is that the legislative attitude towards electronic communication in administrative federal law is expectant. The law is only amended when this is strictly necessary. Practical solutions seem to be preferred over and above legislative ones.

5.8 Electronic communication versus traditional communication

In American administrative law paper-based communication is still the normal way of doing business. Although the administrative law system allows for some forms of electronic communication, e.g. in the form of e-filing, and notwithstanding the paper-reduction policies and the e-government initiatives, electronic communication does not have the same legal standing as paper-based communications have. The way agencies and departments have been trying to tackle this leeway in electronic communication up until recently is to mimic the features of paper-based communication electronically (e-filing and e-signatures using paper-based authentications). The ultimate legal recognition of electronic communication still seems to be a long way off.

5.9 Conclusions and main findings

Drawing conclusions based on the case studies of the IRS and USPTO is, on the one hand, very difficult because the US federal administrative law system differs to a great extent from most European administrative law systems. Some developments are however interesting for the issues at hand. First of all, the US government has official policies on both paper reduction and e-government which have (had) substantial consequences for the introduction, handling and status of electronic communication in administrative law. As a result of these policies both the IRS and USPTO are very actively trying to make their services available to the public electronically. The USPTO has nearly managed to make all of its services available electronically. Most of the electronic communication concerns the initial stages of the agency's or department's decision-making process. In most cases e-filing has been made possible. Subsequent communication, in most cases, is still paper-based due to privacy or confidentiality restrictions. The IRS is looking into the possibilities of allowing their clients to waive their rights of full confidentiality and privacy protection in exchange for more expedient electronic communication. The USPTO engages in 'electronic' follow-up communication if the client has indicated his/her desire to do so.

The approach to the problem of electronic communication in federal administrative law seems to be predominantly practical. The legislative attitude towards electronic communication in administrative federal law is expectant. The law is only amended when this is strictly necessary, e.g. in the case of allowing electronic signatures for trade mark applications. Practical solutions seem to be preferred over and above legislative ones.

Chapter 6
ANALYSIS

Chapter 6
ANALYSIS

6.1 INTRODUCTION

In the foregoing chapters we have provided an overview and analysis of legislative developments in administrative procedural law in four countries: France, Germany, Norway and the United States. We discussed the developments in these countries as well as the approach taken in amending the law to facilitate electronic administrative communication. What can we learn from the regulatory projects in these countries? What differences become clear when comparing the choices made abroad with the situation in The Netherlands?

6.2 PRESENT SITUATION

6.2.1 On-line communication: use and ambitions

The analysis of the situation in all four countries shows that administrative agencies use the Internet for their day-to-day communications with citizens and companies. In all countries, on-line communication was introduced in order to improve the service rendered to citizens and businesses. A closer look shows that the prime aim of the respective governments is restricted to facilitating the on-line availability of government information, the Internet accessibility to all government bodies, the simplification of administrative procedures and the avoidance of the physical presence of citizens or companies. At present, an administrative decision is not handled electronically and subsequently communicated on-line. Thus, electronic communication remains restricted to making forms available on-line but subsequently requiring these to be printed out, completed and sent by post. Even in the United States, generally acknowledged as

J.E.J. Prins (Ed.), E-Government and its Implications for Administrative Law

the leader in electronic government facilities, only very few government bodies allow the on-line communication of a final administrative decision.

The situation differs among the four countries regarding the effect of these policy plans on the speed with which the required amendments of the Public Administration Act are proposed and implemented.

In France, it does not appear that any specific legislative action will be taken in the near future, despite the various general e-government ambitions that have been launched over the past three years. On 13 June 2001, the French cabinet finally presented the long-awaited text of the proposal. The draft Information Society Law (*Project de Loi sur la Société de l'Information*) comprises 50 articles, divided into five principal chapters: 1) assuring citizens' access to digital information; 2) assuring freedom in on-line communication; 3) promoting electronic commerce; 4) assuring the development of the digital network; 5) the prevention of cyber crime.[1] This omnibus law, however, contains no specific proposals to amend the administrative procedure legislation in order to facilitate electronic decisions.

The absence of any substantive discussion on the development of electronic decisions in the French administration is in fact quite emblematic of its specific position. An appropriate legal framework is just the second step in implementing the taking of electronic administrative decisions. The first necessary step is a strong political will to commit administrative agents to adapt to modern changes and technology. Only such a will can overcome the difficulty the French administration has in considering the citizen as a "client" rather than as a dependent individual. That the improvement of the position of citizens should be the driving force of administrative concerns, is quite a new concept in France. In this respect, the French administration, although it is trying to improve its relations with citizens, is still far away from the official goals that have been declared in general policies.

The German situation is characterised by the fact that due to the Federal system, the majority of the interaction between citizens and the public administration takes place at the local or regional level. Almost all states are about to offer on-line access to land registers and indeed other states

[1] Available at: <http://www.lsi.industrie.gouv.fr>.

are planning to do so. Hamburg has now launched a pilot-project with the first instance fiscal court, making it possible to file a suit electronically and Bremen offers the on-line ordering of personal registration certificates, including a payment function. At the federal level, current on-line services for citizens include job-seeking services, credit handling for student scholarships, income tax declarations, a distributing system for geographical data and a statistics shop. It is clear that, in contrast to France, the widespread and accelerating development toward electronic government has heightened the pressure on the German legislature to provide the necessary legal amendments and thus day-to-day practice has certainly fuelled the developments surrounding the amendment of the administrative procedure law.

The same applies to Norway. Although no empirical studies are available on the present use of the Internet by government agencies, clearly the Internet is used on a large scale, both at a central and a local level. The widespread use of the Internet by government agencies is a key ambition under the Action Plan for Electronic Government 1999-2001.[2] The realisation of this ambition is however hindered by the lack of an adequate legal framework, which prompted the Norwegian government to decide to amend, by means of a Bill published on 31 August 2001, the Public Administration Act and to introduce additional Draft Regulations to enhance the security of electronic communication.

Contrary to what most people would expect at first sight, in the field of e-government the United States is definitely not the clear leader in the early stages of e-government, as an editorial review in the Government Finance Review puts it.[3] The highly decentralised and varied operational practices of the different governmental agencies and departments are key factors for this leeway. The 1999 Report *Integrated Service Delivery* (Governments Using Technology to Serve the Citizen) of the Intergovernmental Advisory Board and the Federation of Government Information Processing Councils concludes that US agencies and departments use a wide variety of approaches to benefit from state of the art ICTs. However,

---

[2] Available at: <http://www.odin.dep.no/aad/norsk/publ/rapporter/002005-990168/index-dok000-b-n-a.html>.

[3] Digital Government on the Internet; Rating e-Gov Websites, *Government Finance Review*, October 2000, p. 54.

integrating electronic, interactive services under one interface is still in progress. One of the emerging trends in the USA is that electronic government applications are beginning to be targeted towards specific citizens' groups like senior citizens and students. Another trend is the definite increase of electronic government services on-line.

As a result of the highly decentralised electronic practices, only a few federal provisions exist on electronic communication in the US. The concept of an electronic decision does not appear in federal legislation. However, this does not mean that electronic decision-making does not exist. The IRS for instance, does deal with a large amount of tax returns using ICTs. Legislation of a general nature regarding electronic communication is only to be found in the Electronic Signatures in Global and National Commerce Act, enacted by Congress on June 30, 2000 (ESIGN). ESIGN facilitates the use of electronic records and signatures in interstate or foreign commerce and to remove uncertainty about the validity of contracts entered into electronically. ESIGN is not only applicable in the private sector but also has a bearing on relations in the public sector. Various legislative initiatives have acknowledged electronic administrative communication at the decentralised level. This report analyses the IRSs and USPTOs initiatives to acknowledge and validate electronic signatures. The Trademark Law case was the only case which led to legislative action. The IRS acceptance of e-signatures was not a matter of law but a matter of fact.

6.2.2 Electronic communication under case law

A highly relevant question in the context of the present status of electronic communication under administrative procedure law, is whether or not a document sent by means of an electronic medium meets the requirement of "written communication" or "handwritten signature'', and, what position the courts have taken in this matter.

In France, no specific case law exists under administrative law as regards the status of electronic communication, such as e-mail. However, as has been indicated in chapter 2 of this study, an administrative decision sent by telex, for instance, has been considered as valid, as well as the refusal of a request for extradition that has been communicated orally. On the other hand, a decision of the Conseil d'Etat has explicitly provided that the signature required on an administrative act should be "handwritten". It therefore seems difficult to draw any safe conclusion from the few judicial examples in order to acknowledge the validity of administrative acts communicated electronically.

In Germany, the courts have given different answers to the afore-mentioned question, whereby the highest administrative court (*Bundesverwaltungsgericht*) and the highest social security court (*Bundessozialgericht*) have responded affirmatively, having ruled that an appeal which is filed by an e-mail-like service meets the requirement of communication "in writing". It could therefore be argued that electronic communication fits in with the legal system, but that the present situation does not render legal amendments superfluous in order to establish the complete certainty that electronic communication is allowed.

The Norwegan courts have not delivered any rulings on the status of ICT-related communication mechanisms. Also in the United States, no case law on the admissibility of e-filing or case law relating to electronic communication by the USPTO or IRS was found during this research project.

6.3 Interplay between administrative law and civil law

Characteristic of the Dutch legal system is that all civil law rules also apply to the public sector (art. 6:162 Civil Code). Hence, all public bodies have to act in accordance with both the rules of the Civil Code as well as specific rules in administrative law. This means that when administrative law does not provide any ruling on a specific topic or interpretation question, the courts may interprete administrative law in the light of the civil law rules. In other words, both systems are seen as complementary. This characteristic of Dutch law is important in situations where no rules on electronic communication are available under administrative law, whereas such rules have been provided under civil law. It also means that amendments to the Public Administration Act do not always need to be highly detailed because they can be interpreted in the light of the civil law rules and case law.

At this point a question arises regarding the extent to which other countries work with a system where public law and private law are seen as complementary, or as alternatives and what this means for the amendment of the Public Administration Act in the light of electronic communication?

From chapter 2 it becomes clear that as a consequence of the general characteristics of French administrative law, there is no formal interaction between administrative law and civil law. Both sets of rules are always understood as alternatives, and not as complementary. However, the gaining importance of electronic material as means of evidence in civil and commercial law, for instance, and the general development of electronic commerce is expected to prevent administrative law from remaining immune to technological developments. Furthermore, the distinction between private and public law seems to be minimised on certain occasions. For instance, when a regulation has been issued apparently concerning the private sector, but no equivalent regulation exists concerning the public sector, it might be possible to argue (not so much on the basis of the law, but from a commitment to realism) that the same developments will eventually characterise the latter. This suggestion seems to apply in particular to the case of electronic signatures.

In Germany, as a matter of principle, public law and civil law have also been considered as being separate for a long time. More recently, however, various scholars have taken the position that they are two parts of the legal system that are interrelated and complement each other. In current laws, however, the separation is still important. Nevertheless, stipulations of civil law can sometimes be applied in the framework of public law and they can influence the interpretation of public law. Civil law is applicable mutatis mutandis when there is a gap in public law regulations that can be appropriately filled by having recourse to civil law rules. This is particularly the case with respect to the law of obligations. It is, however, as mentioned in chapter 3, not the case regarding the formal legal requirements of "written declarations" (*Schriftform*). Civil law can also be "applied" to the extent that it expresses general rules of the legal system and can also be applied in a public law context, e.g. the rule of good faith. This might be relevant under specific circumstances in communication, be it traditional or electronic.

Chapter 4 shows that the Norwegian system lacks a close interaction between civil law and administrative law. It thus greatly differs from the system in the United States, where the interaction between civil law and administrative law is very intense. The US administrative law system developed on the basis of US civil law and has strong roots in the common law tradition. Over the past decades, however, US administrative law has specialized dramatically. Administrative law now has its own character and is considered to be more and more like 'public law' in continental law systems. Most administrative litigation, however, is – ultimately – handled by the ordinary courts and various principles and applicable legislation stem from a civil law origin.

6.4 General versus detailed

From the present Dutch proposal for a Bill, it is clear that the legislature has opted for a simple amendment of the General Administrative Law Act (Awb). It has been proposed that a limited set of provisions should be introduced at the general level, thus acknowledging the possibility to issue an electronic administrative communication (besluit). The specifics are left to more detailed Draft Regulations (dealing, among other things, with additional security measures) as well as the relevant statutes that cover specific topics (such as the environmental statutes, etc.). This means that all topic-specific statutes will in the future be amended when such specific regulations are deemed necessary. Is this approach in line with the approach taken in the surveyed countries? Precisely what issues are regulated at the general legislative level and what issues are to be regulated at the sub-level of more specific legislation?

The above questions are difficult to answer as far as the French situation is concerned. As has been mentioned in chapter 2, the French government has provided no indication whatsoever that it intends to amend the administrative procedure law in order to allow electronic communication. Furthermore, considering the absence of any discussion on this point, it is impossible to determine what a possible e-proof administrative law would look like. However, it seems that if such were the case, the usual procedure would apply: a law would determine the general rules (among which would also be a general requirement of careful electronic communication), while a decree would determine the specific conditions under which electronic communication would be fulfilled. Here mention should also be made of the position of the Conseil d'Etat. Due to the fact that the French administrative system is essentially regulated by judge-made law, and more specifically by the decisions handed down by the Conseil d'Etat, the expected development could be that the Conseil d'Etat would itself first accept administrative decisions to be communicated electronically. It has done so in relation to decisions communicated by telex, for instance, which is a frequent event in daily administrative practice (see above under 6.2.2).

In Germany, the answer to the question whether amendments are made by means of a general stipulation, affecting all specific stipulations in administrative law or by the revision of all pertinent specific stipulations is closely linked to the nature of the German administrative law system. The federal system and the widespread distribution of procedural and especially formal requirements makes a joint effort at all administrative levels and an efficient coordination of all legislative activities crucial to fostering electronic communication between citizens and public administrations. Now officials at the federal as well as the state level have started to closely cooperate with one another in a joint working group to amend the administrative procedure law. As described in chapter 3, in German administrative law, general requirements are laid down in the general Public Administration Act (VwVfG), being complemented or modified by numerous requirements in specific laws. As far as electronic communication affects a general type of administrative decision such as the "Verwaltungsakt" which has traditionally been defined and regulated in the general VwVfG, there is hardly an alternative to amending these general laws in the long run. As far as unprecedented general questions of electronic communication are concerned, for reasons of systematical consistency, they are to be regulated at this level as well. At the level of specific laws, two different approaches have been discussed. The requirements which are basically identical even though they are laid down in specific laws such as the requirement of communication "in writing" can be amended either by means of a general stipulation, or on a case-by-case basis. Requirements which are different in the respective specific laws, by their very nature can only be specifically amended. While at the outset, most comments favoured a step-by-step approach, federal and state ministers have decided to amend all the laws at the same time, enabling the amendment of the identical requirements in specific laws by means of a general provision as a default solution taking into consideration the specific needs of individual specific laws by amending them at the same time. Thus far, only the amendments to the (general) federal Public Administration Act (VwVfG-E), with provisions similar to those of the social security and tax procedure Acts, and of numerous specific tax laws seem to have been spelled out. Besides, a general decision on which procedures are considered to be suitable for electronic communication has not yet been made. Some of the specific amendments to the tax laws already ban electronic communication, however.

In Norway, the legislature has decided to amend the Public Administration Act. The prime objective of the proposed amendments of 31 August 2001 is to remove the present legal obstacles to electronic communication by simply altering the present definitions or inserting new definitions. Clearly, the Norwegian legislative project follows the functional approach chosen in the UNCITRAL Model Law on Electronic Commerce. At the Public Administration Act level it is also made clear whether or not electronic communication is allowed in specific administrative proceedings. In addition to changing the problematic terms and definitions of the Public Administration Act, the legislature will introduce a set of Draft Regulations for the use of electronic signatures and encryption in the public sector. Hence, the specific details of electronic communication of administrative decisions are laid down in secondary legislation.

Chapter 5 shows that the point of reference for the judicial review of administrative acts by agencies in the administrative law system of the US is not, as is the case in many continental law systems, the administrative decision, rule or order, but the agency and the way it has (ab)used its powers. Hence, the majority of the legislative developments to allow electronic administrative communication are to be found at a decentralised level of the agencies. The general Public Administration Act (APA) does not touch upon the subject of electronic communication. Regulatory provisions relating to electronic communication are even hardly to be found in substantive administrative law. Most of the law regarding electronic communication is found in specific acts dealing with the tasks and powers of agencies. In addition, it becomes clear that the legislative attitude towards the advent of the electronic age in administrative law seems to be a predominantly practical one. Both the IRS and USPTO have managed to upgrade their services by using different forms of electronic communications without making substantial changes to the law.

6.5 Rules on careful communication

Amending administrative procedure law alone in order to allow electronic communication will not suffice. As known, electronic communication can be distinguished by various unprecedented features, which despite their fascination and dismay, people and organisations cannot tackle by means of the traditional paradigms because the well-known paradigms have all developed along the lines of physical and local bounds of space and time. These confinements have, however, lost their meaning in a society that is characterised by virtual and distance communication and interaction. The trustworthiness which is obvious in conventional communication, no longer readily exists in electronic communication. For instance, electronic communication can mean that without proper additional security measures an http-address (URL) is not as reliable as a physical address; to verify someone's identity from a passport or driver's licence is not possible virtually; changes in a paper document are more easily detected than in a digital document; confidentiality of information is more easily guaranteed in a physical encounter (e.g. in a dialogue with a civil servant) than in a virtual encounter. These reliabilities, however, are of essential importance for the success of an electronic government. Thus, one of the key challenges in fostering electronic communication is therefore the establishment of sufficient trust between people who communicate by means of electronic facilities. In addition to the trustworthiness of the communication channel and the electronic communication itself, attention should be given to the trustworthiness of the information used and the procedure followed.

An attempt has been made to enhance trust in electronic communication by using technologies such as the use of cryptographic applications; digital certificates to ensure the authenticity of the communication partners; digital signatures and time-stamps to secure the authenticity of documents; encryption to secure the security of information. The question then arises how and to what extent these and other means for building trust can be incorporated into a legal framework for electronic administrative communication.

For the reasons mentioned above, no indication can be provided as regards the additional reliability measures which will be implemented in France.

In Germany rules on reliable electronic communication are included in internal, but nonetheless legally binding rules ("*Dienstanweisungen*", "*Verwaltungsvorschriften*"). Typically, they contain rules on the competent authorities for technical and organisational matters, the establishment and use of mailboxes, the field of application of e-mail communication, formal requirements in e-mail communication, cases in which encryption is required, archiving and documentation as a printout and, last but not least, general references to matters of network security such as how to deal with suspicious mails, the danger of viruses, etc. In addition, they regularly stipulate general rules on paper-based communication which are applicable mutatis mutandis. In their present form, the rules focus very much on e-mail communication, thereby making them technology dependent. It is expected that the rules will be extended to other forms of electronic communication as soon as they become more widespread. The following rules should be mentioned at this point:

- the rules require the establishment of a central e-mail mailbox for every agency as well as the establishment of individual mailboxes for every employee;
- these mailboxes are to be checked at least once a day;
- as a general rule, electronic communication is considered as having been received as soon as it is actually received or retrievable. With respect to an electronically transmitted administrative decision ("Verwaltungsakt") the proposed amendments to the administrative procedure law stipulate that it is deemed to have been received on the day after the message was transmitted as opposed to the third day after handing it over to the mail service with respect to written communications. However, for traditional as well as for electronic communication this is not valid if the "Verwaltungsakt" was received later or was not received at all. There is no specification regarding the moment an electronic document is sent. As regards the term 'transmitted' and 'transfer', this implies the reception of the communication within the reach of the receiver. However, in cases of doubt, the public administration bears the burden of proof as regards the actual reception. All other regulations containing legal fictions of reception implicitly demand paper-based communication but they will be modified along with the comprehensive administrative law amendments;

- the time of reception must be registered for incoming mail;
- misguided e-mails are to be forwarded to the proper receiver;
- e-mails should be deleted as soon as possible unless they are to be filed or they are considered to be of permanent relevance;
- for reasons of legal uncertainty, external e-mail communication is usually not admitted or at least not fostered as far as matters of legal significance are concerned. However, as has already been indicated this will change as soon as an electronic signature is available. As far as electronic communication is relevant to an administrative procedure or any other procedure documented in a paper-based file, usually a printout is required for the paper-based file;
- all communications containing information which is subject to rules on privacy (mainly data related to an individual) should be encrypted;
- a notification to the sender, confirming the receipt of the document by the public administration is required with respect to communications which lack formal requirements (e.g. communication required "in writing"). However, as was discussed in chapter 3, notification was also required by a lower administrative court in a case in which it was evident to the agency that the intended content of the message was missing.

As mentioned in section 6.4, the proposed amendments to the general legal framework (that is at the level of the administrative procedure law) also contain a stipulation on careful communication. This requires a public administration to notify the sender if an electronically transmitted document cannot be handled. It also has to specify the valid technical requirements in this notification.

Norway also proposes to include *Regulations on electronic communication with and within the public administration.* To provide for the binding effect of these Regulations, the Bill proposes the inclusion of a new Paragraph 15a in the Public Administration Act. It reads:

> "Paragraph 15a (Electronic Communication)
> The King may prescribe regulations regarding electronic communication between administrative agencies and the public, electronic handling of cases and communication inside the administrative agencies, inter alia regarding:

a) which electronic address or information service to use;
b) signing, authentication, the securing of integrity and confidentiality;
c) receipt of the submission of an electronic message;
d) technical requirements for the products, services and standards which may be used;
e) the right of administrative agencies to block a user who misuses data designated for signing, authentication, the securing of integrity and confidentiality, and on what constitutes misuse."

In comparison to the aforementioned German rules, one notes that the Norwegian legislature focuses on security requirements (among which are electronic signatures) and in particular pays less attention to issues surrounding the specifics of the electronic communication (such as the time of receipt and notification). The following Draft Regulations are proposed in Norway in relation to security and electronic signatures:

- the generation and distribution of electronic signatures and the relevant services should be left to the market;
- a permanent comittee should be established to evaluate systems and to coordinate the use of electronic signatures;
- no specific requirements as regards security are introduced at a general level. Determining the required level of security as well as the specific measures to be implemented is left to the relevant government agency and is to be determined according to the specific circumstances of the communication and the content of the message;
- in case a user of an electronic communication facility does not meet the required security level, the administration shall notify the sender and give advise on how the situation could be rectified;
- the government agency is required to provide encryption or other facilities in order to protect the privacy and security of the electronic communication. The public body must inform the user of the availability of such facilities;
- when an encrypted electronic message cannot be decrypted by the government agency, it should refuse such a message;
- all electronic communication is, in combination with an electronic signature, to be kept for filing purposes. Furthermore, all other information which is considered necessary for reasons of the trustworthiness of the electronic communication should be kept.

In addition to these security-related requirements, the proposed Draft Regulations contain the following provisions on the communication itself:

- electronic communication of administrative decisions is possible, provided this is done with the consent of the individual (citizen);
- the procedure for the electronic communication of administrative decisions is as follows: the individual is informed that the decision is available from a certain information system and is informed how to access this system;
- if the electronic version of the decision has not been accessed by the individual within seven days, a paper copy of the decision is to be sent.

Clearly, the above provisions make the procedure highly dependent on the technology implemented, since it requires a facility to gain the relevant knowledge as to whether a citizen has indeed accessed the system containing the electronic decision.

In the United States, no general rules have been implemented to safeguard electronic communication by administrative agencies. It appears that the agencies deal with this topic on a rather ad hoc basis, meaning that they provide a practical solution when a specific problem arises. In the case of the IRS and USPTO not all the legal details seem to have been elaborated. Legal problems do not always occur at the moment of a first application or tax return (first e-file moment) but when the agency needs to reply (by confirming the receipt of the e-file) or the citizen is given the agency's decision. At that point, administrative officers are confronted with specific problems. One such problem at present under consideration is the status of e-mail communication. Privacy and confidentiality problems also arise. The IRS admits it would like to send more documents by e-mail than is possible at the moment, but privacy and confidentiality demands prohibit the extended use of e-mail communication in this respect. The IRS is currently investigating the possibilities of 'waivers' whereby taxpayers wave some privacy and confidentiality rights in exchange for expedient e-mail communication with the tax authorities. However, during the interview the spokesperson did have a strong reticence towards 'waivers'. It is, in his view, a sign of weakness on behalf of the IRS not to be able to safeguard all privacy and confidentiality demands in e-mail communications.

A real solution would be preferable. The USPTO encounters similar problems. They send electronic filing receipts and final decisions by electronic mail. The electronic filing receipts do not have any legal standing. Final decisions are sent by ordinary or electronic mail, depending on the recipient's desire. This does not give rise to many problems. Time-limits and deadlines for lodging objections begin to run at the moment when the final decision – or any other message – is sent by USPTO, not at the moment when the addressee receives the message.

6.6 Electronic signatures

The Dutch government is considering using the possibility provided under the European Directive on Electronic Signatures to implement specific national requirements for electronic signatures concerning administrative operations governed by administrative law. Have the surveyed countries also considered using this possibility and if so: what specific requirements will be introduced? To what extent are they specifically introduced in the light of the amendments and requirements on electronic administrative procedures? Will these requirements be laid down in specific legislation?

In Germany, the legislature requires the use of an advanced electronic signature in those situations where the present legislation requires a '*Verwaltungsakt*' to be in writing. In contrast to an earlier draft, the German legislature refrains in the draft issued in July 2001 from imposing additional requirements in general for all electronic *Verwaltungsakten* which substitute *Verwaltungsakten* in writing. Consequently, the general rule of § 3 a VwVfG-E will apply and a qualified electronic signature will be a substitute for a statutorily required *Verwaltungsakt* in writing. § 37a VwVfG-E of the most recent draft does, however, explicitly allow for additional specific requirements for electronic signatures and their certificates in specific laws or regulations with respect to both the durable checkability and the technical and administrative security. The Ministry of the Interior is empowered to regulate the details of those requirements by rule-making (Rechtsverordnung). Besides, § 37 sub. 3a VwVfG-E also stipulates that either the main certificate or the attributed certificates, belonging to the signature, display the agency ("Behörde") which issued the

Verwaltungsakt. Since the German Electronic Signature Act only admits electronic signatures for individuals, this requires that the certificate of the acting official contains information on his professional character as an employee with this agency. Even though it is reasonable to make the official character of a message transparent and to prohibit abuse by including information on the official character in the certificate, the stipulation seems to be too restrictive. Contrary to the proposal, it appears to be sufficient to inform the recipient about the legal entity in the capacity of which the official is admitted to act (e.g. "state (name)") instead of the precise agency. This would allow a higher degree of flexibility for human resource management and would make the key management of administrations cheaper.

In Norway, the legislature has not proposed making use of art. 3 sub. 7 of the European Directive with respect to requirements concerning administrative operations governed by administrative law. The argument of the government is that, at present, it sees no necessity to introduce specific requirements. It first wants to see how practices will evolve and whether such problems will arise that the introduction of a higher degree of certainty when using electronic signatures is required.

Chapter 5 reveals that both US agencies researched have introduced some form of electronic signature. The IRS introduced a system in 2001 that contains a self-selected, five digit personal identification number (PIN), together with two 'shared secrets' (tax liability and the previous year's adjusted gross income) and the taxpayer's name and Social Security number. These items will together constitute a valid signature. This purely technical solution for electronic communication only applies, however, to first part of the communication between the IRS and the taxpayers, the filing of the initial tax return-file. All other forms of communication between the IRS and its clients are paper-based. The strict rules and policies on confidentiality and privacy leave no other options at present.

Whereas the solution of the IRS has no legal basis, the issue of (electronic) identification of e-filers in the case of the USPTO did result in limited – secondary – legislative activity. In 1999, § 2.33 section d of the (37 CFR, part II) Trademark Law Treaty Implementation Act was amended in order to make electronic signatures of electronic trade mark and patent files possible. The agency offers filers a customer number and a digital certificate to sign the application and uses a digital certificate to ensure that transmissions are encrypted from the applicant's PC all the way to USPTO's electronic mailroom. The agency uses the latest public key infrastructure (PKI) technology to guarantee the security of electronic applications. EFS has a built-in validation function to help applicants adhere to USPTO rules and to avoid mistakes of form that can cause delays.

6.7 Traditional versus electronic communication

With the introduction of electronic communication, the question arises whether there can be discrimination of means of access, e.g.: can a situation arise where access to electronic communication is the exclusive medium to communicate with a public body? Various other questions arise in this respect. Does a country favour a general right to obtain paper-based information? And: is a public body required to communicate in a specific type of electronic communication or in writing if the citizen or other addressee informs the public body that a transmitted document is inappropriate for his or her use?

In France, a general principle of administrative law is that of equality, meaning that all citizens, encompassing individuals as well as legal entities, must be similarly treated by the administration. As a consequence, a decision by the administration to limit its communications with individuals or companies to on-line forms of communication might contradict this principle of equality, as it may operate in a discriminatory way. However, a glance at the relevant policy documents shows a different attitude. The 2000 report, discussed in chapter 2, on the evolution of téléprocédures in France takes it for granted that it is undesirable to discriminate between both forms of communication. Electronic communication should be able to compete with traditional forms of communication. In other words, it should always be up to the citizen to decide to switch from traditional forms of communication to an electronic form, because of positive reasons, and not because of an impossibility to have recourse to a substantive procedure. The report, however, also argues that by maintaining paper-based procedures the administration should avoid excluding citizens and companies from using electronic communication forms.

It is interesting to note that from May 1st, 2001, it is now compulsory for companies with a turnover of at least FF 100 million to make exclusive use of electronic communication means to transmit their company tax return, their VAT return, and their VAT payment. It is not surprising that such a procedure is performed exclusively on-line by such companies. The risk of discrimination then seems to be quite small for such companies. With high turnovers one may presume that they will avail themselves of the necessary computer systems to carry out this transmission.

Based on the above, the conclusion could thus be that both mediums of communication should remain available when exclusion or unfairness might result from making electronic communication the exclusive way of communicating with the administration. On the other hand, if no such risk of exclusion applies, the rule may be to impose electronic communication as the exclusive method of communication.

In Germany, the law is very restrictive with regard to exclusive access to services of the public administration. As far as there are any comments on this issue by scholars, at least exclusive electronic access to public administration is considered unconstitutional, violating the principle of equality as well as the due process clause, and the principles of the democratic and social welfare state. The proposed amendment to the Public Administration Act stipulates that the public administration is obliged to send the document either in an electronic form suitable for the recipient or as a paper document in case the recipient asserts that an electronic document is unsuitable for further processing. This corresponds to the tradition of ensuring access to public administration for everybody. Even with respect to tenders which are only relevant for enterprises, Germany neither favours nor has legally introduced the possibility of exclusive electronic communication although the opportunity has been created by EU law.

The amendment also stipulates that the transmission of electronic documents in administrative procedures is permitted if and to the extent that access has been provided. Hence, in Germany the public administration is not forced to accept electronic documents unless it has decided to do so and has installed the technical infrastructure for this purpose. Of course, it also implies that the public administration is not obliged to provide access at all. Also, the public administration may determine technical requirements which have to be fulfilled for the valid submission of electronic documents. Correspondingly, if a recipient notifies the public administration that an electronically transmitted document cannot be handled, the public administration is then obliged to send the document either in an electronic form which is suitable for the recipient or as a paper document.

Chapter 3 on the German situation, demonstrates that there is currently an ongoing discussion as regards the possible remedies for discrimination between different types of access and communication. A "public access infrastructure", consisting, for example, of easily accessible public terminals as are currently being planned by many local governments[4], could be a remedy for undue discrimination. As actual access does not only presuppose technical access but also sufficient media competence on the part of the users, there could be an argument in favour of supplementary obligations for public administrations to provide for appropriate advice and support. With regard to discrimination at the "pricing" level, there have not been any specific regulations, nor have there been any cases as yet. Since electronic services which are subject to a fee have only recently been launched, it cannot be concluded that this issue will not become relevant. In any event, a closer examination of the administrative law governing the determination of fees by the public administration has shown that there is ample discretion for public administrations to price electronic and paper-based access differently.

The situation in the United States shows that electronic communication has not taken over from paper-based communication. In American administrative law paper-based communication is still the normal way of doing business. Although the administrative law system allows for some forms of electronic communication, e.g. in the form of e-filing, and notwithstanding the paper reduction policies and the e-government initiatives, electronic communication does not have the same legal standing as paper-based communications have. The way agencies and departments have been trying to tackle this problem of electronic communication up until recently is to mimic the features of paper-based communication electronically (e-filing and e-signatures using paper-based authentications). The ultimate legal recognition of purely electronic communication does not appear to be realistic within the foreseeable future.

---

[4] Cf. the short versions of the Media@Komm applications on the CD-ROM supplement of Kubicek et al., *Multimedia@Verwaltung*.

APPENDICES

APPENDIX 1

Stand: 16. Juli 2001

Entwurf
eines
Dritten Gesetzes zur Änderung verwaltungsverfahrensrechtlicher Vorschriften (3. VwVfÄndG)

A. Problem und Ziel

Der Gesetzentwurf soll die rechtsverbindliche elektronische Kommunikation zwischen Bürger und Verwaltung ermöglichen. Dazu sind entsprechende Änderungen in den verwaltungsverfahrensrechtlichen Gesetzen des Bundes notwendig. Das Vorhaben ist ein wesentlicher Schritt zur Modernisierung der Verwaltung auf dem Wege zur Verwirklichung der Bürgergesellschaft.

B. Lösung

Die Verwaltungsverfahrensgesetze des Bundes (Verwaltungsverfahrensgesetz, Sozialgesetzbuch X, Abgabenordnung) und die Fachgesetze werden für die Möglichkeit der rechtsverbindlichen elektronischen Kommunikation geöffnet. Der Gesetzentwurf enthält die hierzu notwendigen Maßgaben und Anpassungen. Dabei wird für den Bürger ein leichter Zugang zur Verwaltung sichergestellt, für die Verwaltung werden Sicherheit und Dauerhaftigkeit ihres elektronischen Handelns gewährleistet.

C. Alternativen

Keine.

D. Kosten

1. Haushaltskosten ohne Vollzugsaufwand

Durch die Einführung und auch die absehbare Zunahme elektronischer Kommunikation werden für die Verwaltung Kosten der Einführung entsprechender Signaturanwendungen entstehen. Die Vorhaltung geeigneter Hard- und Software gehört bereits heute im Wesentlichenzum Ausstattungsstandard und muss um Komponenten zur Unterstützung von Anwendungen mit qualifizierten elektronischen Signaturen ergänzt werden. Dieses lässt sich teilweiseim Rahmen der üblichen Austauschzyklen oder der Einführung elektronsicher Verwaltungsdienstleistungen realisieren. Den Kosten steht ein erhebliches Rationalisierungs- und Einsparungspotential gegenüber. Im Bereich des Bundes dürften die Auswirkungen daher zuvernachlässigen sein.

2. Vollzugsaufwand.

Vollzugsaufwand entsteht nicht.

E. Sonstige Kosten

Sonstige Kosten (z.B. Kosten für die Wirtschaft, Kosten für die sozialen Sicherungssysteme, Auswirkungen auf das Preisniveau, insbesondere das Verbraucherpreisniveau) entstehennicht. Vielmehr erleichtert das Gesetz Wirtschaft und Bürgern den Zugang zu Verwaltungsbehörden unter Nutzung kostensparender Informationstechnik, daher ist von Kostenreduktionen für Wirtschaft und Bürger auszugehen.

Der Bundestag hat mit Zustimmung des Bundesrates das folgende Gesetz beschlossen:

Artikel 1

Änderung des Verwaltungsverfahrensgesetzes

Das Verwaltungsverfahrensgesetz in der Fassung der Bekanntmachung vom 21. September 1998 (BGBl. I S. 3050) wird wie folgt geändert:

Die Inhaltsübersicht wird wie folgt geändert:

a) In der Überschrift zu Teil 1 werden nach dem Wort "Zuständigkeit," die Wörter "elektronische Kommunikation" eingefügt.

b) Nach der Angabe "§ 3 Örtliche Zuständigkeit" wird die Angabe "§ 3a Elektronische Kommunikation" eingefügt.

c) Nach der Angabe "§ 34 Beglaubigung von Unterschriften" wird die Angabe "§ 34a Beglaubigung von elektronischen Dokumenten" eingefügt.

d) Nach der Angabe "§ 37 Bestimmtheit und Form des Verwaltungsaktes" wird die Angabe "§ 37a Zusätzliche Anforderungen an elektronische Verwaltungsakte" eingefügt.

1. In der Überschrift zu Teil 1 werden nach dem Wort "Zuständigkeit," die Wörter "elektronische Kommunikation," eingefügt.

2. Nach § 3 wird folgender § 3a eingefügt:

"§ 3a
Elektronische Kommunikation

(1) Die Übermittlung elektronischer Dokumente ist zulässig, soweit ein Zugang hierfür eröffnet ist.

(2) Eine durch Rechtsvorschrift angeordnete Schriftform kann, soweit nicht Rechtsvorschriften etwas anderes bestimmen, durch die mit einer qualifizierten elektronischen Signatur im Sinne des Signaturgesetzes verbundene elektronische Form ersetzt werden. Die Signatur mit einem Pseudonym ersetzt nicht die Schriftform. Bei grenzüberschreitenden Diensten zu einem anderen Mitgliedstaat der Europäischen Union oder zu einem anderen Vertragsstaat des Abkommens über den europäischen Wirtschaftsraum genügt die Form des Satzes 1, auch wenn Rechtsvorschriften zusätzliche Anforderungen an eine qualifizierte elektronische Signatur stellen.

(3) Ist ein der Behörde übermitteltes elektronisches Dokument für sie zur Bearbeitung nicht geeignet, hat sie dies dem Absender unverzüglich mitzuteilen. Sie hat dabei die für sie geltenden technischen Rahmenbedingungen zu benennen. Macht ein sonstiger Empfänger der Behörde gegenüber geltend, dass ein von ihr übermitteltes elektronisches Dokument für ihn zur Bearbeitung nicht geeignet sei, hat die Behörde ihm das Dokument erneut in einem geeigneten elektronischen Format oder als Schriftstück zuzusenden."

3. § 14 Abs. 6 Satz 1 wird wie folgt gefasst:

"(6) Bevollmächtigte und Beistände können vom Vortrag zurückgewiesen werden, wenn sie hierzu ungeeignet sind; vom mündlichen Vortrag können sie nur zurückgewiesen werden, wenn sie zum sachgemäßen Vortrag nicht fähig sind."

4. § 15 wird wie folgt geändert:

a) Satz 2 wird durch folgende neue Sätze 2 und 3 ersetzt:

"Unterlässt er dies, so gilt ein an ihn gerichtetes Schriftstück am siebenten Tage nach der Aufgabe zur Post als zugegangen; ein elektronisch übermitteltes Dokument gilt am Tage nach der Übermittlung als zugegangen. Dies gilt nicht, wenn feststeht, dass das Dokument den Empfänger nicht oder zu einem späteren Zeitpunkt erreicht hat."

b) Der bisherige Satz 3 wird Satz 4.

5. In § 23 Abs. 2 Satz 1 wird das Wort "Schriftstücke" durch das Wort "Dokumente" ersetzt.

6. In § 26 Abs. 1 Satz 2 Nr. 2 wird das Wort "schriftlich" gestrichen.

7. Nach § 34 wird folgender § 34a eingefügt:

"§ 34a
Beglaubigung von elektronischen Dokumenten

(1) Die Beglaubigung nach den §§ 33 und 34 kann auch in elektronischer Form erfolgen. Das hierzu erstellte elektronische Dokument ist mit einer dauerhaft überprüfbaren Signatur nach § 37a des zuständigen Bediensteten der Behörde zu verbinden.
Aus dem der Signatur zugehörigen Zertifikat müssen sich die nach § 33 Abs. 3 oder § 34 Abs. 3 notwendigen Inhalte der Beglaubigung ergeben.

(2) Elektronische Dokumente können ebenfalls nach den §§ 33 und 34 beglaubigt werden. Bei der Beglaubigung nach § 33 muss der Beglaubigungsvermerk neben den nach § 33 Abs. 3 notwendigen Inhalten die Angabe enthalten,
1. wer das Dokument elektronisch signiert hat,
2. wann diese Signatur erfolgt ist,
3. welche Zertifikate mit welchen Daten dieser Signatur zugrunde lagen.

Bei der Beglaubigung nach § 34 tritt die mit dem Dokument verbundene qualifizierte elektronische Signatur an die Stelle der Unterschrift. § 34 Abs. 2 findet keine Anwendung; den Anforderungen des § 34 Abs. 3 Nr. 2 kann durch Anerkennung der Signatur als eigener genügt werden."

8. § 37 wird wie folgt geändert:

a) Absatz 2 wird wie folgt geändert:

aa) In Satz 1 wird nach dem Wort "schriftlich" das Wort "elektronisch" eingefügt.

bb) In Satz 2 werden nach dem Wort "schriftlich" die Wörter "oder elektronisch" eingefügt.

cc) Es wird folgender Satz 3 angefügt:

"Ein elektronischer Verwaltungsakt ist unter denselben Voraussetzungen schriftlich zu bestätigen; § 3a Abs. 2 findet insoweit keine Anwendung."

b) An Absatz 3 werden folgende Sätze 2 und 3 angefügt: "Entsprechendes gilt für den elektronischen Verwaltungsakt. Ist für einen Verwaltungsakt durch Rechtsvorschrift eine Schriftform vorgeschrieben, so muss bei einem elektronischen Verwaltungsakt auch das der Signatur zugrunde liegende qualifizierte Zertifikat oder ein zugehöriges qualifiziertes Attributzertifikat die erlassende Behörde erkennen lassen."

9. Nach § 37 wird folgender § 37a eingefügt:

"§ 37a
Zusätzliche Anforderungen an elektronische Verwaltungsakte

Für einen Verwaltungsakt in elektronischer Form, dessen Schriftlichkeit durch Rechtsvorschrift vorgeschrieben ist, können durch Rechtsvorschriften zusätzliche Anforderungen an die qualifizierte elektronische Signatur im Sinne des Signaturgesetzes und das ihr zugrundeliegende qualifizierte Zertifikat hinsichtlich
1. deren dauerhafter Überprüfbarkeit und
2. deren technischer und administrativer Sicherheit

gestellt werden. Das Bundesministerium des Innern kann die Einzelheiten zur Erfüllung dieser zusätzlichen Anforderungen durch eine Rechtsverordnung mit Zustimmung des Bundesrates regeln."

10. § 39 wird wie folgt geändert:

a) Absatz 1 Satz 1 wird wie folgt gefasst:

"Ein schriftlicher, elektronischer sowie ein entsprechend bestätigter Verwaltungsakt ist mit einer Begründung zu versehen."

b) In Absatz 2 Nr. 2 wird das Wort "schriftliche" gestrichen.

11. § 41 wird wie folgt geändert:

a) Absatz 2 wird wie folgt gefasst:

"Ein schriftlicher Verwaltungsakt, der durch die Post im Inland übermittelt wird, gilt mit dem dritten Tage nach der Aufgabe zur Post als bekannt gegeben. Ein Verwaltungsakt, der elektronisch übermittelt wird, gilt am Tage nach der Übermittlung als bekannt gegeben. Dies gilt nicht, wenn der Verwaltungsakt nicht oder zu einem späteren Zeitpunkt zugegangen ist; im Zweifel hat die Behörde den Zugang des Verwaltungsaktes und den Zeitpunkt des Zugangs nachzuweisen."

b) In Absatz 4 Satz 1 werden nach dem Wort "schriftlichen" die Wörter "oder elektronischen" eingefügt.

12. In § 42 Satz 3 wird das Wort "Schriftstückes" durch das Wort "Dokumentes" ersetzt.

13. In § 44 Abs. 2 Nr. 1 werden nach dem Wort "schriftlich" die Wörter "oder elektronisch" eingefügt.

14. In § 66 Abs. 2 wird das Wort "schriftliches" durch die Wörter "schriftlich oder elektronisch vorliegendes" ersetzt.

15. In § 69 Abs. 2 Satz 5 werden nach dem Wort "schriftlich" die Wörter "oder elektronisch" eingefügt.

16. In § 71c Abs. 1 Satz 2 werden nach dem Wort "schriftlich" die Wörter "oder elektronisch" eingefügt.

Artikel 2
§ 1
Änderung des Ersten Buches Sozialgesetzbuch

Das Erste Buch Sozialgesetzbuch – Allgemeiner Teil – (Artikel I des Gesetzes vom 11. Dezember 1975, BGBl. I S. 3015), zuletzt geändert durch ..., wird wie folgt geändert:

1. In der Inhaltsübersicht wird nach der Angabe zu § 36 die Angabe "§ 36a Elektronische Kommunikation" eingefügt.

2. Nach § 36 wird folgender § 36a eingefügt:

"§ 36a
Elektronische Kommunikation

(1) Die Übermittlung elektronischer Dokumente ist nur mit Zustimmung des Empfängers zulässig.

(2) Eine durch Rechtsvorschrift angeordnete Schriftform kann, soweit nicht Rechtsvorschriften etwas anderes bestimmen, durch die mit einer qualifizierten elektronischen Signatur im Sinne des Signaturgesetzes verbundene elektronische Form ersetzt werden. Die Signatur mit einem Pseudonym ersetzt nicht die Schriftform. Bei grenzüberschreitenden Diensten zu einem anderen Mitgliedstaat der Europäischen Union oder zu einem anderen Vertragsstaat des Abkommens über den Europäischen Wirtschaftsraum genügt die Form des Satzes 1, auch wenn Rechtsvorschriften zusätzliche Anforderungen an eine qualifizierte elektronische Signatur stellen.

(3) Ist ein der Behörde übermitteltes elektronisches Dokument für sie zur Bearbeitung nicht geeignet, teilt sie dies dem Absender unter Angabe der für sie geltenden technischen Rahmenbedingungen unverzüglich mit. Macht ein Empfänger der Behörde gegenüber geltend, dass ein von ihr übermitteltes elektronisches Dokument für ihn zur Bearbeitung nicht geeignet ist, übermittelt die Behörde ihm das Dokument erneut in einem geeigneten elektronischen Format oder als Schriftstück.

(4) Die Spitzenverbände der Träger der Sozialversicherung können für die öffentlich-rechtliche Verwaltungstätigkeit der Träger der Sozialversicherung einen Zertifizierungsdienst nach dem Signaturgesetz betreiben, wenn sie der Aufsicht einer obersten Bundesbehörde unterstehen und auf Dauer die Ausübung dieser Tätigkeit sichergestellt ist."

§ 2
Änderung des Zehnten Buches Sozialgesetzbuch

Das Zehnte Buch Sozialgesetzbuch – Sozialverwaltungsverfahren und Sozialdatenschutz – in der Fassung der Bekanntmachung vom 18. Januar 2001 (BGBl. I S. 130), zuletzt geändert durch ..., wird wie folgt geändert:

1. Die Inhaltsübersicht wird wie folgt geändert:

   a) Nach der Angabe zu § 30 wird die Angabe "§ 30a Beglaubigung von elektronischen Dokumenten" eingefügt.

   b) Nach der Angabe zu § 33 wird die Angabe "§ 33a Zusätzliche Anforderungen an elektronische Verwaltungsakte" eingefügt.

2. § 13 Abs. 6 Satz 1 wird wie folgt gefasst:

   "Bevollmächtigte und Beistände können vom Vortrag zurückgewiesen werden, wenn sie hierzu ungeeignet sind; vom mündlichen Vortrag können sie nur zurückgewiesen werden, wenn sie zum sachgemäßen Vortrag nicht fähig sind."

3. § 14 wird wie folgt gefasst:

"Ein Beteiligter ohne Wohnsitz oder gewöhnlichen Aufenthalt, Sitz oder Geschäftsleitung im Inland hat der Behörde auf Verlangen innerhalb einer angemessenen Frist einen Empfangsbevollmächtigten im Inland zu benennen. Unterlässt er dies, gilt ein an ihn gerichtetes Schriftstück am siebenten Tage nach der Aufgabe zur Post als zugegangen; ein elektronisch übermitteltes Dokument gilt am Tage nach der Übermittlung als zugegangen. Dies gilt nicht, wenn feststeht, dass das Dokument den Empfänger nicht oder zu einem späteren Zeitpunkt erreicht hat. Auf die Rechtsfolgen der Unterlassung ist der Beteiligte hinzuweisen."

4. In § 19 Abs. 2 Satz 1 wird jeweils das Wort "Schriftstücke" durch das Wort "Dokumente" ersetzt.

5. In § 21 Abs. 1 Satz 2 Nr. 2 wird das Wort "schriftliche" gestrichen.

6. Nach § 30 wird folgender § 30a eingefügt:

"§ 30a

Beglaubigung von elektronischen Dokumenten

(1) Die Beglaubigung nach den §§ 29 und 30 kann auch in elektronischer Form erfolgen. Das hierzu erstellte elektronische Dokument ist mit einer dauerhaft überprüfbaren Signatur nach § 33a des zuständigen Bediensteten der Behörde zu verbinden.
Aus dem der Signatur zugehörigen Zertifikat müssen sich die nach § 29 Abs. 3 oder § 30 Abs. 3 notwendigen Inhalte der Beglaubigung ergeben.

(2) Elektronische Dokumente können ebenfalls nach den §§ 29 und 30 beglaubigt werden. Bei der Beglaubigung nach § 29 muss der Beglaubigungsvermerk neben den nach § 29 Abs. 3 notwendigen Inhalten die Angaben enthalten,
1. wer das Dokument elektronisch signiert hat,

2. wann diese Signatur erfolgt ist.
3. welche Zertifikate mit welchen Daten dieser Signatur zu Grunde lagen.

Bei der Beglaubigung nach § 30 tritt die mit dem Dokument verbundene qualifizierte elektronische Signatur an die Stelle der Unterschrift. § 30 Abs. 2 findet keine Anwendung; den Anforderungen des § 30 Abs. 3 Nr. 2 kann durch die Anerkennung der Signatur als eigener genügt werden."

7. § 33 wird wie folgt geändert:

a) Absatz 2 wird wie folgt geändert:

aa) In Satz 1 wird nach der Angabe "schriftlich," die Angabe "elektronisch," eingefügt.

bb) In Satz 2 werden nach dem Wort "schriftlich" die Wörter "oder elektronisch" eingefügt.

cc) Folgender Satz 3 wird angefügt:

"Ein elektronischer Verwaltungsakt ist unter denselben Voraussetzungen schriftlich zu bestätigen; § 36a Abs. 2 des Ersten Buches findet insoweit keine Anwendung."

b) Dem Absatz 3 werden folgende Sätze angefügt:

"Entsprechendes gilt für den elektronischen Verwaltungsakt. Ist für einen Verwaltungsakt durch Rechtsvorschrift eine Schriftform vorgeschrieben, muss bei einem elektronischen Verwaltungsakt auch das der Signatur zugrunde liegende qualifizierte Zertifikat oder ein zugehöriges qualifiziertes Attributzertifikat die erlassende Behörde erkennen lassen."

8. Nach § 33 wird folgender § 33a eingefügt:

"§ 33a
Zusätzliche Anforderungen an elektronische Verwaltungsakte

Bei einem Verwaltungsakt in elektronischer Form, dessen Schriftlichkeit durch Rechtsvorschrift vorgeschrieben ist, können durch Rechtsvorschriften zusätzliche Anforderungen an die qualifizierte elektronische Signatur im Sinne des Signaturgesetzes und das ihr zugrunde liegende qualifizierte Zertifikat hinsichtlich
1. deren dauerhafter Überprüfbarkeit und
2. deren technischer und administrativer Sicherheit
gestellt werden. Das Bundesministerium für Arbeit und Sozialordnung kann für die in den §§ 19, 19b, 22 bis 24, 28 und 29 des Ersten Buches genannten Sozialleistungsbereiche die Einzelheiten zur Erfüllung dieser zusätzlichen Anforderungen durch Rechtsverordnung mit Zustimmung des Bundesrates regeln."

9 § 35 wird wie folgt geändert:

a) Absatz 1 Satz 1 wird wie folgt gefasst:

"Ein schriftlicher, elektronischer sowie ein entsprechend bestätigter Verwaltungsakt ist entsprechend zu begründen."

b) In Absatz 2 Nr. 2 wird das Wort "schriftliche" gestrichen.

c) In Absatz 3 werden nach dem Wort "schriftlich" die Wörter "oder elektronisch" eingefügt.

10. § 37 wird wie folgt geändert:

a) Absatz 2 wird wie folgt gefasst:

"(2) Ein schriftlicher Verwaltungsakt, der durch die Post im Inland übermittelt wird, gilt mit dem dritten Tage nach der Aufgabe zur Post als bekannt gegeben. Ein Verwaltungsakt, der elektronisch übermittelt wird, gilt am Tage nach der Übermittlung als bekannt gegeben. Dies gilt nicht, wenn der Verwaltungsakt nicht oder zu einem späteren Zeitpunkt zugegangen ist; im Zweifel hat die Behörde den Zugang des Verwaltungsaktes und den Zeitpunkt des Zugangs nachzuweisen."

b) In Absatz 4 Satz 1 werden nach dem Wort "schriftlichen" die Wörter "oder elektronischen" eingefügt.

11. In § 38 Satz 3 wird das Wort "Schriftstückes" durch das Wort "Dokumentes" ersetzt.

12. In § 40 Abs. 2 Nr. 1 werden nach dem Wort "schriftlich" die Wörter "oder elektronisch" eingefügt.

Artikel 3
Änderung der Abgabenordnung

Die Abgabenordnung vom 16. März 1976 (BGBl. I S. 613, BGBl. 1977 I S. 269), zuletzt geändert durch Gesetz vom ...
(BGBl. I S. ...), wird wie folgt geändert:

1. § 80 Abs. 6 Satz 1 wird wie folgt gefasst:

"Bevollmächtigte und Beistände können vom Vortrag zurückgewiesen werden, wenn sie hierzu ungeeignet sind; vom mündlichen Vortrag können sie nur zurückgewiesen werden, wenn sie zum sachgemäßen Vortrag nicht fähig sind."

2. § 87 Abs. 2 Satz 1 wird wie folgt gefasst:

"Werden bei einer Finanzbehörde in einer fremden Sprache Anträge gestellt oder Eingaben, Belege, Urkunden oder sonstige Dokumente vorgelegt, kann die Finanzbehörde verlangen, dass unverzüglich eine Übersetzung vorgelegt wird."

3. Nach § 87 wird folgender § 87a eingefügt:

"§ 87a
Elektronische Kommunikation

(1) Die Übermittlung elektronischer Dokumente ist zulässig, soweit ein Zugang hierfür eröffnet ist. Ein elektronisches Dokument ist zugegangen, sobald die für den Empfang bestimmte Einrichtung es in für den Empfänger bearbeitbarer Weise aufgezeichnet hat. Übermittelt die Finanzbehörde Daten, die dem Steuergeheimnis unterliegen, sind diese Daten zu verschlüsseln.

(2) Ist ein der Finanzbehörde übermitteltes elektronisches Dokument für sie zur Bearbeitung nicht geeignet, hat sie dies dem Absender unverzüglich mitzuteilen. Sie hat dabei die für sie geltenden technischen Rahmenbedingungen zu benennen. Macht ein Empfänger der Finanzbehörde gegenüber geltend, dass ein von ihr übermitteltes elektronisches Dokument für ihn zur Bearbeitung nicht geeignet sei, hat die Finanzbehörde ihm das Dokument erneut in einem geeigneten elektronischen Format oder als Schriftstück zuzusenden.

(3) Ist durch Gesetz für Anträge, Erklärungen oder Mitteilungen an die Finanzbehörden die Schriftform vorgeschrieben, kann, soweit sich aus dem Gesetz nichts anderes ergibt, die Schriftform durch die elektronische Form ersetzt werden. In diesem Fall muss der Antragsteller, Erklärende oder Mitteilende dem Text seinen Namen hinzufügen und das elektronische Dokument mit einer qualifizierten elektronischen Signatur nach dem Signaturgesetz versehen. Die Signierung mit einem Pseudonym (§ 5 Abs. 3 Satz 1 und § 7 Abs. 1 Nr. 1 des Signaturgesetzes) ersetzt nicht die Schriftform.

(4) Ist durch Gesetz für Verwaltungsakte oder sonstige Maßnahmen der Finanzbehörden die Schriftform vorgeschrieben, kann, soweit sich aus dem Gesetz nichts anderes ergibt, die Schriftform durch die elektronische Form ersetzt werden. In diesem Fall muss das elektronische Dokument die erlassende Finanzbehörde erkennen lassen und mit einer qualifizierten elektronischen Signatur nach dem Signaturgesetz versehen werden. Für von der Finanzbehörde aufzu-

nehmende Niederschriften gilt Satz 1 nur, wenn dies durch Gesetz ausdrücklich zugelassen ist.

(5) Ist ein elektronisches Dokument Gegenstand eines Beweises, wird der Beweis durch Vorlegung oder Übermittlung der Datei angetreten; befindet diese sich nicht im Besitz des Beweisführers, gelten die §§ 422 bis 432 der Zivilprozessordnung entsprechend. Der Anschein der Echtheit eines mit einer qualifizierten elektronischen Signatur nach dem Signaturgesetz übermittelten Dokuments, der sich aufgrund der Prüfung nach dem Signaturgesetz ergibt, kann nur durch Tatsachen erschüttert werden, die ernstliche Zweifel daran begründen, dass das Dokument mit dem Willen des Signaturschlüs-selInhabers übermittelt worden ist.

(6) Bis zum 31. Dezember 2006 kann abweichend von Absatz 3 Satz 2 die qualifizierte elektronische Signatur mit Einschränkungen nach Maßgabe einer Rechtsverordnung nach § 150 Abs. 6 eingesetzt werden."

4. § 93 wird wie folgt geändert:

a) Absatz 4 Satz 1 wird wie folgt gefasst:

"Der Auskunftspflichtige kann die Auskunft schriftlich, elektronisch, mündlich oder fernmündlich erteilen."

b) Absatz 5 Satz 2 wird wie folgt gefasst:

"Hierzu ist sie insbesondere befugt, wenn trotz Aufforderung eine schriftliche Auskunft oder eine Auskunft in elektronischer Form mit qualifizierter elektronischer Signatur nach dem Signaturgesetz nicht erteilt worden ist oder eine schriftlich oder in elektronischer Form mit qualifizierter elektronischer Signatur nach dem Signaturgesetz erteilte Auskunft nicht zu einer Klärung des Sachverhalts geführt hat."

5. § 119 wird wie folgt gefasst:

"§ 119
Bestimmtheit und Form des Verwaltungsaktes

(1) Ein Verwaltungsakt muss inhaltlich hinreichend bestimmt sein.

(2) Ein Verwaltungsakt kann schriftlich, elektronisch, mündlich oder in anderer Weise erlassen werden. Ein mündlicher Verwaltungsakt ist schriftlich oder in elektronischer Form mit qualifizierter elektronischer Signatur nach dem Signaturgesetz zu bestätigen, wenn hieran ein berechtigtes Interesse besteht und der Betroffene dies unverzüglich verlangt.

(3) Ein schriftlich oder elektronisch erlassener Verwaltungsakt muss die erlassende Behörde erkennen lassen. Ferner muss er die Unterschrift oder die Namenswiedergabe des Behördenleiters, seines Vertreters oder seines Beauftragten enthalten; dies gilt nicht für einen Verwaltungsakt, der formularmäßig oder mit Hilfe automatischer Einrichtungen erlassen wird."

6. § 121 wird wie folgt geändert:

   a) Absatz 1 wird wie folgt gefasst:

      "(1) Ein schriftlicher, elektronischer sowie ein entsprechend bestätigter Verwaltungsakt ist mit einer Begründung zu versehen, soweit dies zu seinem Verständnis erforderlich ist."

   b) Absatz 2 Nr. 2 wird wie folgt gefasst:

      "2. soweit demjenigen, für den der Verwaltungsakt bestimmt ist oder der von ihm betroffen wird, die Auffassung der Finanzbehörde über die Sach- und Rechtslage bereits bekannt oder auch ohne Begründung für ihn ohne weiteres erkennbar ist,"

7. § 122 wird wie folgt geändert:

   a) Nach Absatz 2 wird folgender Absatz 2a eingefügt:

"(2a) Ein elektronisch übermittelter Verwaltungsakt gilt einen Tag nach Abschluss des Übermittlungsvorgangs bei der Behörde als bekannt gegeben, außer wenn er nicht oder zu einem späteren Zeitpunkt zugegangen ist; im Zweifel hat die Behörde den Zugang des Verwaltungsaktes und den Zeitpunkt des Zugangs nachzuweisen."

b) In Absatz 4 Satz 1 wird das Wort "schriftlichen" gestrichen.

c) In Absatz 5 Satz 1 wird das Wort "schriftlicher" gestrichen.

8. § 123 Satz 2 wird wie folgt gefasst:

"Unterlässt er dies, so gilt ein durch die Post übermittelter Verwaltungsakt einen Monat nach Aufgabe zur Post und ein elektronisch übermittelter Verwaltungsakt einen Tag nach Abschluss des Übermittlungsvorgangs bei der Behörde als bekannt gegeben, es sei denn, dass feststeht, dass der Verwaltungsakt den Empfänger nicht oder zu einem späteren Zeitpunkt erreicht hat."

9. § 125 Abs. 2 Nr. 1 wird wie folgt gefasst:

"1. der schriftlich oder elektronisch erlassen worden ist, die erlassende Finanzbehörde aber nicht erkennen lässt,"

10. § 129 Satz 3 wird wie folgt gefasst:

"Wird zu einem schriftlich ergangenen Verwaltungsakt die Berichtigung begehrt, ist die Finanzbehörde berechtigt, die Vorlage des Schriftstücks zu verlangen, das berichtigt werden soll."

11. § 150 wird wie folgt geändert:

a) Absatz 1 wird wie folgt geändert:

aa) Nach Satz 1 wird folgender Satz eingefügt:

"§ 87a ist nur anwendbar, soweit aufgrund eines Gesetzes oder einer nach Absatz 6 erlassenen Rechtsverordnung die Steuererklärung auf maschinell verwertbarem Datenträger oder durch Datenfernübertragung übermittelt werden darf."

bb) Der bisherige Satz 2 wird Satz 3.

b) Absatz 6 Nummer 5 wird wie folgt gefasst:

"5. die Haftung von Dritten für Steuern oder Steuervorteile, die aufgrund unrichtiger Erhebung, Verarbeitung oder Übermittlung der Daten verkürzt oder erlangt werden,"

12. § 202 Abs. 1 wird wie folgt geändert:

a) Nach Satz 1 wird folgender Satz eingefügt:

"Wird der Prüfungsbericht elektronisch übermittelt, bedarf es abweichend von § 87a Abs. 4 Satz 2 keiner elektronischen Signatur."

b) Die bisherigen Sätze 2 und 3 werden Sätze 3 und 4.

13. § 203 Abs. 2 Satz 3 wird wie folgt gefasst:

"§ 202 Abs. 1 Satz 2 gilt entsprechend; § 201 Abs. 1 und § 202 Abs. 2 gelten nicht."

14. § 224a Abs. 2 Satz 1 wird wie folgt gefasst:

"Der Vertrag nach Absatz 1 bedarf der Schriftform; die elektronische Form ist ausgeschlossen."

15. § 244 Abs. 1 Satz 3 wird wie folgt gefasst:

"Schuldversprechen und Bürgschaftserklärungen sind schriftlich zu erteilen; die elektronische Form ist ausgeschlossen."

16. Dem § 309 Abs. 1 wird folgender Satz angefügt:

"Die elektronische Form ist ausgeschlossen."

17. Dem § 324 Abs. 2 wird folgender Satz angefügt:

"Die elektronische Form ist ausgeschlossen."

18. § 356 wird wie folgt gefasst:

"§ 356
Rechtsbehelfsbelehrung

(1) Ergeht ein Verwaltungsakt schriftlich oder elektronisch, so beginnt die Frist für die Einlegung des Einspruchs nur, wenn der Beteiligte über den Einspruch und die Finanzbehörde, bei der er einzulegen ist, deren Sitz und die einzuhaltende Frist in derselben Form belehrt worden ist.

(2) Ist die Belehrung unterblieben oder unrichtig erteilt, so ist die Einlegung des Einspruchs nur binnen eines Jahres seit Bekanntgabe des Verwaltungsaktes zulässig, es sei denn, dass die Einlegung vor Ablauf der Jahresfrist infolge höherer Gewalt unmöglich war oder schriftlich oder elektronisch darüber belehrt wurde, dass ein Einspruch nicht gegeben sei. § 110 Abs. 2 gilt für den Fall höherer Gewalt sinngemäß."

19. § 366 wird wie folgt gefasst:

"§ 366
Form, Inhalt und Bekanntgabe der Einspruchsentscheidung

Die Einspruchsentscheidung ist schriftlich zu erteilen, zu begründen, mit einer Rechtsbehelfsbelehrung zu versehen und den Beteiligten bekannt zu geben."

Artikel Bundespräsidialamt
Artikel Deutscher Bundestag
Artikel Bundesrat
Artikel Bundeskanzleramt
Artikel AA
Artikel BMI

§ X
Weitere Änderung des Verwaltungsverfahrensgesetzes

Das Verwaltungsverfahrensgesetz in der Fassung der Bekanntmachung vom 21. September 1998 (BGBl. I S. 3050) wird wie folgt geändert:

1. In § 15 Satz 1 werden die Wörter "Geltungsbereich dieses Gesetzes" durch das Wort "Inland" ersetzt.

2. In § 45 Abs. 2 wird das Wort "Abschluß" durch die Wörter "Abschluss der letzten Tatsacheninstanz" ersetzt.

3. In § 49a Abs. 3 Satz 1 werden die Wörter "mit 3 vom Hundert über dem jeweiligen Diskontsatz der Deutschen Bundesbank" durch die Wörter "mit fünf Prozentpunkten über dem Basiszinssatz nach § 1 des Diskontsatz-Überleitungs-Gesetzes vom 9. Juni 1998 (BGBl. I S. 1242)" ersetzt.

4. In § 61 Abs. 1 wird Satz 3 und 4 gestrichen.

Artikel BMJ
Artikel BMF

§ 1
Änderung des Grunderwerbsteuergesetzes

Das Grunderwerbsteuergesetz in der Fassung der Bekanntmachung vom 26. Februar 1997 (BGBl. I S. 418), zuletzt geändert durch ... (BGBl. I ...), wird wie folgt geändert:

1. § 18 Abs. 1 wird wie folgt geändert:

   a) In Satz 1 wird nach dem Wort "Finanzamt" das Wort "schriftlich" eingefügt.

   b) Nach Satz 1 wird folgender neuer Satz 2 eingefügt:

      "Eine elektronische Übermittlung der Anzeige ist ausgeschlossen."

   c) Der bisherige Satz 2 wird Satz 3.

2. § 19 Abs. 5 Satz 2 wird wie folgt gefasst:

   "Sie sind schriftlich abzugeben."

3. Dem § 22 Abs. 2 wird folgender Satz angefügt:

   "Das Finanzamt hat die Bescheinigung schriftlich zu erteilen."

§ 2
Änderung des Versicherungsteuergesetzes

Das Versicherungsteuergesetz in der Fassung der Bekanntmachung vom 10. Januar 1996 (BGBl. I S. 22), zuletzt geändert durch ... (BGBl. I S. ...), wird wie folgt geändert:

1. § 8 Abs. 5 Satz 3 wird wie folgt gefasst:

   "Der Versicherungsnehmer hat innerhalb von fünfzehn Tagen nach Ablauf des Monats, in dem das Versicherungsentgelt gezahlt worden ist, eine eigenhändig unterschriebene Steueranmeldung abzugeben und die selbstberechnete Steuer zu entrichten."

2. In § 10 Abs. 1 Satz 3 wird nach dem Wort “Angaben” das Wort “schriftlich” eingefügt.

§ 3
Änderung der Ausführungsbestimmungen zum Rennwett- und Lotteriegesetz

Die Ausführungsbestimmungen zum Rennwett- und Lotteriegesetz in der im Bundesgesetzblatt Teil III, Gliederungsnummer 611-14-1, veröffentlichten bereinigten Fassung, zuletzt geändert durch ... (BGBl. I S. ...), werden wie folgt geändert:

1. In § 34 wird das Wort “schriftlich” gestrichen.

2. Dem § 35 wird folgender Satz angefügt:

   “Eine elektronische Übermittlung ist ausgeschlossen.”

3. In § 45 Abs. 3 wird vor den Wörtern “bei dem Finanzamt” das Wort “schriftlich” eingefügt.

4. In § 46 Abs. 2 Satz 2 wird nach dem Wort “Anzeigen” das Wort “schriftlich” eingefügt.

§ 4
Änderung des Feuerschutzsteuergesetzes

Das Feuerschutzsteuergesetz in der Fassung der Bekanntmachung vom 10. Januar 1996 (BGBl. I S. 18), zuletzt geändert durch ... (BGBl. I S. ...), wird wie folgt geändert:

1. § 8 Abs. 4 Satz 3 wird wie folgt gefasst:

   “Der Versicherungsnehmer hat spätestens am fünfzehnten Tag nach Ablauf des Monats, in dem das Versicherungsentgelt gezahlt worden ist, eine Steueranmeldung nach amtlich vorgeschriebenem Vordruck abzugeben und die selbstberechnete Steuer zu entrichten."

2. In § 9 Abs. 1 Satz 3 wird nach dem Wort "Angaben" das Wort "schriftlich" eingefügt.

§ 5
Änderung des Kraftfahrzeugsteuergesetzes

Das Kraftfahrzeugsteuergesetz in der Fassung der Bekanntmachung vom 24. Mai 1994 (BGBl. I S. 1102), zuletzt geändert durch ... (BGBl. I S. ...), wird wie folgt geändert:

1. In § 3a Abs. 3 Satz 1 wird vor dem Wort "Antrag" das Wort "schriftlichen" eingefügt.

2. In § 4 Abs. 1 Satz 1 wird vor dem Wort "Antrag" das Wort "schriftlichen" eingefügt.

3. In § 10 Abs. 1 Satz 1 wird vor dem Wort "Antrag" das Wort "schriftlichen" eingefügt.

4. In § 10 Abs. 2 Satz 1 wird vor dem Wort "Antrag" das Wort "schriftlichen" eingefügt.

5. In § 11 Abs. 2 Satz 3 wird vor dem Wort "angezeigt" das Wort "schriftlich" eingefügt.

6. In § 11 Abs. 4 Satz 1 Nr. 1 Buchst. a wird vor dem Wort "Antrag" das Wort "schriftlichen" eingefügt.

§ 6
Änderung der Kraftfahrzeugsteuer-Durchführungsverordnung

Die Kraftfahrzeugsteuer-Durchführungsverordnung in der Fassung der

Bekanntmachung vom 24. Mai 1994 (BGBl. I S. 1144), zuletzt geändert durch ... (BGBl. I S. ...), wird wie folgt geändert:

1. In § 3 Abs. 2 werden nach dem Wort "Steuererklärung" die Wörter "nach Absatz 1" eingefügt.

2. In § 4 Satz 1 wird vor dem Wort "Antrag" das Wort "schriftliche" eingefügt.

3. § 7 Abs. 1 wird wie folgt geändert:

   a) In Satz 1 wird vor dem Wort "geltend" das Wort "schriftlich" eingefügt.

   b) In Satz 2 wird vor dem Wort "anzuzeigen" das Wort "schriftlich" eingefügt.

4. § 11 wird wie folgt geändert:

   a) Nach Satz 1 wird folgender Satz eingefügt:
   "Eine elektronische Übermittlung ist ausgeschlossen."

   b) Der bisherige Satz 2 wird Satz 3.

5. § 14 wird wie folgt gefasst:

   "(1) Ansprüche auf Erstattung der Steuer, die sich aufgrund des § 12 Abs. 2 Nr. 3 des Gesetzes ergeben, sind unter Rückgabe der Steuerkarte bei der Stelle schriftlich geltend zu machen, die die Steuer festgesetzt hat. Elektronische Übermittlungen sind ausgeschlossen.

   (2) Als Tag der Beendigung der Steuerpflicht gilt der Tag, an dem der Steuerschuldner die Steuerkarte zurückgibt. § 5 Abs. 4 Satz 2 des Gesetzes gilt sinngemäß."

§ 7
Änderung der Stromsteuer-Durchführungsverordnung

Die Stromsteuer-Durchführungsverordnung vom 31. Mai 2000 (BGBl. I S. 794) wird wie folgt geändert:

1. Dem § 3 wird folgender Satz angefügt:

   "Eine elektronische Übermittlung der Erlaubnis ersetzt die Schriftform nicht."

2. Dem § 9 Abs. 1 wird folgender Satz angefügt:

   "Eine elektronische Übermittlung der Erlaubnis ersetzt die Schriftform nicht."

§ 8
Änderung der Mineralölsteuer-Durchführungsverordnung

Die Mineralölsteuer-Durchführungsverordnung vom 15. September 1993 (BGBl. I S. 1602),
zuletzt geändert durch ...(BGBl. I S. ...), wird wie folgt geändert:

1. Dem § 6 Abs. 1 wird folgender Satz angefügt:

   "Eine elektronische Übermittlung der Erlaubnis ersetzt die Schriftform nicht."

2. Dem § 19 Abs. 1 wird folgender Satz angefügt:

   "Eine elektronische Übermittlung der Erlaubnis ersetzt die Schriftform nicht."

Artikel BMWi

Artikel BMVEL

Artikel BMA

§ 1
Änderung des Vierten Buches Sozialgesetzbuch

Das Vierte Buch Sozialgesetzbuch – Gemeinsame Vorschriften für die Sozialversicherung – (Artikel I des Gesetzes vom 23. Dezember 1976, BGBl. I S. 3845), zuletzt geändert durch ..., wird wie folgt geändert:

1. Die Inhaltsübersicht wird wie folgt geändert:

   a) Nach der Angabe zu § 110 werden folgende Angaben eingefügt:

   "Siebter Abschnitt

   Aufbewahrung von Unterlagen

   § 110a Aufbewahrungspflicht

   § 110b Rückgabe, Vernichtung und Archivierung von Unterlagen

   § 110c Verwaltungsvereinbarungen, Verordnungsermächtigung

   § 110d Beweiswirkung"

   b) Die bisherige Angabe "Siebter Abschnitt" wird durch die Angabe "Achter Abschnitt" ersetzt.

2. § 28f Abs. 4 Satz 2 wird wie folgt gefasst:

   "Dies gilt auch für Arbeitgeber, die den Gesamtsozialversicherungsbeitrag an mehrere Betriebskrankenkassen oder landwirtschaftliche Krankenkassen zu zahlen haben, gegenüber dem jeweiligen Bundesverband."

3. Dem § 93 Abs. 3 wird folgender Satz 3 angefügt:

"Für die Aufnahme von Anträgen auf Leistungen der gesetzlichen Rentenversicherung im automatisierten Verfahren ist das Versicherungsamt ausschließlich zuständig, in dessen Bezirk der Versicherte seine alleinige Wohnung oder seine Hauptwohnung hat."

4. Nach § 110 wird folgender neuer Abschnitt eingefügt:

"Siebter Abschnitt

Aufbewahrung von Unterlagen

§ 110a

Aufbewahrungspflicht

(1) Die Behörde bewahrt Unterlagen, die für ihre öffentlich-rechtliche Verwaltungstätigkeit, insbesondere für die Durchführung eines Verwaltungsverfahrens oder für die Feststellung einer Leistung, erforderlich sind, nach den Grundsätzen ordnungsmäßiger Aufbewahrung auf.

(2) Die Behörde kann an Stelle der schriftlichen Unterlagen diese als Wiedergabe auf einem Bildträger oder auf anderen dauerhaften Datenträgern aufbewahren, soweit dies unter Beachtung der Grundsätze der Wirtschaftlichkeit und Sparsamkeit den Grundsätzen ordnungsmäßiger Aufbewahrung entspricht. Nach den Grundsätzen ordnungsmäßiger Aufbewahrung von auf Datenträgern aufbewahrten Unterlagen ist insbesondere sicherzustellen, dass

1. die Wiedergabe auf einem Bildträger oder die Daten auf einem anderen dauerhaften Datenträger
   a) mit der diesen zu Grunde gelegten schriftlichen Unterlage bildlich und inhaltlich vollständig übereinstimmen, wenn sie lesbar gemacht werden, und über diese Übereinstimmung ein Nachweis geführt wird,
   b) während der Dauer der Aufbewahrungsfrist jederzeit verfüg-

bar sind und unverzüglich bildlich und inhaltlich unverändert lesbar gemacht werden können,

2. die Ausdrucke oder sonstigen Reproduktionen mit der schriftlichen Unterlage bildlich und inhaltlich übereinstimmen und
3. als Unterlage für die Herstellung der Wiedergabe nur dann der Abdruck einer Unterlage verwendet werden darf, wenn die dem Abdruck zu Grunde liegende Unterlage bei der Behörde nicht mehr vorhanden ist.

Die Sätze 1 und 2 gelten auch für die Aufbewahrung von Unterlagen, die nur mit Hilfe einer Datenverarbeitungsanlage erstellt worden sind, mit der Maßgabe, dass eine bildliche Übereinstimmung der Wiedergabe auf dem dauerhaften Datenträger mit der erstmals erstellten Unterlage nicht sichergestellt sein muss.

(3) Können aufzubewahrende Unterlagen nur in der Form einer Wiedergabe auf einem Bildträger oder als Daten auf anderen dauerhaften Datenträgern vorgelegt werden, sind, soweit die Akteneinsicht zu gestatten ist, bei der Behörde auf ihre Kosten diejenigen Hilfsmittel zur Verfügung zu stellen, die erforderlich sind, die Unterlagen lesbar zu machen. Soweit erforderlich, ist die Behörde verpflichtet, die Unterlagen ganz oder teilweise auszudrucken oder ohne Hilfsmittel lesbare Reproduktionen beizubringen; die Behörde kann Ersatz ihrer Aufwendungen in angemessenem Umfang verlangen.

(4) Absatz 2 gilt für Unterlagen, die als Wiedergabe auf einem Bildträger aufbewahrt werden, wenn diese Wiedergabe nach dem [einsetzen: Tag des Inkrafttretens dieses Gesetzes] durchgeführt wird.

§ 110b
Rückgabe, Vernichtung und Archivierung von Unterlagen

(1) Unterlagen, die für eine öffentlich-rechtliche Verwaltungstätigkeit einer Behörde nicht mehr erforderlich sind, können nach Maßgabe der Absätze 2 und 3 zurückgegeben oder vernichtet wer-

den. Die Anbietungs- und Übergabepflichten nach den Vorschriften des Bundesarchivgesetzes und der entsprechenden gesetzlichen Vorschriften der Länder bleiben unberührt. Satz 1 gilt insbesondere für

1. Unterlagen, deren Aufbewahrungsfristen abgelaufen sind,
2. Unterlagen, die nach Maßgabe des § 110a Abs. 2 als Wiedergabe auf einem maschinell verwertbaren dauerhaften Datenträger aufbewahrt werden und
3. der Behörde vom Betroffenen oder von Dritten zur Verfügung gestellte Unterlagen.

(2) Unterlagen, die einem Träger der gesetzlichen Rentenversicherung von Versicherten, Antragstellern oder von anderen Stellen zur Verfügung gestellt worden sind, sind diesen zurückzugeben, soweit sie nicht als Ablichtung oder Abschrift dem Träger auf Anforderung von den genannten Stellen zur Verfügung gestellt worden sind; werden die Unterlagen anderen Stellen zur Verfügung gestellt, sind sie von diesen Stellen auf Anforderung zurückzugeben.

(3) Die übrigen Unterlagen im Sinne von Absatz 1 können vernichtet werden, soweit kein Grund zu der Annahme besteht, dass durch die Vernichtung schutzwürdige Interessen des Betroffenen beeinträchtigt werden.

§ 110c
Verwaltungsvereinbarungen, Verordnungsermächtigung

(1) Die Spitzenverbände der Träger der Sozialversicherung und die Bundesanstalt für Arbeit vereinbaren gemeinsam unter besonderer Berücksichtigung der schutzwürdigen Interessen der Betroffenen das Nähere zu den Grundsätzen ordnungsmäßiger Aufbewahrung im Sinne des § 110a, den Voraussetzungen der Rückgabe und Vernichtung von Unterlagen sowie die Aufbewahrungsfristen für Unterlagen. Die Vereinbarung kann auf bestimmte Sozialleistungsbereiche beschränkt werden; sie ist von den beteiligten Spitzenverbänden abzuschließen. Die Vereinbarungen bedürfen der

Genehmigung der beteiligten Bundesministerien.

(2) Soweit Vereinbarungen nicht getroffen sind, wird die Bundesregierung ermächtigt, durch Rechtsverordnung mit Zustimmung des Bundesrates unter besonderer Berücksichtigung der schutzwürdigen Interessen der Betroffenen

1. das Nähere zu bestimmen über
   a) die Grundsätze ordnungsmäßiger Aufbewahrung im Sinne des § 110a,
   b) die Rückgabe und Vernichtung von Unterlagen,
2. für bestimmte Unterlagen allgemeine Aufbewahrungsfristen festzulegen.

§ 110d
Beweiswirkung

Ist eine Unterlage nach § 110a Abs. 2 auf anderen dauerhaften maschinell verwertbaren Datenträgern als Bildträgern aufbewahrt und

1. die Wiedergabe mit einer dauerhaft überprüfbaren qualifizierten elektronischen Signatur im Sinne des Signaturgesetzes dessen versehen, der die Wiedergabe auf dem dauerhaften Datenträger hergestellt hat, oder
2. bei urschriftlicher Aufzeichnung des Textes nur in gespeicherter Form diese mit einer dauerhaft überprüfbaren qualifizierten elektronischen Signatur im Sinne des Signaturgesetzes dessen versehen ist, der den Text elektronisch signiert hat,

können der öffentlich-rechtlichen Verwaltungstätigkeit die Daten auf diesem dauerhaften Datenträger zu Grunde gelegt werden, soweit nach den Umständen des Einzelfalles kein Anlass ist, ihre sachliche Richtigkeit zu beanstanden."

5. Der bisherige Siebte Abschnitt wird Achter Abschnitt.

§ 2
Änderung des Sechsten Buches Sozialgesetzbuch

Das Sechste Buch Sozialgesetzbuch – Gesetzliche Rentenversicherung – (Artikel 1 des Gesetzes vom 18.Dezember 1989, BGBl. I S. 2261, 1990 I S. 1337), zuletzt geändert durch ...,
wird wie folgt geändert:

1. In der Inhaltsübersicht werden die Angabe "Drittes Kapitel Organisation und Datenschutz" durch die Angabe "Drittes Kapitel Organisation, Datenschutz und Datensicherheit", die Angabe "Zweiter Abschnitt Datenschutz" durch die Angabe "Zweiter Abschnitt Datenschutz und Datensicherheit" ersetzt und nach der Angabe zu § 151 die Angabe "§ 151a Antragstellung im automatisierten Verfahren beim Versicherungsamt" eingefügt.

2. Die Überschrift vor § 125 wird wie folgt gefasst:

   "DRITTES KAPITEL
   Organisation, Datenschutz und Datensicherheit"

3. Die Überschrift vor § 147 wird wie folgt gefasst:

   "Zweiter Abschnitt
   Datenschutz und Datensicherheit"

4. § 148 Abs. 3 Satz 1 wird wie folgt geändert:

   Nach den Wörtern "Bundesanstalt für Arbeit," wird das Wort "und" durch ein Komma ersetzt und nach den Wörtern "betraut ist," werden die Wörter "und Versicherungsämter und Gemeindebehörden, soweit sie mit der Aufnahme von Anträgen auf Leistungen der gesetzlichen Rentenversicherung betraut sind," eingefügt.

5. In § 150 Abs. 4 Satz 2 werden nach den Wörtern "Deutsche Post AG" die Wörter ", für die Versicherungsämter und Gemeindebehörden" angefügt.

6. Nach § 151 wird folgender § 151a eingefügt:

"§ 151a
Antragstellung im automatisierten Verfahren beim Versicherungsamt

(1) Für die Aufnahme von Leistungsanträgen beim Versicherungsamt oder der Gemeindebehörde und für die nachfolgende Übermittlung der Anträge an den Träger der Rentenversicherung kann ein automatisiertes Verfahren eingerichtet werden, das es dem Versicherungsamt oder der Gemeindebehörde ermöglicht, die für das automatisierte Verfahren erforderlichen Daten der Versicherten, die ihre alleinige Wohnung oder ihre Hauptwohnung im Bezirk des Versicherungsamtes oder im Gebiet der Gemeinde haben, aus Dateien der Träger der Rentenversicherung gemäß § 149 Abs. 1 oder der Datenstelle der Rentenversicherungsträger gemäß § 150 Abs. 2 abzurufen.

Sofern aus datenschutzrechtlichen Gründen eine weitere Konkretisierung der zu übermittelnden Daten für notwendig gehalten wird, bietet sich mit Absatz 2 nachfolgende, den Absatz 1 ergänzende Variante an:

(2) Aus dem Versicherungskonto nach § 149 Abs. 1 dürfen nur folgende Daten übermittelt werden:
1. Staatsangehörigkeit,
2. Familienstand und früherer Name des Versicherten,
3. Anschrift sowie Telefon- und Faxnummer,
4. Bankverbindung,
5. Daten zum Zuzug aus dem Ausland,
6. Daten zum Stand der Kontoklärung und gegebenenfalls zu früheren Rentenantragstellungen,
7. Daten zum Bezug einer Hinterbliebenenrente sowie
8. im Falle eines Versorgungsausgleichs Angaben zum früheren Ehegatten.

Aus der Stammsatzdatei nach § 150 Abs. 2 dürfen nur folgende Da-

ten zur Verfügung gestellt werden:

1. Name, Vorname, Vorsatzwort zum Namen, Geburtsname und Geburtsort,

2. Bereichsnummer des aktuellen Kontoführers,

3. voraussichtlich für die Antragsbearbeitung zuständiger Rentenversicherungsträger.

(2) *((3))* Für die Einrichtung des automatisierten Verfahrens ist ein Sicherheitskonzept, das insbesondere die nach § 78a des Zehnten Buches erforderlichen technischen und organisatorischen Maßnahmen enthalten muss, von den Trägern der Rentenversicherung und dem Verband Deutscher Rentenversicherungsträger im Einvernehmen mit dem Bundesamt für Sicherheit in der Informationstechnik zu erstellen. Die Einrichtung und Änderung des Verfahrens bedarf im Einzelfall der vorherigen Zustimmung der jeweiligen Aufsichtsbehörde. Die Träger der Rentenversicherung und der Verband Deutscher Rentenversicherungsträger müssen das Sicherheitskonzept im Falle sicherheitserheblicher Veränderungen, spätestens jedoch alle drei Jahre nach erstmaliger Einrichtung des Verfahrens aktualisieren und der jeweiligen Aufsichtsbehörde vorlegen. Die Aufsichtsbehörde kann die Fortführung des Verfahrens untersagen, wenn sie das Sicherheitskonzept nicht mehr für ausreichend hält."

§ 3
Weitere Änderung des Zehnten Buches Sozialgesetzbuch

Das Zehnte Buch Sozialgesetzbuch – Sozialverwaltungsverfahren und Sozialdatenschutz –, zuletzt geändert durch Artikel 2 § 2 dieses Gesetzes, wird wie folgt geändert:

1. In § 50 Abs. 2a wird die Angabe "mit 3 vom Hundert über dem jeweiligen Diskontsatz der Deutschen Bundesbank" (ab 1.1.2002: "mit 3 vom Hundert über dem jeweiligen Basiszinssatz der Deutschen Bundesbank") durch die Wörter "mit fünf Prozentpunkten über dem Basiszinssatz nach § 1 des Diskontsatz-Überleitungs-

Gesetzes vom 9. Juni 1998 (BGBl. I S. 1242)" ersetzt.

2. In § 60 Abs. 1 werden die Sätze 3 und 4 gestrichen.

§ 4
Änderung des Sozialgerichtsgesetzes

Wird nach Abstimmung mit den BMJ-Formulierungen zur VwGO nachgereicht

Artikel BMVg

Artikel BMFSFJ

Artikel BMG

Artikel BMVBW

Artikel BMU

Artikel BMBF

Artikel BMZ

Artikel X
Rückkehr zum einheitlichen Verordnungsrang

Die auf den Artikeln ... bis ... beruhenden Teile der dort geänderten Rechtsverordnungen können auf Grund der jeweils einschlägigen Ermächtigungen durch Rechtsverordnung geändert werden.

Artikel XX
Neubekanntmachung

Das Bundesministerium des Innern kann den Wortlaut des Verwaltungsverfahrensgesetzes in der vom Inkrafttreten dieses Gesetzes an geltenden Fassung im Bundesgesetzblatt bekannt machen.

Artikel XXX
Inkrafttreten

Dieses Gesetz tritt am Tage nach der Verkündung in Kraft.

Begründung

A. Allgemeiner Teil:

I. Ausgangslage

Die Entwicklung der Informations- und Kommunikationstechnik stellt die Modernisierung der Verwaltung vor neue Aufgaben. Inhalte jeder Art, insbesondere auch Willenserklärungen, können weltweit, schnell und grundsätzlich ohne Qualitätsverlust übermittelt werden. Es sind zwei miteinander verknüpfte Aufgabenstellungen identifizierbar: Im Rahmen der fortschreitenden Verwirklichung der Bürgergesellschaft ist die Kommunikation zwischen Bürger und Verwaltung weiter zu verbessern. Hierzu sind für den Bürger übliche Standards der Informations- und Kommunikationstechnik auch durch die Verwaltung bereitzustellen. Gleichzeitig müssen auch für die Verwaltung die Vorteile der Informationstechnik weiter nutzbar gemacht werden, um die Potentiale zur Kostensenkung und Produktivitätssteigerung ausschöpfen zu können. Beide Aufgabenstellungen setzen voraus, dass einerseits Hindernisse für die elektronische Übermittlung von rechtsverbindlichen Erklärungen so weit wie möglich beseitigt werden und andererseits die Rechtssicherheit im elektronischen Rechtsverkehr durch einen verlässlichen gesetzlichen Rahmen gestärkt wird.

II. Ziel und Gegenstand des Gesetzentwurfs

1. Mit dem vorliegenden Gesetzentwurf wird das gesamte Verwaltungsverfahrensrecht des Bundes für die Entwicklungen des modernen Rechtsverkehrs geöffnet. Bürger und Verwaltung sollen grundsätzlich in allen Fachgebieten und jeder Verfahrensart elektronische Kommunikationsformen gleichberechtigt neben der Schriftform und der mündlichen Form rechtswirksam verwenden können. Wirtschaft und Bürger erhalten dadurch eine einfache zusätzliche Möglichkeit des Zugangs zur Verwaltung.

2. Der das Verwaltungsverfahrensrecht prägende Grundsatz der Nichtförmlichkeit des Verwaltungshandelns (§ 10 VwVfG, § 9 SGB X) erlaubt schon heute die Anwendung elektronischer Verfahren. Gleichwohl sind rechtliche Änderungen und Ergänzungen notwendig, um die rechtsverbindliche elektronische Kommunikation zwischen Bürger und Verwaltung durchgängig zu ermöglichen. Der Grundsatz der Nichtförmlichkeit wird von einer Reihe von Schriftformerfordernissen eingeschränkt. Diese werden in Rechtsvorschriften ausdrücklich durch unterschiedliche Begriffe, wie "schriftlich", "schriftliche Form", "Schriftform" bestimmt oder durch Formulierungen wie "Unterschrift", "Unterschriftenliste", "Niederschrift", vorausgesetzt.

   Der Begriff der Schriftform im Verwaltungsrecht verlangt nicht stets die eigenhändige Unterzeichnung eines Dokuments, seine konkrete Bedeutung erschließt sich erst durch die Auslegung der jeweiligen gesetzlichen Bestimmungen. Elektronische Dokumente entsprechen dabei den Schriftformerfordernissen des Verwaltungsrechts durch nicht ohne Weiteres. Ihnen fehlt insoweit die Verkörperung durch unmittelbar lesbare Schriftzeichen. Vollelektronischer Verkehr zwischen Bürger und Verwaltung erfordert deshalb eine Regelung, die die elektronische Form der Schriftform gleich stellt.

3. Der Gesetzentwurf berücksichtigt, dass elektronische Daten auf ihrem Weg durch offene Netze für den Empfänger unerkennbar verändert werden können und es daher eines sicheren Rahmens zur elektronischen Authentifizierung des Kommunikationspartners und Überprüfung der Integrität der übermittelten Daten bedarf. Die hierzu notwendigen Bedingungen regelt das Signaturgesetz (Artikel 1 des Gesetzes über Rahmenbedingungen für elektronische Signaturen und zur Änderung weiterer Vorschriften vom 16. Mai 2001 [BGBl. I S. 876]). Die Vorschriften des Gesetzentwurfs knüpfen daher, wo dies erforderlich ist, an die Regelungen des Signaturgesetzes an.

   Mit den sich aus der Richtlinie 1999/93/EG des Europäischen Parlaments und des Rates vom 13. Dezember 1999 über gemeinschaftliche Rahmenbedingungen für elektronische Signaturen (ABl.

EG 2000 Nr. L 13 S. 12) ergebenden Anforderungen ist der Gesetzentwurf kompatibel. Änderungen des deutschen Rechts, die durch die Richtlinie über gemeinschaftliche Rahmenbedingungen für elektronische Signaturen veranlasst werden, sind durch das Signaturgesetz umgesetzt worden. Sie werden daher durch die Bezugnahme auf das Signaturgesetz bereits berücksichtigt. Der Gesetzentwurf macht auch von der durch Art. 3 Abs. 7 der Richtlinie eröffneten Möglichkeit, den Einsatz elektronischer Signaturen im öffentlichen Bereich möglichen zusätzlichen Anforderungen zu unterwerfen, im Rahmen der dies national umsetzenden Regelung des § 1 Abs. 3 Signaturgesetz Gebrauch, soweit dies erforderlich ist.

III. Die wesentlichen Änderungen im Überblick

1. In die Verwaltungsverfahrensgesetze werden Generalklauseln eingeführt, die die Gleichwertigkeit einer durch Rechtsvorschrift angeordneten Schriftform und der mit einer qualifizierten elektronischen Signatur verbundenen elektronischen Form bestimmen (§ 3a Abs. 2 Satz 1 VwVfG, § 36a Abs. 2 Satz 1 SGB I, § ... AO). Die Anforderung der qualifizierten elektronischen Signatur wurde wie im Bereich des Zivilrechts (§§ 126 ff. BGB) gewählt, um eine der Schriftform in etwa gleichwertige Beweisqualität zu erzielen. Die neue Regelung gilt grundsätzlich im gesamten Anwendungsbereich des Verwaltungsverfahrensrechts; sie erfasst nicht nur die Schriftformerfordernisse im Verwaltungsverfahrensgesetz, dem Zehnten Buch Sozialgesetzbuch und der Abgabenordnung, sondern auch im gesamten Fachrecht.

   Wird die Schriftform durch eine elektronische Alternative ersetzt, muss diese der schriftlichen Form entsprechendes leisten können. Dies ist auch bei der Generalklausel zu berücksichtigen. Hinsichtlich der verschiedenen Funktionen der Schriftlichkeit und der Funktionsäquivalenz einer mit einer qualifizierten elektronischen Signatur verbundenen elektronischen Form wird auf die Begründung des Entwurfs eines Gesetzes zur Anpassung der Formvorschriften des Privatrechts und anderer Vorschriften an den modernen Rechtsgeschäftsverkehr (BT-Drs. 14/4987, S. 15 ff.) verwiesen. Die dort angesprochenen Funktionen der Schriftlichkeit haben im Verwaltungsverfahrensrecht – je nach Fachgebiet – unterschiedliche Bedeutung und unterschiedliches Gewicht. Auch im Verwaltungsverfahrensrecht gilt aber: Ohne qualifizierte elektronische Signatur hat ein elektronisches Dokument nicht die der Schriftform entsprechende Funktionalität. Deshalb greift der Gesetzentwurf auf die mit der Signaturgesetznovelle 2001 neu definierten qualifizierten elektronischen Signaturen zurück.

Elektronische Dokumente unterscheiden sich von schriftlichen Dokumenten bei Entstehung, Handhabung und Übermittlung. Bei vollelektronischer Arbeitsweise hat das elektronische Dokument die Funktion des Originals, das vollständig, inhaltlich richtig und authentisch sein muss. Die Verwendung elektronischer Signaturen erlaubt einen entsprechenden Nachweis. Ohne eine solche hat ein elektronisches Dokument im allgemeinen nur eine geringe Beweisqualität.

Ein elektronisches Dokument mit einer qualifizierten elektronischen Signatur weist eine erheblich höhere Sicherheit vor Fälschung und Verfälschung auf als eine herkömmliches Dokument mit eigenhändiger Unterschrift. In Signaturschlüssel-Zertifikaten oder in Attribut-Zertifikaten können alle Funktionen, Zuständigkeiten, Rechte usw. von Behördenmitarbeitern ausgewiesen werden (z.B. Referatsleiter für ... und/oder Prokura-Berechtigung bis ...). Auch Dienstsiegel können elektronisch abgebildet werden. Für bestimmte Funktionen (z.B. automatische Empfangsbestätigungen bei elektronischen Eingängen) können gesonderte Signaturschlüssel, die durch entsprechende Zertifikate auf die jeweilige Anwendung beschränkt sind, eingesetzt werden.
Die Generalklausel entspricht inhaltlich der durch das Gesetz zur Anpassung der Formvorschriften des Privatrechts und anderer Vorschriften an den modernen Rechtsgeschäftsverkehr eingefügten Regelung des § 126a BGB. Sie berücksichtigt jedoch die vom Privatrecht abweichenden Bedingungen öffentlichrechtlicher Verwaltungstätigkeit.

Die qualifizierte elektronische Signatur nach § 2 Nr. 3 Signaturgesetz bildet im Einklang mit dem europäischen Recht den Standard für rechtsverbindliches elektronisches Handeln sowohl des Bürgers als auch der Verwaltung, soweit eine Rechtsvorschrift bislang schriftliches Handeln forderte. Im Übrigen kann der Bürger jede Form elektronischer Kommunikation nutzen. Er erhält damit einen einfachen und schnellen Zugang zu der Verwaltung; gleichzeitig werden die schutzwürdigen Interessen des Bürgers und der Verwaltung bei rechtlich bedeutsamen Sachverhalten, die elektronische Authentifizierung des Kommunikationspartners und Überprüfung der Integrität der übermittelten Daten vornehmen zu können, wirkungsvoll gesichert.

2. Bei Verwaltungsakten, bei denen durch Rechtsvorschrift eine Schriftform vorgeschrieben ist, eröffnet der Gesetzentwurf die Möglichkeit, höhere Anforderungen an die elektronische Alternative zu stellen. Hier können die dauerhafte Überprüfbarkeit der qualifizierten elektronischen Signatur sowie Nachweise zur technischen und administrativen Sicherheit verlangt werden. Einzelheiten regelt eine Rechtsverordnung. Diese Sonderregelung (§ 37a VwVfG, § 33a SGB X, § ... AO) verdrängt insoweit die Generalklausel (§ 3a Abs. 2 Satz 1 VwVfG, § 36a Abs. 2 Satz 1 SGB I, § ... AO).

3. Wenn auch einfache Formen elektronischer Kommunikation genügen sollen (E-Mail ohne qualifizierte elektronische Signatur), bedarf es einer ausdrücklichen Regelung. Hierzu verwendet der Gesetzentwurf das Begriffspaar "schriftlich oder elektronisch".

4. Zur Beschreibung jeglicher Erscheinungsform elektronischer Dokumente, also nicht nur als Alternative zur gesetzlich angeordneten Schriftlichkeit, verwendet der Gesetzentwurf das Wort "elektronisch" als Oberbegriff.

5. Die elektronische Kommunikation soll allein davon abhängen, dass entsprechende Empfangsmöglichkeiten vorhanden und der Öffentlichkeit gewidmet worden sind. Damit werden die legitimen Interessen sowohl der Bürger als auch der Verwaltung gewahrt. Die

Ausgestaltung der elektronischen Kommunikation bleibt dabei jeder Behörde überlassen. Sie ist auch frei darin, wie sie elektronische Eingänge im internen Geschäftsgang bewältigt. Die Behörde kann deren Bearbeitung vollelektronisch fortsetzen bis hin zum elektronischen Bescheid. Sie kann aber ebenso jeden Eingang ausdrucken und ihn sodann in herkömmlicher Weise als Original auf Papier weiterbearbeiten.

6. Kein Änderungsbedarf zur Ermöglichung einer vollelektronischen Arbeitsweise der Verwaltung besteht im Hinblick auf den Urkundsbegriff, die Beweiseignung elektronischer Dokumente, die Einsichtnahme in elektronische Dokumente und die Berichtigung von offensichtlichen Unrichtigkeiten in elektronischen Dokumenten.

Im Sinne des Verwaltungsrechts ist Urkunde jede verkörperte Gedankenerklärung, Akten in diesem Sinne sind nach bestimmten Ordnungsgesichtspunkten in geeigneter Form zusammengestellte Urkunden. Ausgehend von diesem weiten Urkunden- und Aktenbegriff lassen sich auch elektronische Dokumente als Urkunden oder Akten verstehen. Dies entspricht der bereits bestehenden Praxis bei der Nutzung elektronischer Daten im Rahmen des "papierarmen Büros". Daher bedarf es im Verwaltungsverfahrensgesetz keiner Änderung des § 5 Abs. 2 Satz 2 und § 26 Abs. 1 Satz 2 Nr. 3.

Elektronische Dokumente sind geeignete Beweismittel im Sinne des § 26 VwVfG. Die Aufzählung der Beweismittel in den Nummern 1 bis 4 ist nicht abschließend.
Die Einsichtnahme in elektronische Dokumente als Bestandteil der Verfahrensakten ist nach § 29 Abs. 3 Satz 2 letzter Halbsatz VwVfG zulässig. Dabei wird in der Praxis dieser Weg der Akteneinsicht im Regelfall nur bei elektronischer Durchführung des Verwaltungsverfahrens eröffnet werden.

Die Berichtigungsmöglichkeiten nach § 42 VwVfG erfassen auch offenbare Unrichtigkeiten in einem elektronischen Dokument.

Keiner zusätzlichen Regelungen bedarf auch der Schutz von Geheimnissen der Beteiligten eines Verwaltungsverfahrens. Die Behörde muss, wie in § 30 VwVfG vorgesehen, die notwendigen Sicherheitsvorkehrungen treffen.

IV. Anpassung der Vorschriften des besonderen Verwaltungsrechts

Die Anpassung der Vorschriften des besonderen Verwaltungsrechts erfolgt ausgehend von den Grundsatzentscheidungen in den Verwaltungsverfahrensgesetzen des Bundes nach den folgenden Regeln:

1. Der vorliegende Gesetzentwurf soll den Bürgern und der Verwaltung die Nutzung elektronischer Kommunikationsmöglichkeiten erleichtern, deshalb werden einfache Möglichkeiten der elektronischen Kommunikation möglichst beibehalten. Gleichzeitig muss sich die Entscheidung für einen elektronischen Standard in einer Norm an der Rechtsverbindlichkeit der jeweiligen Handlung orientieren. Sie spiegelt daher gleichsam die Interessen von Bürger und Verwaltung an der Sicherheit und Dauerhaftigkeit des entsprechenden Vorgangs.

2. Verwaltungsakte, für die durch Gesetz die Schriftlichkeit angeordnet ist, entfalten vielfach über lange Zeiträume hinweg Rechtswirkungen. Sind sie in elektronischer Form ergangen, so muss ihre – formelle – Richtigkeit gegebenenfalls noch nach vielen Jahren geprüft werden können. Entscheidend ist dabei vor allem die Überprüfbarkeit der Integrität des Dokuments, deshalb wird hier entsprechend der Regelung des § 37a VwVfG regelmäßig eine "dauerhaft überprüfbare Signatur" notwendig sein. "Dauerhaft überprüfbare Signaturen" sind qualifizierte elektronische Signaturen im Sinne von § 2 Nr. 3 Signaturgesetz, die entsprechend der Regelung des § 1 Abs. 3 Signaturgesetz besonderen Anforderungen genügen müssen. Diese Signaturen und die qualifizierten Zertifikate, auf denen sie beruhen, müssen im Rahmen der Möglichkeiten des Standes der Technik dauerhaft, also so langfristig wie möglich, überprüfbar sein. Um den Geltungsanspruch entsprechender schrift-

licher Verwaltungsakte abbilden zu können, ist vor dem Hintergrund des derzeitigen Standes der Technik eine Online Prüfung der Integrität und Authentizität für mindestens dreißig Jahre erforderlich. Staatliches Handeln muss transparent sein, seine Rechtmäßigkeit muss gesichert sein. Deshalb muss die technische und administrative Sicherheit der für diese Zwecke verwendeten Signaturen und Zertifikate umfassend prüfbar sein. Die Einhaltung der notwendigen Maßnahmen, um diese Sicherheit auch permanent sicherzustellen, muss regelmäßig geprüft werden können. Diese Anforderungen werden im Rahmen einer Rechtsverordnung in ihren Einzelheiten geregelt.

3. Jedoch können auch Verwaltungsakte, deren Schriftform durch Gesetz vorgeschrieben ist, von nur kurzer zeitlicher Bedeutung sein. Dies kommt insbesondere in verschiedenen Bereichen der Leistungsverwaltung in Betracht, hier verbleibt es für entsprechende Verwaltungsakte bei den qualifizierten elektronischen Signaturen nach § 3a Abs. 2 VwVfG.

4. Allgemeine Schriftformerfordernisse in Verwaltungsverfahren, die rechtsverbindliches Handeln des Bürgers verlangen, können aufgrund der Generalklausel des § 3a Abs. 2 VwVfG stets durch eine mit einer qualifizierten elektronischen Signatur verbundenen elektronischen Form ersetzt werden.

5. Soweit der Schriftform im jeweiligen Normkontext über z.B. den Dokumentations- und Nachweischarakter hinaus, keine eigenständige, vor allem rechtliche Bedeutung zukommt, etwa auch mündliche Erklärungen zulässig sind, wird durch die Ergänzung des Begriffs "schriftlich" zum Begriffspaar "schriftlich oder elektronisch" die Möglichkeit der Nutzung auch einfacher elektronischer Kommunikation eröffnet. So werden einfache Auskünfte der Verwaltung ebenso wie entsprechende Anfragen der Bürger regelmäßig durch den Austausch von E-Mails erfolgen können.

6. Daneben sind jedoch auch Fallgestaltungen denkbar, wo aufgrund der besonderen Bedeutung des Rechtsaktes die elektronische Form –

zumindest gegenwärtig – ausgeschlossen bleiben soll. Dies ist etwa für die ausfertigende Unterzeichnung von Gesetzen durch den Bundespräsidenten vorgesehen.

V. Gesetzgebungskompetenz
Hinsichtlich aller Materien, für die dem Bund die Sachkompetenz zukommt, kann er – als Annex – das Verwaltungsverfahren mitregeln. Zum Verwaltungsverfahren gehört auch die bei diesem zu beachtenden Formbestimmungen.

VI. Finanzielle Auswirkungen
Durch die Einführung und auch die absehbare Zunahme elektronischer Kommunikation werden für die Verwaltung Kosten der Einführung entsprechender Signaturanwendungen entstehen. Die Vorhaltung geeigneter Hard- und Software gehört bereits heute im Wesentlichen zum Ausstattungsstandard und muss um Komponenten zur Unterstützung von Anwendungen mit qualifizierten elektronischen Signaturen ergänzt werden. Dieses lässt sich teilweise im Rahmen der üblichen Austauschzyklen oder der Einführung elektronsicher Verwaltungsdienstleistungen realisieren. Den Kosten steht ein erhebliches Rationalisierungs- und Einsparungspotential gegenüber. Im Bereich des Bundes dürften die Auswirkungen daher zu vernachlässigen sein. Besonderer Vollzugsaufwand entsteht nicht. Sonstige Kosten (z.B. Kosten für die Wirtschaft, Kosten für die sozialen Sicherungssysteme, Auswirkungen auf das Preisniveau, insbesondere das Verbraucherpreisniveau) entstehen nicht. Vielmehr erleichtert das Gesetz Wirtschaft und Bürgern den Zugang zu Verwaltungsbehörden unter Nutzung kostensparender Informationstechnologie, daher ist von Kostenreduktionen für Wirtschaft und Bürger auszugehen.

B. Besonderer Teil:

Zu Artikel 1 – Änderung des Verwaltungsverfahrensgesetzes

Zu Nummer 1 (Inhaltsübersicht VwVfG)

Bei den Änderungen handelt es sich um Folgeänderungen zu Nummer 3 (§ 3a), Nummer 8 (§ 34a) und Nummer 10 (§ 37a).

Zu Nummer 2 (Überschrift des Teils 1)

Mit der Änderung wird die Überschrift des Teils 1 des Gesetzes an die Einfügung des § 3a angepasst. Um den generellen Geltungsanspruch der Norm deutlich darzustellen, wird deren Überschrift in die Überschrift des Teils 1 einbezogen.

Zu Nummer 3 (§ 3a)

§ 3a regelt in Absatz 1 die Zulässigkeit der Übermittlung elektronischer Dokumente. Absatz 2 enthält eine Generalklausel, nach der eine gesetzlich angeordnete Schriftform unter Beachtung bestimmter Voraussetzungen durch die elektronische Form ersetzt werden kann. In Absatz 3 ist eine Bestimmung für das Verfahren bei fehlgeschlagener elektronischer Kommunikation vorgesehen.

Zu § 3a Abs. 1:
Die neuen Kommunikationstechniken sind noch nicht flächendeckend verbreitet. Der Gesetzentwurf vermeidet deshalb Regelungen, die einen rechtlichen oder tatsächlichen Zwang auf Bürger und/oder Behörde zur Schaffung der Voraussetzungen für eine moderne elektronische Kommunikation ausüben könnten. Statt dessen ist die Möglichkeit zur Verwendung neuer Technologien eröffnet worden, "soweit" Bürger und Behörde die Voraussetzungen hierfür bereits geschaffen haben. Jedenfalls bei Behörden ist grundsätzlich von der Eröffnung eines entsprechenden Zugangs auszugehen, wenn eine E-Mail-Adresse im Briefkopf angegeben wird oder ein Internetangebot ohne ausdrücklichen Vorbehalt vorhanden ist.

Zu § 3a Abs. 2 Satz 1:
Ein elektronisches Dokument, das mit einer qualifizierten elek-

tronischen Signatur verbunden ist, soll gesetzlich angeordneten Schriftformerfordernissen genügen. Dieser Grundsatz gilt im gesamten Anwendungsbereich des Verwaltungsverfahrensgesetzes. Ausnahmen bedürfen einer gesonderten Regelung.

Die Schriftform hat, sei es kumulativ, sei es zum Teil,

- eine Abschlussfunktion, d.h. sie bringt das Ende der Erklärung zum Ausdruck,
- eine Perpetuierungsfunktion, d.h. sie gewährleistet die fortdauernde Wiedergabe der Erklärung in einer Urkunde mit der Möglichkeit zur Überprüfung,
- eine Identitätsfunktion, d.h. sie ermöglicht es, den Erklärenden zu erkennen,
- eine Echtheitsfunktion, d.h. sie gewährleistet die inhaltliche Zuordnung der Erklärung zum Erklärenden,
- eine Verifikationsfunktion, d.h. sie dient der Überprüfbarkeit der Echtheit der Erklärung,
- eine Beweisfunktion, d.h. sie ist zum Nachweis der Erklärung geeignet,
- eine Warnfunktion, d.h. der Erklärende wird auf die rechtliche Verbindlichkeit der Erklärung hingewiesen und vor Übereilung geschützt.

Der Verweis auf die qualifizierte elektronische Signatur im Sinne des Signaturgesetzes stellt für den Bereich der elektronischen Kommunikation die genannten Funktionen in ihrer Gesamtheit sicher. Eine elektronische Signatur kann mit einem Siegel für ein elektronisches Dokument verglichen werden. Signiert wird mittels eines privaten kryptographischen Schlüssels, der mathematisch erzeugt wird. Diesem korrespondiert ein öffentlicher Schlüssel zur jederzeit möglichen Überprüfung der Signatur. Die Schlüsselpaare sind einmalig; sie werden durch anerkannte Stellen natürlichen Personen fest zugeordnet. Das beglaubigende Signaturschlüssel-Zertifikat ist ein signiertes elektronisches Dokument, das den jeweiligen öffentlichen Schlüssel sowie den Namen der ihm zugeordneten Person enthält. Dieser sog. Signaturschlüssel-Inhaber erhält das Zertifikat und kann es signierten Daten zu deren Überprüfung beifügen. Das Zertifikat ist daneben über öffentlich erreichbare Telekommunikationsverbindungen jederzeit für jeden nachprüfbar. Nach heutigem Stand der Technik erfolgt die Speicherung der relevanten Daten auf einer Chipkarte, die nur mit einer PIN und in der Regel in einem Chipkartenleser eines Personal-Computers eingesetzt werden kann.

Zu § 3a Abs. 2 Satz 2:
Das Signaturgesetz erlaubt die Zuordnung von Signaturen an Personen unter einem Pseudonym. In solchen Fällen lassen sich die mit der Verwendung einer qualifizierten elektronischen Signatur bezweckten Funktionen nicht sicherstellen. Deshalb werden solche Signaturen von der Gleichwertigkeit ausgenommen.

Zu § 3a Abs. 2 Satz 3:
Die qualifizierte elektronische Signatur nach EU-Mindeststandard ist bei der elektronischen Kommunikation des Bürgers mit Behörden grundsätzlich ausreichend. Falls durch besondere gesetzliche Regelung eine qualifizierte elektronische Signatur nach § 2 Nr. 2 Signaturgesetz gefordert wird, darf diese nach Artikel 3 Abs. 7 Satz 3 der EU-Richtlinie 1999/93/EG bei grenzüberschreitenden Diensten für den Bürger kein Hindernis darstellen. Satz 3 trägt dem dadurch Rechnung, dass bei solchen grenzüberschreitenden Diensten dem nationalen Erfordernis einer Signatur im Sinne von § 37a VwVfG (entspricht derzeit vor allem qualifizierten elektronischen Signaturen mit Anbieter-Akkreditierung nach § 15 Abs. 1 Signaturgesetz) ausnahmsweise auch eine qualifizierte elektronische Signatur nach EU-Mindeststandard genügt. Soweit ausländische Signaturen nach § 23 Abs. 2 Signaturgesetz den Anforderungen an eine dauerhaft überprüfbare qualifizierte elektronische Signatur entsprechen, sind sie diesen gleichgestellt.

Zu § 3a Abs. 3:
Angesichts der Vielfalt der neuen technischen Möglichkeiten ist es möglich, dass die verwendeten Kommunikationsmethoden zueinander nicht kompatibel sind, so dass entweder Bürger oder Behörde übermittelte elektronische Dokumente nicht lesen und damit nicht

bearbeiten können. Im Rahmen des Verwaltungsrechtsverhältnisses, das Bürger und Verwaltung durch ihre Kommunikation schaffen, kann von den Partnern erwartet werden, den jeweils anderen darüber zu unterrichten, dass die von ihm gewählte Form der elektronischen Kommunikation nicht möglich ist, die übermittelten Zeichen nicht lesbar sind.

Die Pflicht der Behörde, unverzüglich, also ohne schuldhaftes Zögern (§ 122 Abs. 1 Satz 1 BGB), mitzuteilen, dass ein Dokument nicht bearbeitet werden kann, besteht nur und ausschließlich gegenüber dem jeweiligen Absender, da regelmäßig nur dieser dasselbe Dokument erneut übermitteln kann. Der Begriff der Bearbeitung ist weit zu verstehen.

Absatz 3 trifft keine Regelung über den Zugang von elektronischen Dokumenten, dieser bestimmt sich vielmehr nach den allgemeinen Grundsätzen.

Zu Nummer 4 (§ 14)

Die Änderung stellt klar, dass wegen Ungeeignetheit Bevollmächtigte und Beistände sowohl vom schriftlichen wie auch vom Vortrag mittels elektronischer Dokumente zurückgewiesen werden können. Gleichzeitig wird das geltende Recht präzisiert, beim mündlichen Vortrag ist eine Zurückweisung nur möglich, wenn der Bevollmächtigte oder Beistand zum sachgemäßen Vortrag nicht in der Lage ist.

Zu Nummer 5 (§ 15)

Die bisherige Fassung des Satzes 2 stellte nur auf Schriftstücke und deren Transportbedingungen ab. Bei der elektronischen Übermittlung ist dagegen die Übermittlungszeit so kurz, dass die Entfernung zum Bestimmungsort bedeutungslos wird. Deshalb kann bei ihr der Zugang spätestens am Tage nach der Übermittlung vermutet werden.

§ 15 Satz 2 ist nur anwendbar, wenn der Behörde der ausländische Wohnsitz oder Aufenthaltsort oder Sitz bekannt ist.

Auch für das Telefax als elektronisch übermitteltes Dokument tritt die durch die Änderung herbeigeführte Zugangsbeschleunigung ein.

Zu Nummer 6 (§ 23)

Das Wort "Schriftstücke" wird durch das Wort "Dokumente" ersetzt. Damit wird klargestellt, dass eine Behörde auch bei fremdsprachigen elektronischen Dokumenten die Vorlage einer Übersetzung verlangen darf.

Zu Nummer 7 (§ 26)

Die Änderung in Absatz 1 Satz 2 Nr. 2 stellt klar, dass die Verwaltung auch elektronische Äußerungen von Beteiligten, Sachverständigen und Zeugen einholen kann.

Zu Nummer 8 (§ 34a)

Schriftdokumente werden etwa zum Zwecke der elektronischen Weiterverarbeitung zunehmend in elektronische Dokumente, umgekehrt aber auch noch signierte elektronische Dokumente in schriftliche umgewandelt werden. In beiden Fällen kann eine Beglaubigung erforderlich sein.

Zu § 34a Abs. 1:
Absatz 1 regelt den Fall der Beglaubigung eines Dokuments bei dessen Überführung von der Papierform in die elektronische Form. Er ermöglicht die Beglaubigung nach den §§ 33 und 34 auch in elektronischer Form. Die Beglaubigung durch die Behörde erfolgt durch eine dauerhaft überprüfbare qualifizierte elektronische Signatur nach § 37a des zuständigen Bediensteten, um dem Interesse an der dauerhaften Nachweisbarkeit der ordnungsgemäßen Beglaubigung Rechnung zu tragen. Die elektronische Beglaubigung eines schriftlichen Dokuments ändert jedoch nichts an den inhalt-

lichen Voraussetzungen für die Beglaubigung nach den § 33 Abs. 3 und § 34 Abs. 3. Diese müssen in vollem Umfang eingehalten werden.

Zu § 34a Abs. 2:
Absatz 2 regelt den entgegengesetzten Fall der Beglaubigung eines Dokuments bei dessen Überführung von der elektronischen Version in die Papierversion. Auch insoweit ist die Beglaubigung nach den §§ 33, 34 möglich. Die allgemeinen Voraussetzungen für eine Beglaubigung bedürfen teilweise jedoch der Modifikation. So treten für den Fall der Beglaubigung nach § 33 neben den Voraussetzungen nach dessen Absatz 3 weitere Anforderungen hinzu. Der Beglaubigungsvermerk muss zusätzlich angeben, wer der Inhaber des mit dem Dokument verbundenen Signaturschlüssels ist, also der Signaturschlüssel-Inhaber im Sinne von § 2 Nr. 9 Signaturgesetz. Zudem muss festgestellt werden, wann die elektronischen Signatur mit dem Dokument verbunden wurde. Daneben ist die Angabe notwendig, welche Zertifikate mit welchen Daten der Signatur zugrunde lagen. Hierdurch kann in Verbindung mit den anderen Angaben die Geltung des Signaturschlüssels überprüft werden; ob der Signaturschlüssel z.B. zum Zeitpunkt seiner Nutzung noch gültig war, das zugehörige Zertifikat entsprechende Rechtshandlungen, ggf. in Verbindung mit Attributzertifikaten ermöglicht. Basis hierfür ist die mit dem zur Beglaubigung vorliegenden Dokument verbundene qualifizierte elektronische Signatur und die dieser zugehörigen Zertifikate. Attributzertifikat ist nach § 5 Abs. 2 Satz 1 Signaturgesetz ein qualifiziertes Zertifikat, das auf Verlangen eines Antragstellers Angaben über seine Vertretungsmacht für eine dritte Person sowie berufsbezogene oder sonstige Angaben zu seiner Person (Attribute) enthält. Dabei gilt das von § 5 Abs. 1 Satz 1 Signaturgesetz formulierte Prinzip, das der Zertifizierungsdiensteanbieter Personen, die ein qualifiziertes Zertifikat beantragen, zuverlässig zu identifizieren hat. Diese Attribute können auch in ein gesondertes qualifiziertes Zertifikat (qualifiziertes Attribut-Zertifikat) aufgenommen werden (§ 7 Abs. 2 Satz 1 Signaturgesetz).

Bei der Beglaubigung von Unterschriften nach § 34 wird regelmäßig eine Überprüfung der Signatur ausreichen. Auch ist aus der Natur der Sache heraus ein Vollzug der Unterschrift vor dem aufnehmenden zuständigen Bediensteten nicht möglich. Dementsprechend wird für diese Voraussetzung der Beglaubigung hier ausgenommen und § 34 Abs. 2 für unanwendbar erklärt. Der Möglichkeit, dass der Bürger vor dem beglaubigenden zuständigen Bediensteten die Signatur als die seine anerkennt, wird durch die Aufnahme eines entsprechenden Hinweises im Beglaubigungsvermerk Rechnung getragen. Im übrigen gelten die Voraussetzungen des § 34 Abs. 3 für den Inhalt des Beglaubigungsvermerks uneingeschränkt.

Zu Nummer 9 (§ 37)

Zu Buchstabe a):
In Absatz 2 Satz 1 werden die Formen, in denen ein Verwaltungakt erlassen werden kann – schriftlich, mündlich oder in anderer Weise – , um die elektronische ergänzt. Zwar kann der elektronisch übermittelte nicht nur als in anderer Weise, sondern auch als schriftlich erlassener Verwaltungsakt verstanden werden, da Schrift im modernen Sprachgebrauch eine allgemeine Bezeichnung für eine Form oder ein Verfahren der Aufzeichnung oder Einprägung von Information (digitaler und analoger) auf oder in einen Träger ist (vgl. *Brockhaus*, Die Enzyklopädie, 20. Aufl., Bd. 19 [1998], Stichwort "Schrift"). Dem Anliegen des Gesetzentwurfs, die elektronische Kommunikationsform rechtswirksam neben den herkömmlichen Formen zu etablieren, wird die gesonderte Aufnahme in den Normtext jedoch in höherem Maße gerecht.

Absatz 2 Satz 2 stellt klar, dass ein mündlicher Verwaltungsakt schriftlich oder elektronisch bestätigt werden kann.

Zu Buchstabe b):
Absatz 3 Satz 2 stellt klar, dass die inhaltlichen Anforderungen an elektronische Verwaltungsakte denen an schriftliche Verwaltungsakte entsprechen. Auch ein elektronischer Verwaltungsakt muss die ausstellende Behörde erkennen lassen und die Namenswiedergabe

des Behördenleiters, seines Vertreters oder seines Beauftragten enthalten. Diese Anforderungen gelten für alle elektronischen Verwaltungsakte.

Zu Nummer 10 (§ 37a)

§ 37a ermöglicht besondere Anforderungen an einen elektronischen Verwaltungsakt, der einer durch materielles Gesetz angeordneten Schriftform genügen soll. Aus Gründen der Rechtssicherheit kann z.B. die Form einer dauerhaft überprüfbaren qualifizierten elektronischen Signatur erforderlich sein. Denn beim Verwaltungsakt kann sich noch nach Jahren oder Jahrzehnten die Notwendigkeit ergeben, auf das mit voller Beweiskraft versehene Original zurückzugreifen. Sind aus fachlichen Gründen die dauerhafte Überprüfbarkeit der qualifizierten elektronischen Signatur oder bestimmte Merkmale der technischen und administrativen Sicherheit geboten, kann das Fachrecht diese besonderen Anforderungen in dem von § 37a vorgegebenen Rahmen anordnen. § 37a verdrängt dann die Generalklausel des § 3a Abs. 2.

Die auf Grund der Ermächtigung des Satzes 2 zu erlassende Verordnung präzisiert den Rahmen des § 37a. Die Verordnung entlastet das Fachrecht von der Bestimmung technischer Einzelheiten und dient der auch aus Gründen der Rechtsklarheit erforderlichen Rechtseinheit. Zugleich ermöglicht die Auslagerung dieser konkretisierenden Regelungen in eine Verordnung die zügige Anpassung an neue technische Entwicklungen und administrative Erfordernisse.

Zu Nummer 11 (§ 39)

Zu Buchstabe a):
Der Begründungszwang ist bei schriftlichen Verwaltungsakten ein Gebot der Rechtsstaatlichkeit. Dies gilt in gleicher Weise dort, wo Formfreiheit herrscht und die Verwaltung aus sonstigen Gründen die Schriftform gewählt hat. Diese Erwägungen treffen auch zu, wenn ein elektronischer Verwaltungsakt übermittelt wird. Die Änderung in

Absatz 1 Satz 1 stellt dies klar.

Zu Buchstabe b):
Die Änderung stellt klar, dass die in Absatz 2 Nr. 2 bestimmet Ausnahme von dem Begründungserfordernis auch bei einem elektronischen Verwaltungsakt gilt.

Zu Nummer 12 (§ 41)

Zu Buchstabe a):
Die bisherige Fassung des Absatzes 2 stellt auf Schriftstücke und deren postalischer Übermittlung im Inland ab. Bei elektronischer Übermittlung ist die Übermittlungszeit so kurz, dass die Entfernung zum Bestimmungsort bedeutungslos wird. Daher kann hier die Beschränkung der Vermutungsregelung auf das Inland wegfallen. Da eine elektronische Übermittlung in der Regel unmittelbar erfolgt, kann bei ihr der Zugang spätestens am Tage nach der Übermittlung vermutet werden. Um Unterschiede bei der Übermittlung zu unterschiedlichen Tageszeiten auszugleichen, wird der Zugang erst am Tag nach der Übermittlung vermutet.

Zu Buchstabe b):
Die Änderung stellt klar, dass die Regelung über die öffentliche Bekanntgabe eines Verwaltungsaktes auch für elektronische Verwaltungsakte gilt.

Zu Nummer 13 (§ 42).

Es handelt sich um eine redaktionelle Folgeänderung zu Nummer 9 Buchstabe a.

Zu Nummer 14 (§ 44)

Es handelt sich um eine redaktionelle Folgeänderung zu Nummer 9 Buchstabe a.

Zu Nummer 15 (§ 66)

Die Änderung stellt klar, dass den Beteiligten auch ein der Behörde elektronisch vorliegendes Gutachten zugänglich gemacht wird.

Zu Nummer 16 (§ 69)

Dem beteiligten Bürger wird ermöglicht, den das förmliche Verwaltungsverfahren abschließenden Verwaltungsakt auch in einfacher elektronischer Form anzufordern.

Zu Nummer 17 (§ 71c)

Im Rahmen von Beratung und Auskunft bei Genehmigungsverfahren können jegliche elektronischen Kommunikationsmittel genutzt werden. Im Hinblick auf die rechtliche Bedeutung dieser Auskünfte ist hier die Verbindung des Textes mit einer qualifizierten elektronischen Signatur nicht notwendig.

Zu Artikel 2 – Änderung des Sozialgesetzbuchs I und X

Auch im Sozialverwaltungsverfahren sollen die sich abzeichnenden neuen Entwicklungen des elektronischen Geschäftsverkehrs genutzt werden können. Dabei sind vorrangig die Interessen aller Beteiligten, insbesondere der hilfesuchenden leistungsberechtigten Bürger, zu berücksichtigen. Es gilt daher nach wie vor, dass jeder Berechtigte die hm zustehenden Sozialleistungen in zeitgemäßer Weise, umfassend und zügig erhalten uss (§ 17 Abs. 1 SGB I). Die Verwaltung muss daher darauf Rücksicht nehmen, inwieweit der Bürger überhaupt in der Lage ist, die Möglichkeiten des modernen elektronischen Rechts- und Geschäftsverkehrs zu nutzen. Das Gleiche muss aber für die Verwaltungsseite gelten, die sich diesen Möglichkeiten nach dem Grundsatz der Wirtschaftlichkeit und Sparsamkeit stellen muss. Es kann daher derzeit nur um die Schaffung der rechtlichen Grundlagen für die Nutzung der Möglichkeiten des modernen elektronischen Rechts- und Geschäftsverkehrs gehen; eine Verpflichtung kann – jedenfalls derzeit – nicht normiert werden. Der Entwurf geht infolgedessen von einer gegenseitigen Einverständniserklärung beider Seiten hinsichtlich der Nutzung elektronischer Übermittlungsformen aus, wobei die Form dieser Einverständniserklärung offen bleiben kann. So kann die Angabe einer E-Mail-Adresse Hinweise hierfür geben; lehnt eine Seite jedoch ab, ist dies vom Betroffenen zu akzeptieren.

Schließlich muss berücksichtigt werden, dass in den einzelnen Sozialleistungsbereichen, für die das Sozialgesetzbuch gilt, unterschiedliche Anforderungen an die Sicherheit und Dauerhaftigkeit von für eine Leistungsgewährung oder Mitgliedschaft ausschlaggebenden Unterlagen zu stellen sind. Insbesondere im Leistungsbereich der lebenslange Leistungen erbringenden gesetzlichen Rentenversicherung ergibt sich die Notwendigkeit, anspruchsbegründende Unterlagen "lebenslang" sicher und gegen Veränderungen dauerhaft geschützt aufzubewahren. Selbst nach dem Tode des Leistungsempfängers können solche Unterlagen noch unentbehrlich sein, wenn Leistungen an Hinterbliebene erbracht werden. Insoweit muss Sicherheit und Dauerhaftigkeit über mehrere Jahrzehnte hinweg gewährleistet werden. Deshalb ist in diesem Bereich auch die Möglichkeit der Aufbewahrung von Unterlagen in elektronischer Form gesetzlich (im Vierten Buch Sozialgesetzbuch, vergleiche Artikel BMA § 1) zu regeln.

Um im Sozialleistungsbereich möglichst alle Verwaltungszuständigkeiten und Tätigkeiten zu erfassen, für die das Sozialgesetzbuch gilt, soll eine Grundsatznorm, die die elektronische Übermittlung grundsätzlich der Schriftform gleichgestellt, ins Erste Buch Sozialgesetzbuch – Allgemeiner Teil aufgenommen werden. Auf diese Weise werden auch weitere schriftliche Erklärungen des Einzelnen gegenüber der Verwaltung erfasst.

Der Datenschutz muss auch im Rahmen elektronischer Verfahren gewahrt bleiben (§ 35 SGB I). Insoweit muss die Behörde die notwendigen Sicherheitsvorkehrungen treffen (vgl. auch § 78a SGB X), z.B. auch durch Verschlüsselung der Texte.

Zu § 1 – Änderung des SGB I

Zu Nummer 1 (Inhaltsübersicht)

Folgeänderung zur Einfügung des § 36a SGB I.

Zu Nummer 2 (§ 36a)

Die Vorschrift stellt wie im Verwaltungsverfahrensrecht des Bundes (vgl. zu Artikel 1 Nr. 3) die elektronische Form der Datenübermittlung der schriftlichen Form unter bestimmten Voraussetzungen gleich; vergleiche im Einzelnen Begründung zu Artikel 1 Nr. 3 und Vorbemerkungen zu Artikel 2.

Absatz 4 lässt es zu, dass die Spitzenverbände der Träger der Sozialversicherung selbst für den jeweiligen Sozialleistungsbereich einen Zertifizierungsdienst i. S. des Signaturgesetzes betreiben, sofern sie der Aufsicht einer obersten Bundesbehörde unterstehen und auf Dauer die Ausübung dieser Tätigkeit sichergestellt ist. Die Regelung soll ein möglichst einfaches Verwaltungshandeln eröffnen.

Zu § 2 – Änderung des SGB X

Zu Nummer 1 (Inhaltsübersicht)

Folgeänderung zur Einfügung der §§ 30a und 33a SGB X

Zu Nummer 2 (§ 13)

Vgl. Begründung zur inhaltsgleichen Änderung in Artikel 1 Nr. 4 (§ 14 VwVfG).

Zu Nummer 3 (§ 14)

Die Neufassung des § 14 regelt den Zugang des Dokuments bei elektronischer Übermittlung; die Regelung erfasst auch das Telefax (vgl. auch Artikel 1 Nr. 5).

Zu Nummer 4 (§ 19)

Vgl. Begründung zur inhaltsgleichen Änderung in Artikel 1 Nr. 6 (§ 23 VwVfG).

Zu Nummer 5 (§ 21)

Vgl. Begründung zur inhaltsgleichen Änderung in Artikel 1 Nr. 7 (§ 26 VwVfG).

Zu Nummer 6 (§ 30a)

Vgl. Begründung zur inhaltsgleichen Änderung in Artikel 1 Nr. 8 (§ 34a VwVfG).

Zu Nummer 7 (§ 33)

Vgl. Begründung zur inhaltsgleichen Änderung in Artikel 1 Nr. 9 (§ 37 VwVfG).

Zu Nummer 8 (§ 33a)

Vgl. Begründung zu § 37a VwVfG (Artikel 1 Nr. 10). Die Ermächtigungsnorm richtet sich in den festgelegten Sozialbereichen an das Bundesministerium für Arbeit und Sozialordnung.

Zu Nummer 9 (§ 35)

Die Änderung in Absatz 1 stellt sicher, dass die Verwaltungsbehörde einen elektronischen Verwaltungsakt auch in elektronischer Form begründen kann, eine Begründung in mündlicher Form ist ausgeschlossen. In den Fällen des Absatzes 2 Nr. 2 soll – wie bisher – die Begründung eines Verwaltungsaktes nur entbehrlich sein, wenn die Auffassung der Behörde auch ohne Begründung ohne weiteres erkennbar ist. Absatz 3 stellt die elektronische der schriftlichen Begründung gleich.

Zu Nummer 10 (§ 37)

Vgl. Begründung zur inhaltsgleichen Änderung in Artikel 1 Nr. 12 (§ 41 VwVfG).

Zu Nummer 11 (§ 38)

Vgl. Begründung zur inhaltsgleichen Änderung in Artikel 1 Nr. 13 (§ 42 VwVfG).

Zu Nummer 12 (§ 40)

Vgl. Begründung zur inhaltsgleichen Änderung in Artikel 1 Nr. 14 (§ 44 VwVfG).

Zu Artikel 3 – Änderung des Abgabenordnung

Allgemeines

Artikel 3 passt die Vorschriften der Abgabenordnung an die Entwicklung der Kommunikationstechnik an und schafft für die Finanzverwaltung die rechtlichen Rahmenbedingungen für eine "elektronische Akte". Soweit die Steuergesetze die Schriftform vorschreiben, sieht § 87a AO als Option hierzu die elektronische Form mit einer qualifizierten elektronischen Signatur vor. Dies gilt sowohl für Anträge, Erklärungen und Mitteilungen der Steuerpflichtigen als auch für Maßnahmen (insbesondere Verwaltungsakte) der Finanzbehörden.

In bestimmten Fällen ist es aber auch künftig erforderlich, ausschließlich an der Schriftform festzuhalten. In der jeweils einschlägigen Vorschrift wird dann die Möglichkeit der elektronischen Form ausdrücklich ausgeschlossen (vgl. die Nummern 14 bis 17 – Änderung der §§ 224a, 244, 309, 324 AO – sowie die Artikel ...). Soweit Anträge, Anzeigen usw. "auf" (nicht "nach") amtlich vorgeschriebenem Vordruck zu stellen bzw. Zu erstatten sind (siehe z.B. § 46 Abs. 3 AO, § 138 Abs. 1 AO, § 50d Abs. 2 EStG), ergibt sich bereits aus dieser Gesetzesformulierung der Ausschluss der elektronischen Übermittlungsform. Zur elektronischen Übermittlung von Steuererklärungen, die in der Regel "nach" amtlich vorgeschriebenem Vordruck abzugeben sind, vgl. die vorgesehene klarstellende Regelung in § 150 Abs. 1 AO.

Zu Nummer 1 (§ 80 Abs. 6 Satz 1)

Die Streichung des Wortes "schriftlichen" in Satz 1 soll bewirken, dass zum Sachvortrag ungeeignete Bevollmächtigte und Beistände auch dann zurückgewiesen werden können, wenn sie für ihren Vortrag nicht die Schriftform, sondern die elektronische Form wählen. Ferner wird klargestellt, dass (vorbehaltlich der weiteren Zurückweisungsgründe nach den Absätzen 5 und 7) der zweite Halbsatz abschließend regelt, unter welchen Voraussetzungen eine Zurückweisung vom mündlichen Vortrag zulässig ist.

Zu Nummer 2 (§ 87 Abs. 2 Satz 1)

Die Ersetzung des Wortes "Schriftstücke" durch "Dokumente" in Satz 1 soll bewirken, dass eine Übersetzung auch dann verlangt werden kann, wenn fremdsprachige Unterlagen nicht schriftlich, sondern elektronisch übermittelt werden.

Zu Nummer 3 (§ 87a)

Zu § 87a Abs. 1:
Satz 1 übernimmt die in § 3a Abs. 1 VwVfG vorgesehene Regelung und trägt der Tatsache Rechnung, dass im Zeitpunkt des Inkrafttretens dieses Gesetzes weder auf Seiten der Steuerpflichtigen noch in der Finanzverwaltung die technischen Möglichkeiten für eine umfassende elektronische Kommunikation gegeben sein dürften. Die Voraussetzung, dass ein "Zugang hierfür eröffnet sein muss", bedeutet aber auch, dass der Steuerpflichtige gegenüber der Finanzverwaltung zu erkennen gegeben haben muss, dass er mit der elektronischen Kommunikation einverstanden ist. Dies gilt insbe-

sondere für die Bekanntgabe belastender Verwaltungsakte. Sollte der Gesetzgeber in einzelnen Steuergesetzen von § 87a AO abweichende Regelungen treffen (z.B. eine Verpflichtung der Finanzbehörden, elektronische Anträge oder Erklärungen entgegenzunehmen), wären diese vorrangig gegenüber § 87a AO.

Satz 2 bestimmt im Wesentlichen analog § 130a Abs. 3 ZPO, wann ein elektronisches Dokument zugegangen ist und somit an den Zugang des Dokuments geknüpfte Rechtsfolgen (z.B. Wahrung einer Antrags- oder Einspruchsfrist) eintreten. Maßgebend ist danach, wann die Empfangseinrichtung das elektronisch übermittelte Dokument in für den Empfänger bearbeitbarer Weise aufgezeichnet hat. Ob und wann der Empfänger das Dokument an seinem Bildschirm aufruft oder sich ausdrucken lässt, ist insoweit unmaßgeblich. Zur (widerlegbaren) Fiktion des Bekanntgabezeitpunktes bei elektronisch übermittelten Verwaltungsakten siehe die vorgesehenen Ergänzungen der §§ 122 und 123 AO.

Satz 3 ordnet eine Verschlüsselung an, wenn die Finanzbehörde auf elektronischem Weg Daten übermittelt, die dem Steuergeheimnis (§ 30 AO) unterliegen.

Zu § 87a Abs. 2:
Analog der in § 3a Abs. 3 VwVfG vorgesehenen Regelung wird bestimmt, wie zu verfahren ist, wenn ein elektronisch übermitteltes Dokument vom Empfänger nicht bearbeitbar ist.

Zu § 87a Abs. 3 bis 5:
Soweit durch Gesetz (weiterhin) die Schriftform vorgeschrieben ist, ermöglichen die Regelungen der Absätze 3 und 4 grundsätzlich eine Übermittlung in elektronischer Form, wenn das Dokument mit einer "qualifizierten elektronischen Signatur" versehen ist. Nach der Definition in § 2 Nr. 3 Signaturgesetz muss es sich somit um eine elektronische Signatur handeln, die

- ausschließlich dem Signaturschlüssel-Inhaber zugeordnet ist,
- die Identifizierung des Signaturschlüssel-Inhabers ermöglicht,
- mit Mitteln erzeugt wurde, die der Signaturschlüssel-Inhaber

unter seiner alleinigen Kontrolle halten kann, und

- mit den Daten, auf die sich bezieht, so verknüpft ist, dass eine nachträgliche Veränderung der Daten erkannt werden kann.

Sie muss zudem auf einem zum Zeitpunkt ihrer Erzeugung gültigen qualifizierten Zertifikat eines Zertifizierungsdiensteanbieters beruhen und mit einer sicheren Signaturerstellungseinheit erzeugt worden sein.

Von der durch § 1 Abs. 3 Signaturgesetz eingeräumten Möglichkeit, den Einsatz qualifizierter elektronischer Signaturen zusätzlichen Anforderungen zu unterwerfen und z.B. das Zertifikat eines freiwillig akkreditierten Zertifizierungsdiensteanbieters (§ 15 Signaturgesetz) zu verlangen, wird kein Gebrauch gemacht. Unter den Voraussetzungen des § 23 Signaturgesetz sind auch ausländische Signaturen anzuerkennen.

Absatz 3 enthält die Regelungen für an die Finanzbehörden zu richtende Anträge, Erklärungen und Mitteilungen, Absatz 4 die "spiegelbildlichen" Regelungen für die Maßnahmen der Finanzbehörden. Absatz 4 Satz 3 bestimmt, dass es für von der Finanzbehörde aufzunehmende Niederschriften (z.B. nach den §§ 95 Abs. 2 Satz 1, 215 Abs. 2, 284 Abs. 3, 291, 315 Abs. 3 AO) grundsätzlich bei der Schriftform verbleibt. Ferner schließt Absatz 3 Satz 3 die – nach dem Signaturgesetz zulässige – Signierung mit einem Pseudonym aus. Im Zeitpunkt des Eingangs von Anträgen oder Erklärungen der Steuerpflichtigen, die Rechtsfolgen auslösen sollen oder können, muss für die Finanzbehörde erkennbar feststehen, wer der Absender ist. Zwar muss aus dem Antrag, der Erklärung oder der Mitteilung der Absender hervorgehen (Absatz 3 Satz 2); dies reicht aber für eine ordnungsgemäße Abwicklung des Besteuerungsverfahrens nicht aus. Soweit nämlich (nach Schaffung der entsprechenden Rechtsgrundlagen in einem Gesetz oder in einer nach § 150 Abs. 6 AO erlassenen Rechtsverordnung) Steuererklärungen ausschließlich in elektronischer Form abgegeben werden können, wird die qualifizierte elektronische Signatur die in einer Vielzahl von Vorschriften (z.B. § 25 Abs. 3 Sätze 4 und 5 EStG, § 18 Abs. 3 Satz

3 UStG, § 14a Satz 3 GewStG) angeordnete eigenhändige Unterschrift ersetzen. Um feststellen zu können, ob eine wirksame Steuererklärung vorliegt und diese auch dem Steuerpflichtigen zurechenbar ist, muss somit bereits im Zeitpunkt des Eingang der Steuererklärung automationsgestützt geprüft werden, ob der Name des Steuerpflichtigen mit dem Namen des im Zertifikat angegebenen SignaturschlüsselIn-habers identisch ist. Im Fall der Signierung mit einem Pseudonym wäre eine derartige Übereinstimmung nicht gegeben. Zwar könnte diese durch eine Anfrage bei der Zertifizierungsstelle (§ 14 Abs. 2 Signaturgesetz) festgestellt werden; derartige Anfragen würden aber das Verfahren zur Bearbeitung der elektronischen Steuererklärungen erheblich beeinträchtigen und zudem Kosten verursachen.

Absatz 5 übernimmt die Regelungen des § 292a ZPO und des § 371 Satz 2 ZPO.

Zu § 87a Abs. 6:
Die bei einer "qualifizierten elektronischen Signatur" erforderliche kostenpflichtige Einschaltung einer Zertifizierungsstelle sowie die unzureichende Verbreitung und Nutzung der dafür erforderlichen sicheren Signaturerstellungseinheit (Kartenleser) dürften zumindest in der nahen Zukunft den angestrebten zügigen Aufbau der elektronischen Kommunikation zwischen den Steuerpflichtigen und der Finanzverwaltung noch erheblich behindern. Insbesondere würde die Weiterentwicklung des Projekts "ELSTER" (Verzicht auf Steuererklärungen in "Papierform") gefährdet.

Es wird daher für eine bis zum 31. Dezember 2006 dauernde Übergangszeit vorgesehen, dass für Anträge, Erklärungen oder Mitteilungen an die Finanzbehörden von den durch das Signaturgesetz vorgegebenen Anforderungen an eine "qualifizierte elektronische Signatur" nach Maßgabe einer nach § 150 Abs. 6 AO zu erlassenden Rechtsverordnung abgewichen werden darf.

Zu Nummer 4 (§ 93)

Zu Buchstabe a):
Absatz 4 Satz 1 wird um die Möglichkeit der elektronischen Auskunftserteilung ergänzt. Im Ergebnis ist somit weiterhin für die Erteilung einer Auskunft grundsätzlich keine bestimmte Form vorgeschrieben.

Zu Buchstabe b):
In Absatz 5 Satz 2 werden die Voraussetzungen für die Anordnung, eine mündliche Auskunft an Amtsstelle zu erteilen, neu festgelegt. Die erste Alternative (Nichterteilung einer schriftlichen Auskunft) wird dahingehend erweitert, dass auch keine Auskunft in elektronischer Form mit qualifizierter elektronischer Signatur vorliegt; die zweite Alternative (keine Klärung des Sachverhaltes) wird um den Fall einer in elektronischer Form mit qualifizierter elektronischer Signatur erteilten Auskunft erweitert.

Zu Nummer 5 (§ 119)

Absatz 1 wird unverändert aus dem bisherigen Recht übernommen.

Absatz 2 und Absatz 3 Satz 1 werden um die Fälle der elektronischen Form ergänzt. Der Verwaltungsakt muss die erlassende Behörde auch dann erkennen lassen, wenn er in "einfacher" elektronischer Form ohne qualifizierte elektronische Signatur erlassen wird. Soweit die Gesetze für Verwaltungsakte die Schriftform vorschreiben und somit den in Absatz 2 Satz 1 aufgestellten Grundsatz der Formfreiheit einschränken (siehe z.B. § 157 Abs. 1 Satz 1 AO), kann unter den Voraussetzungen des § 87a AO der Verwaltungsakt grundsätzlich auch elektronisch mit einer qualifizierten elektronischen Signatur übermittelt werden.

Absatz 3 Satz 2 übernimmt die bisher im ersten Satz des Absatzes 4 enthaltene Regelung. Auf die bisherige Vorschrift des zweiten Satzes des Absatzes 4, nach der bei formularmäßig oder mit Hilfe automatischer Einrichtungen erlassenen Verwaltungsakten zur

Inhaltsangabe ggfs. Schlüsselzeichen verwendet werden können, wird im Interesse der Bürgerfreundlichkeit verzichtet. Zudem wurde diese Regelung nur zur Anpassung an das Verwaltungsverfahrensgesetz in die Abgabenordnung aufgenommen und hat in der Finanzverwaltung keine praktische Bedeutung erlangt.

Zu Nummer 6 (§ 121)

Zu Buchstabe a):
Absatz 1 wird um die elektronische Form ergänzt. Die Begründungspflicht gilt sowohl für Verwaltungsakte, die in "einfacher" elektronischer Form erlassen werden, als auch für Verwaltungsakte, die mit einer qualifizierten elektronischen Signatur (§ 87a Abs. 4 AO) versehen sind.

Zu Buchstabe b):
In Absatz 2 Nr. 2 wird das dort überflüssige Wort "schriftliche" gestrichen.

Zu Nummer 7 (§ 122)

Zu Buchstabe a):
Der neue Absatz 2a regelt (nach dem Grundgedanken des Absatzes 2), wann ein elektronisch übermittelter Verwaltungsakt als bekannt gegeben gilt. Die Vorschrift gilt sowohl für eine Übermittlung mit qualifizierter elektronischer Signatur (§ 87a Abs. 4 AO) als auch für Fälle einer "einfachen" elektronischen Übermittlung. Für die Widerlegung der Vermutung zum Zeitpunkt des Zugangs ist § 87a Abs. 1 Satz 2 AO von Bedeutung.

Zu Buchstaben b) und c):
Die Hinweise in Absatz 4 Satz 1 und in Absatz 5 Satz 1 auf einen "schriftliche", Verwaltungsakt sind an diesen Stellen entbehrlich und werden daher zur Rechtsbereinigung gestrichen.

Zu Nummer 8 (§ 123 Satz 2)

Analog § 122 Abs. 2a AO wird geregelt, wann ein elektronisch übermittelter Verwaltungsakt als bekannt gegeben gilt.

Zu Nummer 9 (§ 125 Abs. 2 Nr. 1)

Die fehlende Erkennbarkeit der Finanzbehörde soll künftig auch dann zur Nichtigkeit des Verwaltungsaktes führen, wenn der Verwaltungsakt in elektronischer Form (mit oder ohne qualifizierter elektronischer Signatur) erlassen wurde.

Zu Nummer 10 (§ 129 Satz 3)

Die Neufassung des Satzes 3 soll klarstellen, dass die Finanzbehörde die Vorlage des zu berichtigenden Schriftstücks nur dann verlangen kann, wenn der zu berichtigende Verwaltungsakt schriftlich erlassen wurde, und somit nicht, wenn die Finanzbehörde zulässigerweise den Verwaltungsakt auf elektronischem Wege bekannt gegeben hat und der Empfänger diesen Verwaltungsakt sich hat ausdrucken lassen.

Zu Nummer 11 (§ 150)

Zu Buchstabe a):
Nach § 150 Abs. 1 Satz 1 AO sind Steuererklärungen nach amtlich vorgeschriebenem Vordruck abzugeben, soweit nicht eine mündliche Steuererklärung zugelassen ist. Aufgrund der Fortschritte in der Computertechnik kann dem Erfordernis, Erklärungen "nach" (nicht "auf") amtlich vorgeschriebenem Vordruck abzugeben, möglicherweise auch durch eine elektronische Übermittlung entsprochen werden, wenn das der Finanzbehörde übermittelte Dokument in seinem Aufbau und Inhalt vollständig dem amtlich vorgeschriebenem Vordruck entspricht. Durch die Ergänzung des Absatzes 1 soll daher klargestellt werden, dass § 87a AO nur anwendbar und eine elektronische Übermittlung von Steuererklärungen nur zulässig ist, soweit ein Gesetz oder eine nach § 150 Abs. 6 AO erlassene Rechtsverordnung dies erlaubt.

Zu Buchstabe b):
Die Ergänzung soll eine Ermächtigungsgrundlage dafür schaffen, in einer Rechtsverordnung nach § 150 Abs. 6 AO eine Haftungsregelung auch für den Fall vorzusehen, dass ein Hersteller eines Programms für die Übermittlung steuerlich relevanter Daten von den Vorgaben der Gesetze abweicht und dadurch solche Daten nicht erhoben werden.

Zu Nummer 12 (§ 202 Abs. 1 Satz 2)

Bei der elektronischen Übersendung eines Außenprüfungsberichts soll keine Verpflichtung bestehen, den Bericht mit einer elektronischen Signatur zu versehen.

Zu Nummer 13 (§ 203 Abs. 2 Satz 3

Analog zur Regelung zum Außenprüfungsbericht (§ 202 AO) soll auch bei einer elektronischen Übermittlung der steuerlich erheblichen Feststellungen einer abgekürzten Außenprüfung auf eine elektronische Signatur verzichtet werden können.

Zu Nummer 14 (§ 224a Abs. 2 Satz 1)

Wegen des Ausnahmecharakters der Regelung und im Hinblick auf die erforderliche Einschaltung der obersten Landesfinanzbehörde und der für kulturelle Angelegenheiten zuständigen obersten Landesbehörde wird für den öffentlich-rechtlichen Vertrag über die Hingabe von Kunstgegenständen an Zahlungs Statt darin festgehalten, dass er nur schriftlich abgeschlossen werden kann.

Zu Nummer 15 (§ 244 Abs. 1 Satz 3)

Um den Schuldner vor übereilten Erklärungen zu schützen, wird analog §§ 766, 780 BGB für Schuldversprechen und Bürgschaftserklärungen daran festgehalten, dass sie ausschließlich schriftlich abgegeben werden können.

Zu Nummer 16 (§ 309 Abs. 1)

Insbesondere wegen der Bedeutung für die Rangfolge einer ausgebrachten Pfändung wird für Pfändungen von Geldforderungen daran festgehalten, dass sie nur schriftlich ergehen dürfen und förmlich zuzustellen sind. Zwar ergibt sich bereits aus dem Gebot der förmlichen Zustellung, dass die Schriftform nicht durch eine elektronische Übermittlung mit qualifizierter elektronischer Signatur (§ 87a Abs. 4 AO) ersetzt werden kann (vgl. § 2 Abs. 1 Satz 1 VwZG); im Hinblick auf Überlegungen, im Verwaltungszustellungsgesetz auch elektronische Übermittlungsformen zuzulassen, erscheint es aber zweckmäßig, bereits jetzt für Pfändungsverfügungen die elektronische Übermittlung ausdrücklich auszuschließen.

Zu Nummer 17 (§ 324 Abs. 2)

Wegen der einschneidenden Wirkungen einer Arrestanordnung und der Bedeutung des Zeitpunkts der Unterschrift für die Zulässigkeit ihrer Vollziehung (Absatz 3 Satz 1) wird die elektronische Übermittlung einer Arrestanordnung nicht zugelassen; siehe auch die Begründung zu Nummer 16.

Zu Nummer 18 (§ 356)

Im Interesse der Rechtssicherheit sollen künftig die Rechtsfolgen einer unterlassenen oder fehlerhaften Rechtsbehelfsbelehrung nicht nur bei schriftlich ergehenden Verwaltungsakten eintreten, sondern auch bei Verwaltungsakten, die in elektronischer Form mit oder ohne qualifizierter elektronischer Signatur erlassen werden. Hieran anknüpfend wird für die Rechtsbehelfsbelehrung die Form vorgeschrieben, in der der Verwaltungsakt ergeht. Für mündlich oder durch schlüssige Handlung bekannt gegebene Verwaltungsakte verbleibt es dabei, dass eine unterlassene oder fehlerhafte Rechtsbehelfsbelehrung keinen Einfluss auf den Lauf der Einspruchsfrist hat.

Zu Nummer 19 (§ 366)

In Anlehnung an § 157 Abs. 1 Satz 1 AO werden die Wörter "schriftlich abzufassen" durch die Wörter "schriftlich zu erteilen" ersetzt, um klarzustellen, dass bei Einspruchsentscheidungen das Schriftformerfordernis sich nicht auf das bei der Finanzbehörde verbleibende "Aktenexemplar" bezieht. Im Übrigen kann die Schriftform durch die elektronische Übermittlung mit qualifizierter elektronischer Signatur ersetzt werden (§ 87a Abs. 4 AO). Satz 2 des bisherigen § 366 AO wird nicht übernommen, da die Einspruchsentscheidung einen Verwaltungsakt darstellt und somit § 122 AO bereits unmittelbar anwendbar ist.

Zu Artikel Bundespräsidialamt

Zu Artikel Deutscher Bundestag

Zu Artikel Bundesrat

Zu Artikel Bundeskanzleramt

Zu Artikel AA

Zu Artikel BMI

Zu § X – Weitere Änderung des Verwaltungsverfahrensgesetzes

Zu Nummer 1 (§ 15)

Redaktionelle Anpassung.

Zu Nummer 2 (§ 45 Abs. 2)

Die derzeitige Fassung des § 45 Abs. 2 VwVfG berücksichtigt nicht hinreichend die Strukturen des Verwaltungsprozesses, wenn sie entgegen § 137 Abs. 2 VwGO die Berücksichtigung nachgeholter Verfahrenshandlungen – und damit tatsächlicher Entwicklungen – noch im Revisionsverfahren anordnet.

Zu Nummer 3 (§ 49a Abs. 3)

Mit der Regelung wird der Zinssatz für Erstattungen nach § 49a VwVfG an die Regelungen des Diskontsatz-Überleitungs-Gesetzes vom 9. Juni 1998 (BGBl. I S. 1242) angepasst.

Zu Nummer 4 (§ 61 Abs. 1)

Das bisherige Genehmigungserfordernis ist im Zuge der Verwaltungsvereinfachungs und Deregulierungsbemühungen von Bund und Ländern als nicht mehr notwendig aufzuheben. Die Bundesregierung setzt damit einen der 183 Vorschläge der Ministerpräsidentenkonferenz zur staatlichen Aufgabenwahrnehmung um.

Zu Artikel BMJ

Zu Artikel BMF

Zu § 1 – Änderung des Grunderwerbsteuergesetzes

Zu Nummer 1 (§ 18 Abs. 1)

Nach § 87a AO (vgl. Artikel ...) wird zukünftig eine vorgeschriebene Schriftform auch durch elektronische Übermittlung mit qualifizierter elektronischer Signatur ersetzt werden können. Um klarzustellen, dass die Anzeigepflicht der Gerichte, Behörden und Notare weder durch einfache elektronische Übermittlung noch durch Übermittlung mit qualifizierter elektronischer Signatur erfüllt werden kann, wird die Schriftlichkeit der Anzeigen vorgeschrieben sowie die Möglichkeit ausgeschlossen, Anzeigen auch elektronisch zu erstatten.

Zu Nummer 2 (§ 19 Abs. 5 Satz 2)

Nach § 87a AO (vgl. Artikel ...) wird zukünftig eine vorgeschriebene Schriftform auch durch elektronische Übermittlung mit qualifizierter elektronischer Signatur ersetzt werden können. Um klarzustellen, dass die Anzeigepflicht der Beteiligten zwar auch in elektronischer

Form, aber nicht durch "einfache" E-Mail erfüllt werden kann, wird die Notwendigkeit, Anzeigen schriftlich zu erstatten, ausdrücklich festgeschrieben (siehe auch Artikel ... Nr. 11 - § 150 Abs. 1 Satz 2 (neu) AO).

Zu Nummer 3 (§ 22 Abs. 2 Satz 3)

Nach § 87a AO (vgl. Artikel ...) wird zukünftig eine vorgeschriebene Schriftform auch durch elektronische Übermittlung mit qualifizierter elektronischer Signatur ersetzt werden können. Um klarzustellen, dass die Unbedenklichkeitsbescheinigung zwar auch in elektronischer Form, aber nicht durch "einfache" E-Mail erteilt werden kann, wird die Notwendigkeit, die Unbedenklichkeitsbescheinigung schriftlich zu erteilen, ausdrücklich festgeschrieben.

Zu § 2 – Änderung des Versicherungsteuergesetzes

Zu Nummer 1 (§ 8 Abs. 5 Satz 3)

Der Versicherungsnehmer soll zur Anmeldung der Steuer den gleichen Formvorschriften unterliegen wie der Versicherer (vgl. § 8 Abs. 1 VersStG).

Zu Nummer 2 (§ 10 Abs. 1 Satz 3)

Für das Verzeichnis der sich auf deutsche Risiken beziehenden Versicherungsverhältnisse soll die elektronische Übermittlung mit qualifizierter elektronischer Signatur ermöglicht werden (vgl. Artikel .. - § 87a AO -).

Zu § 3 – Änderung der Ausführungsbestimmungen zum Rennwett- und Lotteriegesetz

Zu Nummer 1 (§ 34)

Aufgrund der Änderung können Mitteilungen der Genehmigungsbehörde auch durch einfache elektronische Post erfolgen.

Zu Nummer 2 (§ 35)

Die elektronische Übermittlung der Anmeldung soll ausdrücklich ausgeschlossen werden, da der Anmeldung die eingeführten Lose beizufügen sind.

Zu Nummer 3 (§ 45 Abs. 3)

Aufgrund der Änderung kann der Erstattungsantrag auch elektronisch mit qualifizierter elektronischer Signatur erfolgen (vgl. Artikel .. - § 87a AO -).

Zu Nummer 4 (§ 46 Abs. 2 Satz 2)

Durch die Einfügung des Wortes "schriftlich" wird ermöglicht, die Anzeigen der Staatslotterien auch elektronisch mit qualifizierter elektronischer Signatur zu übermitteln (vgl. Artikel .. - § 87a AO -).

Zu § 4 – Änderung des Feuerschutzsteuergesetzes

Zu Nummer 1 (§ 8 Abs. 4 Satz 3)

Der Versicherungsnehmer soll zur Anmeldung der Steuer den gleichen Formvorschriften unterliegen wie der Versicherer (vgl. § 8 Abs. 1 FeuerschStG).

Zu Nummer 2 (§ 9 Abs. 1 Satz 3)

Für das Verzeichnis der sich auf deutsche Risiken beziehenden Versicherungsverhältnisse soll die elektronische Übermittlung mit qualifizierter elektronischer Signatur ermöglicht werden (vgl. Artikel .. - § 87a AO -).

Zu § 5 – Änderung des Kraftfahrzeugsteuergesetzes

Nach § 87a AO (vgl. Artikel ...) wird zukünftig eine vorgeschriebene Schriftform auch durch elektronische Übermittlung mit qualifizierter elektronischer Signatur ersetzt werden können. Es wird klargestellt, dass die Erklärungen, Anträge und Anzeigen zwar auch in elektronischer Form, aber nicht durch einfache elektronische Post möglich sind.

Zu § 6 – Änderung der Kraftfahrzeugsteuer-Durchführungsverordnung

Zu Nummern 1 bis 3 (§ 3 Abs. 2, § 4 Abs. 1, § 7 Abs. 1)

Nach § 87a AO (vgl. Artikel ...) wird zukünftig eine vorgeschriebene Schriftform auch durch elektronische Übermittlung mit qualifizierter elektronischer Signatur ersetzt werden können. Es wird klargestellt, dass die Erklärungen, Anträge und Anzeigen zwar auch in elektronischer Form, aber nicht durch einfache elektronische Post möglich sind.

Zu Nummern 4 und 5 (§ 11, § 14)

Nach § 87a AO (vgl. Artikel ...) wird zukünftig eine vorgeschriebene Schriftform auch durch elektronische Übermittlung mit qualifizierter elektronischer Signatur ersetzt werden können. Für Erklärungen und Anträge nach den §§ 11, 14 soll die elektronische Übermittlung jedoch ausgeschlossen werden.

Zu § 7 – Änderung der Stromsteuer-Durchführungsverordnung

Zu Nummer 1 (§ 3)

Versorger im Sinne des § 2 Nr. 1 des Stromsteuergesetzes können an andere Versorger steuerfrei Strom leisten. Der von der Zollverwaltung ausgestellte Erlaubnisschein stellt für den leistenden Versorger Rechtssicherheit darüber her, dass er Strom an einen Versorger leistet und im Rahmen dieser Leistung keine Stromsteuer entsteht, für die er selbst Steuerschuldner wird. Für die Erlaubnis soll daher ausschließlich die Schriftform vorbehalten bleiben.

Zu Nummer 2 (§ 9 Abs. 1)

Die Erteilung einer Erlaubnis zur steuerbegünstigten Entnahme von Strom gemäß § 9 Abs. 4 des Stromsteuergesetzes hat konstitutive Wirkung für die Anwendung des ermäßigten Stromsteuersatzes. Versorger, die Strom an Letztverbraucher leisten, benötigen Rechtssicherheit darüber, welcher Steuersatz für den von ihnen geleisteten Strom anzuwenden ist. Diese Rechtssicherheit kann nur dadurch hergestellt werden, dass dem Inhaber einer Erlaubnis zur steuerbegünstigten Entnahme von Strom von der Zollverwaltung ein schriftlicher Erlaubnisschein zur Vorlage beim Versorger ausgestellt wird.

Zu § 8 – Änderung der Mineralölsteuer-Durchführungsverordnung

Die §§ 6, 9, 12a, 13 und 19 der Mineralölsteuer-Durchführungsverordnung regeln den Bezug von Mineralöl unter Steueraussetzung oder Steuerbegünstigung. Die hierzu ausgestellten Erlaubnisscheine sind wie diejenigen im Stromsteuerrecht (siehe Artikel ...) die Nachweise der Bezugsberechtigung. Der abgebende Betrieb (Herstellungsbetrieb, Lager oder Verwalter) wird im Falle einer Abgabe von unversteuertem oder steuerbegünstigtem Mineralöl an einen Nichtberechtigten selbst Steuerschuldner. Somit wird durch die Vorlage des Erlaubnisscheins beim abgebenden Betrieb Rechtssicherheit hergestellt. Für alle diese Erlaubnisscheine soll auch künftig die Schriftform zur Gewährleistung der Rechtssicherheit vorbehalten bleiben. Dieser Vorbehalt wird durch die vorgeschlagenen Ergänzungen des § 6 Abs. 1 und des § 19 Abs. 1 erreicht. Aufgrund entsprechender Verweisungen auf § 6 gilt dieser Vorbehalt auch in den Fällen der §§ 9, 12a und 13.

Zu Artikel BMWi

Zu Artikel BMVEL

Zu Artikel BMA

Zu Artikel BMA

Zu § 1 – Änderung des SGB IV

Mit der Neuregelung in den §§ 110a – 110d SGB IV soll die Verwaltungstätigkeit der vom ierten Buch Sozialgesetzbuch erfassten Träger öffentlicher Verwaltung – also der Sozialversicherung einschließlich der Bundesanstalt für Arbeit – insoweit entlastet werden, als in diesem Bereich insbesondere die Möglichkeiten der elektronischen Datenverarbeitung auch für die Aufbewahrung von Unterlagen eröffnet werden sollen. Es geht nicht um eine Verpflichtung der Sozialleistungsträger, sondern – wie bereits für die Wirtschaft im Handelsgesetzbuch oder in der Abgabenordnung normiert – um die Eröffnung eines neuen Weges der Aktenaufbewahrung. Außerdem soll der Bundesregierung die Ermächtigung erteilt werden, die Dauer der Aufbewahrung von Unterlagen unter Berücksichtigung gesetzlich vorgegebener Maßstäbe zu regeln. Auch hier soll aber den Trägern der Vorrang eingeräumt werden, die notwendigen Regelungen im Vereinbarungswege gemeinsam zu treffen.

Außerdem soll in § 28f Abs. 4 SGB IV eine Vereinfachung im Gesamtsozialversicherungsbeitragseinzugsverfahren für Arbeitgeber geschaffen werden.

In § 93 SGB IV wird eine Regelung aufgenommen, die die Aufnahme von Rentenanträgen eines Versicherten durch die Versicherungsämter und Gemeindebehörden im automatisierten Verfahren ermöglichen soll.

Zu Nummer 2 (§ 28f Abs. 4 Satz 2)

Auch für den Bereich der landwirtschaftlichen Krankenkassen hat sich in der Praxis die Notwendigkeit gezeigt, Beitragsnachweise über den Bundesverband der landwirtschaftlichen Krankenkassen an die zuständige Einzugsstelle einzureichen. Dem soll durch Ergänzung des § 28f Abs. 4 Satz 2 SGB IV entsprochen werden.

Zu Nummer 4 (§ 110a ff.)

Zu § 110a Abs. 1:
In Absatz 1 soll die Verpflichtung der Träger öffentlicher Verwaltung zur Aufbewahrung von Unterlagen für ihre öffentlich-rechtliche Verwaltungstätigkeit normiert werden. Unterlagen z. B. für das (interne) Rechnungswesen werden nicht erfasst; eine Regelungskompetenz des Bundes ist insoweit in § 78 SGB IV enthalten. Nur Unterlagen, die für die eigene öffentlich-rechtliche Verwaltungstätigkeit erforderlich sind, sind aufzubewahren.

Zu § 110a Abs. 2:
In Absatz 2 soll der Verwaltung die Möglichkeit eröffnet werden, die modernen Alternativen einer Aktenaufbewahrung zu nutzen und damit die Originalakten zu vernichten oder der Archivierung zuzuführen; es wird keine Verpflichtung geschaffen. Insbesondere durch die Nutzung der Möglichkeiten elektronischer Datenverarbeitung für Zwecke der Aufbewahrung ist eine erhebliche Verwaltungskostenersparnis zu erwarten. Die Regelung erfasst sowohl die Aufbewahrung von Unterlagen auf Papier (Sätze 1 und 2) als auch die von lediglich auf elektronischer Basis erstellten Unterlagen (Satz 3).

Absatz 2 Satz 1 lässt die Aufbewahrung von schriftlichen Unterlagen (auf "Papier") auf einem Bildträger oder auf einem anderen dauerhaften Datenträger zu. Bildträger sind hierbei Mikrofilme oder Mikrofiches. Dauerhafte Datenträger sind Speichermedien, deren Inhalt wegen der besonderen Art der Speicherung nicht oder nur mit unverhältnismäßig hohem Aufwand geändert oder gelöscht werden kann. Die Aufbewahrung ist unter Beachtung der Grundsätze der Wirtschaftlichkeit und Sparsamkeit vorzunehmen; dies dürfte insbesondere für kleine Verwaltungsträger von Bedeutung sein. Im Übrigen sind bei der Aufbewahrung von Unterlagen die Grundsätze ordnungsmäßiger Aufbewahrung zu beachten. Die wichtigsten Grundsätze sind in Absatz 2 Satz 2 aufgeführt. Ergänzend sind die Leistungsträger zu einer Sachregelung aufgerufen. Darüber hinaus kann gemäß § 110c SGB IV in einer Rechtsverordnung der Bundesregierung Weitergehendes festgelegt werden; dabei ist davon auszugehen, dass den Leistungsträgern auf Grund ihrer größeren Sachnähe in weitem Umfang der Vorrang zukommt.

Die Grundsätze ordnungsmäßiger Aufbewahrung orientieren sich an der Bedeutung der zur Aufbewahrung bestimmten Unterlagen für die öffentlich-rechtliche Verwaltungstätig keit der Behörde, z.B. für die Bewilligung einer Sozialleistung. Sie müssen berücksichtigen, dass es Zweck der im Vordergrund stehenden elektronischen Aufbewahrung ist, die Verwaltung insbesondere von der Papierflut der Unterlagen zu entlasten. Diese Entlastung ist aber nur zu erreichen, wenn die "Urschrift", insbesondere in Papierform, aus dem Bereich der Verwaltung entfernt werden darf. Dies setzt wiederum voraus, dass die Wiedergabe auf Bildträger oder auf einem anderen dauerhaften Datenträger bei späterem Abruf einen vollständigen "urschrift"-getreuen Ausdruck oder eine sonstige entsprechende Reproduktion garantiert. Wegen der grundsätzlichen Bedeutung insbesondere der inhaltlichen Gestaltung der "Urschrift" z.B. für eine spätere Leistungsbewilligung und der zugelassenen Vernichtung der "Urschrift" müssen die Grundsätze ordnungsmäßiger Aufbewahrung entsprechend ausgestaltet sein; ein späterer Abgleich von "Urschrift" und Reproduktion ist wegen des Fehlens der "Urschrift" ausgeschlossen.

Ist die Unterlage nur auf einem maschinell verwertbaren Datenträger erstellt worden, kann auf eine bildliche Übereinstimmung von zu Grunde gelegter Unterlage und Wiedergabe verzichtet werden, da eine der "Urschrift" auf Papier vergleichbare bildliche Gestaltung nie vorgelegen hat.

Zu § 110a Abs. 3:
Die Regelung des Absatzes 3 verpflichtet die Behörden, dem einzelnen die Möglichkeit an die Hand zu geben, Unterlagen auch bei deren elektronischer Speicherung bei der Behörde einsehen zu können. Will der einzelne eine Abschrift oder Ablichtung davon, richtet sich dies nach § 25 Abs. 5 SGB X. Danach kann die Behörde Aufwendungsersatz nur in angemessenem Umfang verlangen, d. h.

angemessen sind die Kosten bei elektronischer Speicherung z.B. nur insoweit, als sie die Kosten der Fertigung einer Ablichtung von Unterlagen aus Papier nicht übersteigen.

Zu § 110a Abs. 4:
Die Regelung des Absatzes 4 soll gewährleisten, dass – im Gegensatz zu den auf anderen Datenträgern aufbewahrten Unterlagen – bereits auf Mikrofilm oder Mikrofiche gespeicherte Unterlagen nicht erneut bearbeitet werden müssen.

Zu § 110b:
Die Vorschrift regelt die Rückgabe, Vernichtung und Archivierung von Unterlagen; sie trifft grundsätzlich keine Verpflichtungen, sondern ermächtigt die Leistungsträger lediglich zu bestimmten Handlungen. Aufbewahrungsfristen selbst werden im Gesetz nicht festgeschrieben; dies bleibt der größeren Sachnähe wegen vorrangig den Trägern nach § 110c Abs. 1 SGB IV überlassen. Solche Fristen können auch durch Rechtsverordnung festgelegt werden (§ 110c Abs. 2 SGB IV). Um dem Zweck der "papierlosen" Aufbewahrung Rechnung zu tragen, ist auch die Vernichtung von Unterlagen vorgesehen. Urschriften, die einem Träger der Rentenversicherung von Versicherten, Antragstellern oder von anderen Stellen zur Verfügung gestellt worden sind, sind diesem vor allem wegen der evtl. "lebenslangen" Bedeutung der Unterlagen für Leistungen in diesem Sozialleistungsbereich zurückzugeben. Werden die Unterlagen anderen Stellen (als Rentenversicherungsträgern) zur Verfügung gestellt, werden sie nur auf Anforderung zurückgegeben. Andere gesetzliche Vorschriften, die längere Aufbewahrungsfristen vorsehen, z.B. nach der Verordnung nach § 78 SGB IV, bleiben unberührt. Dies gilt auch für die Vorschriften über die Archivierung von Unterlagen. Ebenso bleiben die datenschutzrechtlichen Bestimmungen, insbesondere § 84 Abs. 2 Satz 2 SGB X, unberührt.

Zu § 110c:
Nach dieser Vorschrift vereinbaren die Spitzenverbände der Versicherungsträger einschließlich der Bundesanstalt für Arbeit gemeinsam die Ausgestaltung. Diese Vereinbarungen bedürfen der

Genehmigung der beteiligten Bundesministerien. Soweit Vereinbarungen nicht getroffen sind, wird die Bundesregierung zum Erlass einer Rechtsverordnung zur näheren Bestimmung der Grundsätze ordnungsmäßiger Aufbewahrung und der Rückgabe und Vernichtung von Unterlagen sowie der Aufbewahrungsfristen für bestimmte Unterlagen ermächtigt. Der Erlass einer Rechtsverordnung unmittelbar im Zusammenhang mit dem Inkrafttreten der gesetzlichen Neuregelung ist nicht ins Auge gefasst, da den Träger über eine entsprechende Vereinbarung der Vortritt gesetzlich eingeräumt ist.

Zu § 110d:
Die Vorschrift regelt die Beweiskraft einer nach den Grundsätzen ordnungsmäßiger Aufbewahrung unter Berücksichtigung besonderer Anforderungen auf anderen dauerhaften Datenträgern als Bildträgern aufbewahrten Unterlage; die aufbewahrte Unterlage soll im Anwendungsbereich des SGB IV grundsätzlich der öffentlich-rechtlichen Verwaltungstätigkeit zu Grunde gelegt werden, soweit nach den Umständen des Einzelfalles kein Anlass ist, ihre sachliche Richtigkeit zu beanstanden.

Zu § 2 – Änderung des SGB VI

Zu Nummer 4 (§ 148)

Die Neuregelung ermöglicht es, Anträge auf Leistungen der Rentenversicherung bei den Versicherungsämtern und Gemeindebehörden auch im automatisierten Verfahren (durch eine Online-Anbindung der Versicherungsämter und Gemeindebehörden an die Datenbestände der Rentenversicherungsträger) zu stellen. Der Datenschutz und die Datensicherheit bei diesem Verfahren wird durch die bereits erfolgte Einbeziehung der Versicherungsämter und Gemeindebehörden in § 35 SGB I und durch den neu eingefügten § 151a SGB VI gewährleistet.

Zu Nummer 5 (§ 150)

Der in § 150 Abs.4 Satz 2 SGB VI enthaltene Hinweis auf die besonderen Voraussetzungen, unter denen die in § 148 Abs. 3 SGB VI genannten Stellen zum Online-Abruf bei der Datenstelle berechtigt sind, muss zur Gewährleistung eines vergleichbaren Datenschutzes und einer vergleichbaren Datensicherheit auch auf die Versicherungsämter und Gemeindebehörden erstreckt werden.

Zu Nummer 6 (§ 151a)

Die neu eingefügte Vorschrift soll die Datensicherheit in der Informationstechnik speziell in der Rentenversicherung, bei der die Integrität der Datenbestände zu den bedeut samsten Grundlagen des Systems gehört, optimieren. Die Formulierung "erforderliche Daten" schränkt den Umfang der Daten, die den antragsaufnehmenden Stellen zur Verfügung gestellt werden, auf ein Mindestmaß ein. Gleichzeitig wird damit sowohl der Teil erfasst, der aus dem Datenbestand der Datenstelle der Rentenversicherungsträger geliefert wird, als auch der Teil, der aus dem Versicherungskonto bei dem aktuellen Kontoführer entnommen wird. Die Führung der Dateien ist in § 150 Abs.2 SGB VI für die Stammsatzdatei geregelt und die Führung des Versicherungskontos bei den Rentenversicherungsträgern im § 149 Abs. 1 SGB VI.

Absatz 2 (falls dieser für erforderlich gehalten wird) *stellt eine Konkretisierung der beim automatisierten Verfahren abzurufenden Daten dar.*

Zudem soll es den Versicherungsämtern und Gemeindebehörden auch nur möglich sein, Daten der Versicherten abzurufen, die nach dem Melderechtsrahmengesetz ihre alleinige bzw. Hauptwohnung im Bezirk des Versicherungsamtes oder im Gebiet der Gemeinde haben.

Zur Erhöhung der Datensicherheit haben die Träger der Rentenversicherung sowie der Verband Deutscher Rentenversicherungsträger für ihren Zuständigkeitsbereich in eigener Verantwortung und unter verbindlicher Beteiligung des Bundesamtes für Sicherheit in der Informationstechnik (BSI) ein Sicherheitskonzept zu erstellen. Das BSI soll beratend und unterstützend schwerpunktmäßig dort mitwirken, wo Sicherheitskonzeptionen entwickelt bzw. der technischen Veränderung angepasst werden. Die Erkenntnisse des BSI sollen vor allem dort fruchtbar gemacht werden, wo es darum geht, Angriffe von Hackern auf die besonders sensiblen Datenbestände der Rentenversicherung abzuwehren, insbesondere die Einschleusung von Viren zu verhindern. Mit der Beteiligung des BSI wird zudem sichergestellt, dass die Datensicherheit bei der bildschirmunterstützten Antragsaufnahme durch die Versicherungsämter und Gemeindebehörden im gesamten Bundesgebiet einheitlich gewährleistet wird.

Die Anpassungen des Sicherheitskonzeptes, insbesondere aufgrund von Veränderungen der technischen Rahmenbedingungen, tragen mit dazu bei, die Datensicherheit nach dem jeweiligen neuesten Stand der Technik zu gewährleisten. Darüber hinaus wird durch die Verpflichtung zur Vorlage der aktualisierten Fassungen der Sicherheitskonzepte bei den Aufsichtsbehörden sichergestellt, dass diese über den Verlauf der sicherheitstechnischen Entwicklung stets informiert sind, um so ggf. regulierend eingreifen zu können.

Für das vorgesehene Verfahren sind die §§ 78a und 79 SGB X anzuwenden. In der nach § 79 Abs. 2 Satz 2 SGB X erforderlichen schriftlichen Festlegung sind insbesondere folgende Punkte zu regeln:

- Beschränkung des Online-Zugriffs auf die in der Praxis tatsächlich benötigten Datenfelder des Versichertenkontos,
- Beschränkung der Zahl der Zugriffsberechtigten bei den Versicherungsämtern und den Gemeinden,
- Dokumentation der Tatsache, des Zeitpunkts und des Inhalts jedes erfolgten Abrufs im Versichertenkonto oder der Akte des Versicherten,
- Lückenlose fortlaufende Protokollierung aller Anrufe,
- Überprüfung der Berechtigung eines Abrufs, wenn innerhalb eines festzulegenden Zeitraums (z.B. 3 Monate) kein Rentenantrag eingeht,

- Kennzeichnung im Versichertenkonto auf Verlangen des Versicherten, die ein OnlineZugriff auf das Konto ausschließt,
- Zugriff nur bei persönlichem Erscheinen des Versicherten und Identifizierung durch einen Lichtbildausweis sowie schriftlicher Antragstellung,
- Hinreichender technischer und organisatorischer Sicherheitsstandard.

Zu § 3 (SGB X)

Zu Nummer 1 (§ 50)

Vgl. Begründung zur inhaltsgleichen Änderung in Artikel BMI Nr. 2.

Zu Nummer 2 (§ 60)

Vgl. Begründung zur inhaltsgleichen Änderung in Artikel BMI Nr. 3.

Zu Artikel BMVg

Zu Artikel BMFSFJ

Zu Artikel BMG

Zu Artikel BMVBW

Zu Artikel BMU

Zu Artikel BMBF

Zu Artikel BMZ

Zu Artikel X

Zu Artikel XX

Zu Artikel XXX

APPENDIX 2

BAYERISCHER STÄDTETAG

Dienstanweisung zur Benutzung und
Behandlung elektronischer Post
"DA elektronische Post"
(Muster)

Stand: Dezember 1999

Hinweis:

Die nachfolgende Musterdienstanweisung zur Benutzung und Behandlung der elektronischen Post (DA elektronische Post) enthält Regelungsvorschläge. Diese können je nach den örtlichen Gegebenheiten übernommen oder entsprechend abgeändert bzw. ergänzt werden. Vor allem in kleineren Verwaltungseinheiten werden nicht alle in der Muster-DA enthaltenen Regelungen erforderlich sein.
Zum Zeitpunkt der Erarbeitung dieser Muster-DA (Dezember 1999) waren einige Entwicklungen im Bereich der elektronischen Post (z.B. Umsetzung der EU-Richtlinie zur digitalen Signatur) noch nicht im Detail absehbar. Die Muster-DA wird deshalb bei Bedarf zu gegebener Zeit angepasst.
Für Hinweise zur Ergänzung dieser Muster-DA sind wir jederzeit dankbar. Sie finden auf dieser Seite die E-Mail-Adressen der Autoren.

Bearbeitet von:
Arbeitsgruppe “DA elektronische Post” des Bayerischen Städtetags

- Richard Stelzer, IuK-Referent des Bayerischen Städtetags (stelzer@bay-staedtetag.de)
- Hans-Volker Winkler, Landeshauptstadt München, Amt für Informations- und Datenverar-beitung, Abt. 5 (hans-volker.winkler@muenchen.de)
- Klaus Diemer, Landeshauptstadt München, Direktorium C/S (klaus.diemer@muenchen.de)
- Manfred Birling, Stadt Königsbrunn, Leiter EDV-Service (manfred.birling@koenigsbrunn.de).

Inhaltsverzeichnis:

Vorbemerkung

Mit der Einführung elektronischer Dienste, wie z.B. E-Mail oder PC-Fax wurden neue Möglichkeiten der Kommunikation eröffnet. Vorteile dieser modernen Kommunikationsformen sind z.B. die Beschleunigung der Verwaltungsabläufe, eine bessere Erreichbarkeit sowie Bürger- und Mitarbeiterfreundlichkeit.

Vor diesem Hintergrund nutzt die Gemeinde[1] ... diese elektronischen Medien zum Austausch von Nachrichten und Dokumenten sowohl im verwaltungsinternen als auch im externen Verkehr.

Um einen reibungslosen, ordnungsgemäßen Betrieb und verwaltungsmäßigen Ablauf o.g. Kommunikationsdienste sicher zu stellen, sind nicht zuletzt wegen der damit verbundenen datenschutzrechtlichen und sicherheitsrelevanten Aspekte entsprechende Regelungen erforderlich. Diese werden in der vorliegenden innerdienstlichen Vorschrift getroffen.

Die Kommunikation mittels elektronischer Post ist ein Bereich, der sowohl technisch als auch organisatorisch zum Teil erst am Anfang seiner Entwicklung steht. Regelungen und Standards zur digitalen Signatur und Verschlüsselung von Nachrichten sind zur Zeit erst im Entstehen und konnten so noch nicht im Detail in dieser Dienstanweisung berücksichtigt werden. Eine Fortschreibung erfolgt zu gegebener Zeit.

1 Allgemeines

1.1 Rechtscharakter

Diese Dienstanweisung ist eine innerdienstliche Vorschrift. Sie ergänzt ...[2]

1.2 Zweck

Zweck der Dienstanweisung ist es, die Nutzung und die Behandlung von elektronischer Post zu regeln.

---

[1] in dieser DA wird der Einfachheit halber nur der Begriff Gemeinde verwendet

[2] z.B. die Allgemeine Dienstanweisung der Gemeinde

1.3 Geltungsbereich

Diese Geschäftsanweisung gilt für ....[3]

1.4 Zuständigkeiten

(1) Um einen geordneten Dienstbetrieb zu gewährleisten, ist eine zentrale Steuerung der elektronischen Postdienste notwendig, die von ....[4] wahrgenommen wird. Für die technische Abwicklung ist ...[5] zuständig.
Die Administration des Mailservers und das Einrichten von Postfächern auf dem Mailserver erfolgt durch ....[6]

(2) Die Dienststellen und Einrichtungen haben für ihren Bereich folgende Regelungen zu treffen:
- Antrag auf Einrichtung von Postfächern bei ....[7]
- Festlegung der E-Mail-Adressen in Abstimmmung mit ....[8]
- Festlegung der Zugriffsberechtigungen (z.B. bei organisationsbezogenen Postfächern)
- Meldung der E-Mail-Adressen und etwaiger Adressänderungen an ....[9]
- Meldung der nicht mehr benötigten Postfächer und E-Mail-Adressen an ....[10]

1.5 Private Nutzung

Die private Nutzung der elektronischen Post ist unzulässig.[11]

---

[3] z.B. alle gemeindlichen Stellen und Eigenbetriebe
[4] zuständige Organisationseinheit angeben
[5] zuständige Organisationseinheit angeben
[6] i.d.R. die mit DV-Aufgaben betraute Organisationseinheit
[7] i.d.R. die mit DV-Aufgaben betraute Organisationseinheit
[8] i.d.R. die mit DV-Aufgaben betraute Organisationseinheit
[9] i.d.R. die mit DV-Aufgaben betraute Organisationseinheit
[10] i.d.R. die mit DV-Aufgaben betraute Organisationseinheit
[11] Hinweis: es ist zur Zeit rechtlich nicht abschließend geklärt, ob die Gemeinde beim Zulassen der privaten Nutzung von elektronischer Post als Anbieter im Sinne des Teledienstegesetzes (TDG) gelten und somit den hohen Anforderungen des Teledienstedatenschutzgesetzes (TDDSG) unterliegen würde (z.B. § 4 TDDSG "Datenschutzrechtliche Pflichten des Anbieters")

2 Voraussetzungen

2.1 Einrichtung

Zur Teilnahme am elektronischen Postverkehr ist es technisch erforderlich, auf dem Mailserver elektronische Postfächer einzurichten und auf den PCs E-Mail-Clients zu installieren.

Es werden eingerichtet:[12]
- ein zentrales Postfach für die Gemeinde
- personenbezogene Postfächer
- Postfächer für Organisationseinheiten

2.2 E-Mail-Adressen

2.2.1 E-Mail-Adresse der Gemeinde

Für die Gemeinde ... wird eine zentrale E-Mail-Adresse eingerichtet. Diese lautet: poststelle@gemeindename.de[13]

2.2.2 Personenbezogene E-Mail-Adressen[14]

Jede Dienstkraft, die über einen an die gemeindliche Netzinfrastruktur angebundenen PC-Arbeitsplatz verfügt, erhält eine E-Mail-Adresse. Diese Adresse ist grundsätzlich nach folgendem Schema aufgebaut:
vorname.nachname@gemeindename.de[15]

Abweichungen sind mit ...[16] abzustimmen.

2.2.3 E-Mail-Adressen für Organisationseinheiten[17]

Für Organisationseinheiten werden E-Mail-Adressen nach folgendem Schema eingerichtet:
Organisationseinheit@gemeindename.de[18]

---

[12] dem jeweiligen Bedarf entsprechend
[13] z.B. poststelle@koenigsbrunn.de
[14] dem jeweiligen Bedarf entsprechend
[15] z.B. hans.muster@koenigsbrunn.de
[16] i.d.R. die mit DV-Aufgaben betraute Organisationseinheit
[17] dem jeweiligen Bedarf entsprechend
[18] z.B. hauptamt@koenigsbrunn.de

3 Rechtliche Aspekte

Elektronische Nachrichten sind grundsätzlich nicht rechtsunerheblich. Sie stellen Willenserklärungen dar und können so Rechtsfolgen auslösen.

Viele Verwaltungs- und Rechtsgeschäfte unterliegen besonderen Formvorschriften, z.B. der Schriftform. Diese wiederum bedingt zur Zeit die eigenhändige Unterschrift. Elektronische Post per E-Mail erfüllt deshalb zur Zeit nicht die Anforderungen an die Schriftform und würde einen Formmangel nach sich ziehen. Allerdings werden derzeit diverse Rechtsvorschriften durch den Gesetzgeber dahingehend überprüft, ob eine digitale Unterschrift eingeführt werden kann. Bis zur rechtlichen Klarstellung können deshalb Erklärungen, die einer besonderen Form bedürfen, nicht per elektronischer Post abgegeben werden.

Gehen rechtserhebliche Erklärungen, die besonderen Formvorschriften unterliegen,[19] per elektronischer Post ein, ist die zuständige Stelle verpflichtet, den Absender unverzüglich auf den Formmangel und die Folgen hinzuweisen.

4 Behandlung elektronischer Post

4.1 Allgemeines

Die bestehenden Regelungen zur Behandlung der Postein- und -ausgänge[20] sind, soweit systembedingt übertragbar, auf E-Mail entsprechend anzuwenden. Hierbei ist die Informationspflicht gegenüber Vorgesetzten zu beachten. Diese hat in geeigneter Form zu erfolgen.

Die Manipulation von E-Mails (z.B. Verfälschung des Absenders oder des Inhalts) ist verboten.

---

[19] z.B. Widerspruch

[20] z.B. Allgemeine Geschäftsanweisung, amtsinterne Regelungen

4.2 Elektronischer Posteingang

4.2.1 Posteingangskontrolle

Der E-Mail-Client soll nach Möglichkeit ständig im Hintergrund aktiv sein, damit der Eingang neuer Nachrichten sofort erkannt wird. Ist dies nicht möglich, ist der Posteinlauf mindestens einmal pro Arbeitstag auf Neueingänge zu überprüfen.

Für das zentrale Postfach der Gemeinde ist ...[21] zuständig. Für die Postfächer der Organisationseinheiten sind verantwortliche Dienstkräfte zu bestimmen. Diese leiten die eingegangene elektronische Post an die zuständigen Stellen bzw. Personen weiter.

4.2.2 Regelung bei Abwesenheit

Bei vorhersehbarer Abwesenheit[22] hat der Vertretene zu veranlassen, daß neu eingehende Post automatisch an den Vertreter weitergeleitet wird.[23]
Bei nicht vorhersehbarer Abwesenheit[24] muss die Weiterleitungsfunktion vom Vertreter veranlasst[25] sowie bereits aufgelaufene Post bearbeitet werden.

4.2.3 Behandlung falsch adressierter Post

Erkennbar falsch adressierte Post ist nach Möglichkeit an die richtige Stelle oder die zentrale Posteinlaufstelle elektronisch weiterzuleiten. Der Absender ist von der Weiterleitung durch E-Mail zu unterrichten (Abgabenachricht). Ist die zuständige Stelle nicht zu ermitteln, erfolgt eine Rücksendung an den Absender.

---

[21] zuständige Organisationseinheit angeben

[22] z.B. Urlaub, Dienstreisen

[23] u.U. empfiehlt sich auch ein automatischer Antworttext an den E-Mail-Absender, in dem auf die Abwesenheit des Empfängers hingewiesen wird bzw. eine andere dienstliche E-Mail-Adresse genannt wird

[24] z.B. plötzliche Erkrankung

[25] z.B. durch Hinweis an den Administrator; möglich ist auch eine Regelung zum Umgang mit Passwörtern (z.B. Hinterlegung bei einer bestimmten Stelle)

4.2.4 Nicht lesbare Post

Ist eine eingegangene Nachricht nicht lesbar, ist die zuständige Anwenderbetreuung zu informieren.

4.2.5 Zweifelhafte E-Mails

Über eingegangene E-Mails, deren Absender oder Inhalt zweifelhaft erscheinen und insbesondere zum Aktivieren von Programmen und sonstigen Eingaben auffordern, ist die zuständige Anwenderbetreuung unverzüglich zu informieren. Diese entscheidet über die weitere Behandlung.

4.2.6 Abonnieren von E-Mails über Mailing-Listen

Das Abonnieren von E-Mails über Mailing-Listen darf nur zu dienstlichen Zwecken erfolgen und muss in jedem Fall auf das notwendige Maß beschränkt werden.

4.2.7 Einsatz eines Virenprüfprogrammes

Wegen der permanenten Virengefahr ist ein ständig zu aktualisierender Virenscanner zwingend zu aktivieren.[26]

4.3 Elektronischer Postausgang

4.3.1 Nutzung der elektronischen Post

Für die tägliche Dienstpost soll soweit wie möglich der elektronische Postverkehr genutzt werden.

Bis zur Einführung der digitalen Signatur sowie bis zum Vorliegen eindeutiger rechtlicher Aussagen (s. hierzu Ziff. 3) dürfen nur solche Dokumente per E-Mail versandt werden, die keinen besonderen Formvorschriften oder Zugangsvoraussetzungen unterliegen.

Die Übermittlung sensibler Daten mittels E-Mail ist nur unter Einsatz geeigneter Verschlüsselungsverfahren zulässig.

[26] in der Praxis haben sich zwei Varianten bewährt: permanente Virenprüfung am Arbeitsplatz oder Virenprüfung direkt am Mailserver vor der Weiterleitung der Nachricht an den Arbeitsplatz

4.3.2 Anlagen in Dateiform (Attachments)

Attachments sind grundsätzlich zulässig. Es ist darauf zu achten, nur die durch gesonderte Festlegung bekanntgegebenen Dateiformate zu verwenden.

Spezielle Dateiformate[27] sollen nur dann versandt werden, wenn bekannt ist, dass der Empfänger diese Dateien auch bearbeiten kann.

Wegen der begrenzten Speicherkapazität des zentralen Mailservers dürfen E-Mails einschließlich eines Dateianhangs grundsätzlich nicht größer als ... MB[28] sein. Abweichungen hiervon sind vorher mit dem Administrator des Mailservers abzustimmen.

Programmdateien dürfen wegen der Virengefahr nur durch die Systemverwaltung versandt werden.

4.3.3 E-Mail-Betreff

E-Mails sind mit einem aussagekräftigen Betreff zu versehen, um dem Empfänger den Überblick über die eingegangenen Nachrichten zu erleichtern.

4.3.4 E-Mail-Attribute

Die Verwendbarkeit von Attributen, wie z.B. Priorität “niedrig”, “normal” und “hoch” sowie Vermerke der Vertraulichkeit, wie “normal”, “persönlich”, “vertraulich” ist von den eingesetzten Mail-Client-Produkten abhängig. Vor allem im externen E-Mail-Verkehr ist deshalb bei der Verwendung von Attributen besondere Sorgfalt geboten.

Einstellungen zur Priorität sind im innerdienstlichen E-Mail-Verkehr auch aus organisatorischen Gesichtspunkten auf das notwendige Maß zu beschränken.

---

[27] z.B. aus Fachanwendungen

[28] eine in der Praxis häufig verwendete Beschränkung ist 2 MB

4.3.5 Gestaltung der E-Mail; Absenderangaben

E-Mails dienen der schnellen Übermittlung von Informationen und unterliegen deshalb keiner besonderen Gestaltungsvorgabe. Sollte eine besondere Gestaltung erforderlich sein, ist der Nachricht ein entsprechender Dateianhang beizufügen.

Die E-Mail muss den Absender[29] und die absendende Behörde/ Dienststelle eindeutig erkennen lassen.[30]
Das Einfügen eingescannter Unterschriften ist nicht zulässig.

4.3.6 Sendeoptionen

Sendeoptionen (z.B. Empfangsbestätigungen) basieren derzeit nicht auf In-ternetstandards. Um Störungen im E-Mail-Betrieb zu vermeiden, sollten diese Optionen deshalb grundsätzlich nicht verwendet werden.[31]

4.4 Ablage

Die Grundsätze einer ordnungsgemäßen Aktenführung gelten sinngemäß auch für ein- und ausgehende elektronische Dokumente. Werden zu einem Vorgang Papierakten geführt, sind die elektronischen Dokumente – soweit diese als geschäftskritisch anzusehen sind – deshalb auszudrucken und zu den jeweiligen Akten zu nehmen.

Erhaltene, nicht als geschäftskritisch anzusehende E-Mails, sind nach Durchsicht zu löschen. Geschäftskritische Nachrichten sind nach den bestehenden Regelungen abzulegen; sie dürfen keinesfalls längerfristig im Mail-Client gespeichert werden.

5 Verzeichnis der E-Mail-Adressen; Verteilerlisten

Alle personen- und organisationsbezogenen E-Mail-Adressen

---

[29] für sensible Bereiche (z.B. Sozialamt) ggf. abweichende Regelung erforderlich

[30] zweckmäßigerweise erfolgt dies automatisiert

[31] bei sensiblen oder wichtigen Nachrichten kann im versandten Nachrichtentext eine Empfangsbestätigung durch den Empfänger erbeten werden

[32] nichtzutreffendes streichen

befinden sich im globalen E-Mail-Verzeichnis. Die Pflege dieses Adressbuches erfolgt zentral/dezentral[32] durch ....[33]. Das Anlegen von "persönlichen Adressbüchern" und Verteilerlisten, über die sich eine größere Zahl von Empfängern bequem zeitgleich erreichen lässt, ist zulässig. Allgemein ist beim Gebrauch von Verteilerlisten zu beachten, dass hierdurch unter Umständen nicht unerhebliche Aktivitäten ausgelöst werden.

6 Protokollierung

Das E-Mail-System führt Protokolldateien über ein- und auslaufende E-Mails. Die Protokolldateien für Internet-Mail werden nur in Fehlerfällen zur Klärung der Ursache nach Rücksprache mit der betroffenen Dienstkraft ausgewertet.[34] Bezüglich der Löschung der Protokolldateien finden die Bestimmungen der einschlägigen Datenschutzgesetze Anwendung.

7 Datenschutz

Bei der Nutzung von E-Mail sind die datenschutzrechtlichen Vorschriften zu beachten.

Die verwaltungsinternen Regelungen zur Einhaltung des Datenschutzes finden entsprechende Anwendung.[35]

8 Mitwirkung der Personalvertretung

Die Personalvertretung wurde in die Erstellung dieser Dienstanweisung eingebunden.[36]

9 Nichteinhaltung der Dienstanweisung

Die Einhaltung dieser Dienstanweisung wird durch ...[37] unter

---

[33] zuständige Organisationseinheit angeben
[34] Einzelheiten sind ggf. in einer besonderen Regelung zu treffen
[35] ggf. Benennung der Regelungen
[36] vgl. Art. 76 BayPVG

Beteiligung der zuständigen Personalvertretung überprüft. Hierbei ist die Systemverwaltung unterstützend tätig. Ein grob fahrlässiger oder vorsätzlicher Verstoß gegen die Vorschriften dieser Dienstanweisung kann bei Arbeitern und Angestellten eine Verletzung ihres Arbeitsvertrages, bei Beamten ein Dienstvergehen darstellen.

10 Inkrafttreten

Diese Dienstanweisung tritt mit Wirkung vom ... in Kraft.

[37] zuständige Organisationseinheit angeben

ABOUT THE AUTHORS

Dr. M. Eifert

Martin Eifert is the author of the chapter on Germany. He was awarded a scholarship from the Deutsche Forschungsgemeinschaft (Habilitandenstipendium) and works at the Hans-Bredow-Institut für Medienforschung, Hamburg. Here he heads the legal research which is the largest Multimedia pilot-project to be funded by the Federal Government (MEDIA@Komm) since 1999. He studied law in Hamburg, Geneva and Berkeley and obtained his Ph.D. at Hamburg University and his LL.M. at the University of California at Berkeley (USA). Martin Eifert has published several articles, mainly in the fields of media and administrative law. At present his research topics include the regulation of the media (from telecommunications to broadcasting), modernization of public administration and Electronic Government. E-mail: m.eifert@hans-bredow-institut.de; website: <http://www.hans-bredow-institut.de>.

Dr. C. Girot

Clarisse Girot is the author of the French part of this study. She is French and studied law at the University of Paris II – Panthéon Assas in France (1989-1993), where she also obtained a degree in Intellectual Property. She then passed the Magister Juris in European and Comparative Law (M.Jur., LL.M.) at Oxford University in Great Britain (1994). Subsequently, she worked with the law firm Barennes & ass. in Paris. In 1996, she started working as an assistant researcher at Tilburg University, The Netherlands, and in March 2001 she was awarded a Ph.D. (*cum laude*) for her thesis on contractual imbalance in the ICT sector. Her fields of research are primarily comparative contract law aspects of Information Technology and the legal aspects of Electronic Commerce. At present she works at the European and International section of the Commission Nationale Informatique et Libertés, which is the French body concerned with the protection of personal data in France. E-mail: cgirot@club-internet.fr (private).

M.M. GROOTHUIS
Marga Groothuis wrote the chapter on Norway and assisted in the research for the US chapter. She has a degree in law from Leiden University, The Netherlands, and gained her LL.M. at Queen Mary and Westfield College in London. From 1995 to 1996 she worked for the Dutch Council of State (Raad van State). In 1997 she became a researcher and lecturer at the Department of Information Technology and Law at Leiden University, where she wrote her Ph.D. thesis on the juridical aspects of electronic government and automatic decision-making. This thesis will be published in the IT*e*R series in 2002. She now works for the Constitutional Affairs and Legislation Department of the Dutch Ministry of the Interior. Her fields of interest include electronic government, administrative and constitutional law.

PROF. DR. J.E.J. PRINS
Corien Prins was the project leader as well as the author of the analyses and conclusions of this study. She is a Professor of Law and Informatization at Tilburg University, where she joined the Centre for Law and Informatization in 1994. She obtained a Ph.D. in law at Leiden University where she also studied Slavic Languages. After receiving her Ph.D. in 1991, she was a Visiting Professor at Hastings Law School in San Francisco, USA. Professor Prins is the editor of several national and international magazines and handbooks. Her research topics currently include (international) regulatory questions surrounding ICT, e-government issues, anonimity and privacy in relation to electronic commerce. E-mail: J.E.J.Prins@kub.nl; website: http://rechten.kub.nl/prins.

DR. W.J.M. VOERMANS
Dr Wim Voermans produced this study's report on the United States. He is a senior lecturer and senior researcher at the Centre for Legislative Studies at Tilburg University. He specializes in legislative studies, and in particular the field that researches the possibilities of computer assistance in legislative drafting. This research resulted in the development of the legislative design and advisory system LEDA which is being used by Dutch ministerial departments. He teaches legislative studies and legislative drafting in many different settings, for example for professionanal legislative drafters in The Netherlands and the Drafting staff within the

European Parliament. Together with his colleague Philip Eijlander, Dr. Voermans wrote a handbook on legislative drafting in 2000 (Wetgevingsleer).

INFORMATION TECHNOLOGY & LAW SERIES

1. E-Government and its Implications for Administrative Law – Regulatory Initiatives in France, Germany, Norway and the United States (The Hague: T.M.C.ASSER PRESS, 2002)
   Editor: J.E.J. Prins / ISBN 90-6704-141-6

Forthcoming

- Remodelling Napster – a multidisciplinary investigation into the economic and legal implications of peer to peer models in the music industry.

- Automated argument assistance for lawyers.

- IT, courts, accountability – an investigation into the implications of IT implementation in courts, introducing a framework for comparative law and applying it to the analysis of court accountability in Europe, Australia, China, Venezuela, Egypt and Iran.

- The three-prong test in cyberspace – an investigation into the legal implications for constraining copyright exceptions in cyberspace.

GPSR Compliance

The European Union's (EU) General Product Safety Regulation (GPSR) is a set of rules that requires consumer products to be safe and our obligations to ensure this.

If you have any concerns about our products, you can contact us on ProductSafety@springernature.com

In case Publisher is established outside the EU, the EU authorized representative is:

Springer Nature Customer Service Center GmbH
Europaplatz 3
69115 Heidelberg, Germany

Batch number: 10844692

Printed by Printforce, the Netherlands